Reading in the Reel World

Reading in the Reel World

Teaching Documentaries and Other Nonfiction Texts

John Golden
Grant High School, Portland, Oregon

National Council of Teachers of English
1111 W. Kenyon Road, Urbana, Illinois 61801-1096

Film photos reprinted from PHOTOFEST (212-633-6330): Figures 1.3 and 1.5 (*The Thin Blue Line*); 1.6 (*Waiting for Guffman*); 1.11 and 3.2a (*Fahrenheit 9/11*); 1.14 (*Nanook of the North*); 1.17 (*Triumph of the Will*); 2.8 and 4.2 (*Mad Hot Ballroom*); 2.11 (*March of the Penguins*); 3.1 and 4.15 (*Bowling for Columbine*); 3.5 (*Touching the Void*); 4.8 (*Born into Brothels*); 4.13 and 4.14 (*Super Size Me*). Figure 1.7 comprises photos by Laura Lull.

Staff Editor: Bonny Graham

Interior Design: Doug Burnett

Cover Design: Diana C. Coe/kō Design Studio

Cover Photograph © Photodisc/GettyImages

NCTE Stock Number: 38756

It is the policy of NCTE in its journals and other publications to provide a forum for the open discussion of ideas concerning the content and the teaching of English and the language arts. Publicity accorded to any particular point of view does not imply endorsement by the Executive Committee, the Board of Directors, or the membership at large, except in announcements of policy, where such endorsement is clearly specified.

Every effort has been made to provide current URLs and e-mail addresses, but because of the rapidly changing nature of the Web, some sites and addresses may no longer be accessible.

Library of Congress Cataloging-in-Publication Data

Golden, John, 1968–
    Reading in the reel world : teaching documentaries and other nonfiction texts/ John Golden.
        p. cm.
    Includes bibliographical references.
    ISBN 0-8141-3875-6
    1. Language arts (Secondary) 2. Language arts (Middle school) 3. Motion pictures in education. I. Title.
    LB1631 .G6193 2006
    428.0071'2—dc22

                                                            2006010766

For my mom, Chris Golden, who always sees the world as it really is, without excuse but with such optimism, regardless of her vision, and for my dad, Dick Golden, who taught me that the real thing in this world will always be family.

Contents

Figures   ix

Foreword
    Alan B. Teasley   xi

Acknowledgments   xv

Introduction   xvii

1. Introduction to Documentary Forms and Techniques   1
    Teaching Nonfiction Film   2
    Defining Nonfiction Film   3
    Parts of a Nonfiction Film   17
    Editing in Nonfiction Film   25
    Styles and Modes of Nonfiction Film   32
    Ethical Issues in Nonfiction Film   40
    History of Nonfiction Film   46
    Other Nonfiction Film Experiences   52
    Putting It All Together: What Next?   70

2. Nonfiction Reading Skills and Strategies   72
    Nonfiction Reading Skills   73
    Reading Strategies   80
    Practice Nonfiction Print Texts   95

3. Nonfiction Writing and Analysis   102
    Analytical Writing Skills   102
    Writing Skills   112
    Practice Nonfiction Print Texts   126

4. Teaching a Complete Film   134
    Spellbound   137
    Mad Hot Ballroom   144
    Girlhood   152
    Hoop Dreams   157
    Amandla! A Revolution in Four Part Harmony 165
    Born into Brothels: Calcutta's Red Light Kids 172
    Night and Fog   184
    Super Size Me   191

Bowling for Columbine   201
The True Meaning of Pictures: Shelby Lee Adams' Appalachia   212
4 Little Girls   221
Six o'Clock News   227
The Thin Blue Line   236
High School and *High School II*   242
The Gleaners and I   252

Appendixes
    A. Glossary of Film Terminology   261
    B. Blank Activity Charts   265
    C. Other Documentaries by Topic   275
    D. Annotated List of Resources   277
    E. Index of Films Discussed   281

Works Cited   283

Author   285

Figures

1.1   Thin line between fiction and nonfiction in *The Thin Blue Line*   5

1.2   Venn diagram of students' distinctions between fiction and nonfiction films   6

1.3   Introductory survey about differences between fiction and nonfiction films   7

1.4   Preparation for a reenactment in *The Thin Blue Line*   8

1.5   Staging of students saying the Pledge of Allegiance   12

1.6   Documentary elements of the mockumentary *Waiting for Guffman*   15

1.7   Imaginary documentary of famous guitarist   19

1.8   Parts of a documentary form   23

1.9   Opening shots from *Born into Brothels*   31

1.10   Modes of nonfiction film chart   36

1.11   Michael Moore inserting himself into *Fahrenheit 9/11*   39

1.12   Ethical dilemmas in nonfiction film   42

1.13   Ethically questionable shots from *Hoop Dreams*   45

1.14   Constructed nature of film as seen in *Nanook of the North*   49

1.15   Check sheet for detecting propaganda   55

1.16   Excerpt from Orwell's *1984*   56

1.17   Staged event for propaganda purposes in *Triumph of the Will*   59

1.18   List of activities focusing on reality TV   66

2.1   Venn diagram compare and contrast strategy   74

2.2   From *Spellbound*   75

2.3   Problem and solution strategy   77

2.4   SOAPStone chart   81

2.5   Using SOAPStone   83

2.6   Levels of Questioning exercise   86

2.7   Using Levels of Questioning   88

2.8   From *Mad Hot Ballroom*   89

2.9   Cornell Notes divisions   91

2.10   Using Cornell Notes   93

2.11   From the opening of *March of the Penguins*   95

3.1   Michael Moore in *Bowling for Columbine*   105

3.2   Contrasting images of President Bush   111

3.3   Introducing pathos, ethos, and logos   113

3.4   Nonfiction film treatment   117

3.5   A reenactment from *Touching the Void*   118

4.1   *Spellbound* character chart   139

4.2   Kids dancing in *Mad Hot Ballroom*   147

4.3   Height difference of kids in *Mad Hot Ballroom*   149

4.4   Dance scene from *Amandla!*   170

4.5   South Africa's national anthem   173

4.6   *Born into Brothels* character chart   176

4.7   Children from *Born into Brothels*   177

4.8   Going to the zoo in *Born into Brothels*   179

4.9   Opening shot from *Night and Fog*   187

4.10   Denying responsibility, from *Night and Fog*   189

4.11   SOAPStone analysis of *Night and Fog*   190

4.12   Previewing survey for *Super Size Me*   192

4.13   Doctor visit in *Super Size Me*   194

4.14   End of the experiment, from *Super Size Me*   200

4.15   Gun giveaway promotion in *Bowling for Columbine*   204

4.16   Archival footage of Columbine High School shootings   207

4.17   Graphic organizer for *The True Meaning of Pictures*   215

4.18   Day 1 note-taking form for *Six o'Clock News*   230

4.19   Days 2 and 3 note-taking form for *Six o'Clock News*   233

4.20   Note-taking form for *High School* and *High School II*   245

4.21   Filmmaker's hand from *The Gleaners and I*   257

Foreword

Alan B. Teasley
Duke University

If you have picked up this remarkable book, I'm assuming two things: you're already interested in film and you have a commitment to connecting students and films in engaging, vital ways. You are almost certainly an English teacher or curriculum leader, though you may work in social studies, science, world languages, philosophy, media literacy, or film and video production. You're initially puzzled by the notion that someone could have written an entire book about teaching with and about documentary films. After all, isn't teaching documentaries pretty much like teaching other films? And don't you already have a book about that?

Boy, are you in for an adventure!

As I write this, I have just completed my third season of serving on the selection committee of the Full Frame Documentary Film Festival in Durham, North Carolina. For the 2006 festival, over a thousand films were submitted; my share for viewing was in the range of 185 films (including shorts and features). Fewer than 70 of the hundreds of films discussed by the committee will screen "in competition" during the four-day festival. If this year's festival turns out like those of previous years, my colleagues and I have already seen the films you will be talking about for the next several years. Some of these films will open at your local independent cinema; some of them will play in the multiplexes (assuming there will be multiplexes much longer); and some of them will be broadcast on public television or one of the premium cable channels. Some of them will be nominated for Academy Awards, or Emmys, or a Peabody or two. Perhaps one or two of them will become certified hits. An increasing percentage of them will be released on DVD (or downloaded, or podcast, or distributed by whatever other means their creators can find or invent).

More important, when you do see them, these films will generate discussions and change behavior. Admit it: after you saw Morgan Spurlock's *Super Size Me*, you reconsidered ordering the McFries. When you and your Republican friends ran into one another at Michael Moore's *Fahrenheit 9/11*, you discovered very quickly that you had seen two different movies. Before Morgan Freeman took that National Geographic gig, you weren't at all curious about the mating habits of Antarctic penguins, yet now you own the DVD of *March of the Penguins*, and your children ask to see it at least once a month.

Documentaries will show you parts of the world and of the human experience that you haven't seen—or even knew to look for. You will repeatedly say to yourself, "Wow! I didn't know that!" You will wonder, "How did they get that footage?" You may also think, "I know I just saw it, but do I believe it?" And one of your cynical friends is sure to say, "Yeah, but there's another side to this story. What did they leave out?" You will argue, debate, and go to the library to get a book about the same subject.

Don't you want this type of experience for your students? Isn't this exactly the sort of critical inquiry we want our students to engage in?

If you, my English teacher colleagues, are anything like me in what attracted you to this profession, I would bet it's because you love literature. Reading fiction and poetry are sacred activities—aren't they?—enriched by the practices of literary analysis, discussion, and writing explications and critiques. We have lumped literature other than fiction, poetry, and drama into that catch-all category of "nonfiction"— dozens of genres collapsed into one and defined by what they are *not*. How bizarre is that, when you think about it? Also, if you are like most secondary English teachers I have known, your curriculum guides, anthologies, and reading lists contain a small proportion of nonfiction. When I think back on the years I taught British literature, I can remember only a few selections that ever made it to class: a bit of Pepys's *Diary*, a snippet from Defoe's *A Journal of the Plague Year*, some Addison and Steele perhaps, or maybe an Orwell essay if we didn't have time for *1984*. Would Swift's "A Modest Proposal" count? It isn't really fiction. . . .

Face it. We English teachers have a prejudice in favor of literary fiction. Even those of us who believe in incorporating film into the curriculum most often teach feature-length fiction films. (I'm not saying that's a bad thing; I've spent many hours advocating adding *Citizen Kane* to the high school canon!)

Clearly, if we are to expand our students' access to a broad range of contemporary discourse, we need help. How do we start? What films can we use? How do we teach them? How do we connect them to reading and writing?

Okay, calm down! John Golden has done a tremendous amount of work for you by writing *Reading in the Reel World*. He includes information on the types and history of documentary films. He discusses the primary ethical issues involved in making and analyzing documentaries. He provides you with sample handouts for helping students decode and interpret nonfiction films. He connects film analysis to nonfiction reading skills and strategies. He shows you exactly how to develop your students' nonfiction writing skills through documentary film study. Finally, he provides you with detailed teaching guides for sixteen documentaries that will engage your students.

In short, he has given you everything you need to get started—whether you want ideas for that unit next month or for an entire course on reading nonfiction films. His ideas are sound and his strategies practical. I think I should warn you, though. His passion for teaching documentaries is contagious. You will rent or purchase the films he describes. You will check the local listings of your cable channels. You will scour the movie listings on Friday for the latest "hot doc." You will announce on a Monday, "Students, today we start our unit on documentary film." They will stare at you slack-jawed. Two weeks later, you will all be amazed by how much you have learned and how much fun you have had in the process.

Acknowledgments

Although coming up with the idea for this book was easy, many people were essential in helping to get it out of my head and into the real world. Just about every halfway decent idea I have comes from some kind of conversation with my wife, Laura Lull; this project would have died before it started if she hadn't recognized something worthwhile in it. Kurt Austin, at NCTE, gave me the green light and the encouragement to go forward with the book even though a year ago it was little more than a wreck. His supportive yet gently insistent e-mails throughout the writing should be collected and analyzed as literature for tone. We are all so lucky to have folks like Kurt and Zarina Hock working so hard to expand the literature of our field.

Once I started writing, I realized that I didn't know half as much about documentaries as I thought I did. Luckily, I took a course in nonfiction film at the Northwest Film Center in Portland from Bushra Azzouz, an extraordinarily talented teacher and gifted filmmaker. I also don't think that I have ever written about film without reflecting on the courses I have taken from Enie Vaisburd, also of the Northwest Film Center, and from Cindy Lucia, now of Rider University.

Thank you so much to the early readers, Cheryl Harris from Texas, and Kris Spurlock and Matt Campeau, colleagues of mine at Grant High School in Portland, who helped me to restructure and reemphasize certain parts of the very rough draft. Throughout the writing, the conversations I had with Cheryl, Gary Cowan of Nashville, Nina Wooldridge of Long Beach, and Joellen Victoreen of San Jose always gave me new ideas that I promptly stole and included here with absolutely no financial compensation for any of them. Dave Lickey, a social studies teacher whose classroom is right below mine, tried his best to distract me each day I tried to write but ended up giving me his tremendous insight into the nature of propaganda, which appears in Chapter 1.

Without the support and understanding of the administration at Grant High School, particularly Toni Hunter and Jeff Spaulding, and the assistance of Tom Spring at crucial deadlines, there's no way I'd have gotten a chance to write these acknowledgments, because I'd still be writing the book. To my students at Grant: you are the absolute best; thank you for your patience with my delays in returning your papers and for allowing me to treat you as guinea pigs. I also could not have completed this book without the support of the College Board's Lola Greene, who is always a champion of new ideas.

I can't express how much it means to me to have Alan Teasley, a huge influence on me as a writer and a teacher, lend his name and words to the foreword. He, along with my good friend and colleague Bill McBride and my former teacher Cindy Lucia, were later readers of the book, and their comments and suggestions improved it immeasurably. Notice, Cindy, that there's no "fish carcass" to be seen in the final.

Thank you to my students Becca Carlson, Jon Coon, Emma Dobbins, Ann Kaleshnik, and Ben Zarov, whose nonfiction pieces are included at the end of Chapters 2 and 3.

There is no possible way you could have understood anything I'd written here without editor Bonny Graham's careful eye for detail and language. Thank you so much, Bonny, and please be sure to fix this sentence to make me sound good here too.

I'm amazed to think how much I learn from my now-four-year-old daughter, Eleanor. Watching her play make-believe and listening to the questions she asks while watching a film like *March of the Penguins* gave so much shape to the ideas behind this project. And, there at the beginning and at the end, Laura: thank you for all your film suggestions, encouragement, and occasional butt kicking. All my love.

Introduction

My three-year-old daughter knows the difference between fiction and nonfiction, and let me tell you, she uses this knowledge like a weapon. When I tell her it's time to wash her hands for dinner, she'll say, "I got a good idea: let's *pretend* I washed my hands already. That sound good?" If I tell her it's time to go to bed, she'll say that she's Cinderella now, and Cinderella "never, ever goes to bed." She tries to escape the real world through fiction, like those of us who play the lottery. But, of course, it doesn't work when I try using the weapon on her. If she wants a treat before dinner and I say, "Let's *pretend* that we're eating ice cream right now," she looks at me like I'm crazy and says, "No, I want a *real* one." Fiction has its own limits.

I worry that my three-year-old daughter may know more about truth and fiction than my sixteen-year-old students. My students have been taught that fiction is something "made up," while nonfiction is, by definition, "the truth." My daughter knows what my students have forgotten: truth is malleable. Sixteen-year-olds call this "lying" or "fiction," and though my daughter knows the difference, she doesn't care. She can switch effortlessly between truth and pretend to suit her purposes, just like—some will claim—Michael Moore. With my daughter, this means that if she can successfully convince me that she is in fact Cinderella, then maybe she won't have to go to bed. To me, this seems healthier than automatically believing that something is true just because it's labeled "nonfiction." To create an effective nonfiction piece, you need to be more persuasive than "true," as we will see throughout this text.

These thoughts have occurred to me lately because it seems that we are entering into a period that could be called a "nonfiction explosion." Recently, documentary films have begun enjoying widespread releases and huge commercial success, relatively speaking. Michael Moore's *Bowling for Columbine* and *Fahrenheit 9/11*, *Super Size Me*, *Spellbound*, *March of the Penguins*, and others have played in multiplexes across the country, rather than only in the art houses of major cities. This is in addition to the prevalence of "reality TV," such as *Survivor*, *The Apprentice*, and *The Bachelor*, shows that are, in fact, serial documentaries. And if you've taken a close look at those standardized tests lately, you'll notice that well over 50 percent of the questions ask students to respond to nonfiction texts.

xviii   Introduction

So, while our students are being overwhelmed with nonfiction media these days, we do very little to instruct them in how to sort out these kinds of texts; we don't teach them to ask critical questions such as "How is this constructed, for what purpose, and from whose point of view?" Students should not read a *New York Times* editorial the same way they read a Hemingway short story. Students need different skills and teachers need to use different strategies to help students read and understand nonfiction texts. In talking with students and teachers, I have found that while the overwhelming majority of the film that students encounter in school is nonfiction (they see an average of nearly three documentaries per month, based on an informal survey), very few students have received any direct instruction in how to "read" documentaries, and they have not learned the ways in which documentaries can construct (or reconstruct) the truth.

When watching a documentary in school, students are generally directed to take notes solely on the information presented in the documentary, not on *how* the information is presented, and this knowledge makes a huge difference. Consider, for example, a documentary that students might see in a science class about global warming. They might be able to write down all of the facts presented, but if students are not asked to be aware of who is interviewed or how the visuals and sound are used, they will not be able to discern a bias or point of view.

I started writing this book just after the 2004 presidential election, and lots of people were still talking about Moore's *Fahrenheit 9/11*, which had as its stated goal to prevent George W. Bush from being reelected, and I heard from many people that this film is not a *documentary* because it's so biased. This comment reveals one of the main reasons I wrote this book: we mistakenly believe that "reality TV" is real and we think that documentaries have to be "objective."

Unlike journalists, documentarians have no need or responsibility to be "fair and balanced" (I put this in quotes so that FOX News doesn't sue me). Like any author, poet, or artist, a nonfiction filmmaker has a point of view and uses a series of techniques to present it effectively. Students will often claim that documentaries are "true" and that the films are designed to be "objective," but by doing so they clearly misread the role of the documentarian; nonfiction filmmakers have no requirement to present an objective truth.

In 2005, the Word of the Year, as determined by the American Dialect Society (ADS), was *truthiness*, which was popularized by Stephen Colbert on his Comedy Central mock news show *The Colbert Report*. Truthiness, according to the ADS, is the "stating [of] concepts or facts one *wishes* or *believes* to be true, rather than concepts or facts *known* to be true" (emphasis added). Or, as Colbert satirically states, "I don't trust books. They're all fact, no heart." Too many nonfiction film-makers and writers would probably agree with Colbert, but without his irony. We need to give our students the power to decode a text's point of view to keep them from falling victim to propaganda or becoming believers in "truthiness."

To this end, the book has four long chapters, each designed to help classroom teachers feel comfortable using documentaries actively in the classroom. Chapter 1 introduces the history, forms, and styles of docu-mentaries as well as the significant issues in teaching documentaries. Regardless of your own knowledge of film studies, this chapter will give you the tools and background to teach nonfiction film. Chapter 2 prac-tices some of the skills (compare/contrast, problem/solutions, and cause/effect) and the strategies (SOAPSTone, Levels of Questions, and Cornell Notes) students need to develop when they read nonfiction print texts. The idea behind this chapter and the next is to practice these skills and strategies with high-interest nonfiction film clips and then transfer these abilities to nonfiction print texts. Chapter 3 presents a series of classroom-tested activities that use documentaries and documentary-related issues to teach such skills as discerning theme, tone, and point of view, as well as practicing and improving persuasive, narrative, and expository writing abilities. The final chapter focuses on teaching a com-plete documentary in the classroom and includes rationales, activities, and assessments for a variety of documentaries appropriate for middle and high school students.

So, at the same time that we are teaching our students how to "read" documentary films, we are also giving them the tools and the ability to read nonfiction print texts. As I asserted in my previous bid for financial independence, *Reading in the Dark: Using Film as a Tool in the English Classroom*, film and print should not be enemies: the skills students use to determine characterization, setting, theme, and so on in film are similar to the skills they use when analyzing print texts. The same applies to nonfiction texts, though the stakes are somewhat higher. While few students believe that the events in, say, *The Lord of the Rings* are real and might somehow affect them, the same cannot be said for a documentary, which is often presented by the teacher and viewed by students as "real" and which often can have direct influence on their lives and the choices they make.

It would be a mistake, then, to see this book solely as a "media studies" text and used only in film units or film classes. Although I think it will be useful and appropriate in those classes, I am an English teacher who just happens to use film to teach the reading and writing skills my students need. Nor do I think that just because we can use film as a way to get students to engage more fully with a print text that we are doing any disservice to film study. In the end, this is a book of strategies for reading the world as it is presented to us, and it is designed to give both students and teachers the power to understand the messages of the world in whatever form they appear.

1 Introduction to Documentary Forms and Techniques

I love documentaries, but I recognize that I am an unrepentant voyeur. Now, I am not publicly confessing to peeking in people's windows, but if a couple is arguing at the table next to me at a restaurant, I absolutely guarantee that I'm going to be looking at them. And I wouldn't be sneaky about it either: I'd stare, lean closer trying to hear better, maybe ask the waiter to give me periodic updates. I hope I'm not alone in this, because if so, you probably just put this book back on the shelf. But I don't think I am, because even if you don't spy as blatantly as I do or haven't seen every episode of *Big Brother*, we all can admit to having a desire to peer into the world around us. This is what documentaries can do for us.

Documentaries take us where we often do not, cannot, or even do not *want* to go; they present the lives of people or subjects with whom we may have little in common, knowledge about, or interest in. We may be happy never knowing the real effects of that McDonald's hamburger we just ate, but a film like *Super Size Me* forces us to reevaluate our own lifestyles. A powerful documentary teaches us about the troubles, joys, pain, and circumstances outside of our own limited experiences and can give us the opportunity to have these reflected back on our own lives. By watching quadriplegics play the brutal game of wheelchair rugby in *Murderball*, we have to reassess everything we thought we knew about people with disabilities, just as when we see the poverty-stricken children of *Born into Brothels* learn to take photographs, we recognize something universal about art. And sometimes documentaries don't take us far geographically but hold up a mirror, showing a world that looks just like our own in a way that reveals something we didn't know was there. During the school year, I spend over half of my waking life in a high school, but the nonfiction film *High School* points out the frightening power structures of which I am a part but that I never really notice. A documentary can take us deep into Appalachia, back to the election of 2004, or inside the criminal justice system, allowing us to become voyeurs while not leaving the safety and security of our movie theaters, living rooms, or classrooms.

Now, a fiction film can do all of these things, but documentaries can do them more powerfully than fiction films because a documentary has a truer sense of connection to the real world. It is easier for me to picture myself as a real person in a documentary than as a character played by Tom Cruise (turn to the photo at the back of the book to see why); nor can I imagine myself in the situation of a *Die Hard* movie as easily as I can in the situation of eating too much McDonald's food, as in *Super Size Me*.

Consider two films about basketball: the fiction film *Hoosiers*, which is about a team in Indiana that goes to the state finals after suffering much adversity, and *Hoop Dreams*, a documentary about two boys in Chicago, one of whom goes to the state finals after suffering much adversity. *Hoosiers* stars Gene Hackman and has an excellent script that nevertheless follows the archetypal Cinderella/underdog story, which means that its end is known and no matter what a great actor he is, Hackman merely approximates the idea of dedicated coach. *Hoop Dreams*, on the other hand, is a window into real lives of people who may want to fit within the archetypal story of *Hoosiers*—and the film is constructed to follow a structure similar to that of *Hoosiers*—but real life intrudes; it's not as neat and tidy as a script, but instead feels more real somehow, because our lives are messy too. When the boys experience triumph, we know that because they are real people, they just as easily might have failed—again, just like us.

Deep down, documentaries are about connections that we make to the images we see on-screen, and these connections are often surprising in ways well beyond a surprise ending in *Psycho* or *The Sixth Sense*. Afterward, we know something new about the world; truths can be revealed. Or maybe I'm just rationalizing my own voyeurism.

Teaching Nonfiction Film

The top four answers I get when I ask students what they typically do as they watch documentaries in class are (1) nothing, (2) sleep, (3) take notes on the facts presented for a quiz afterward, and (4) fill in the blanks of a premade worksheet on the facts presented in the film. The concept behind *Reading in the Reel World*, however, asks that students do more than this as they watch. In addition to keeping track of the facts and the story, they should be looking at *how* the film tells its story. How has it constructed reality? What message is it trying to deliver? What is the filmmaker's point of view? What is he or she doing to persuade us of this point of view? In order to examine documentaries in this way, students need to be exposed to some of the key elements of nonfiction film-making. To summarize what you will encounter in this first chapter, my suggestions for teaching documentaries to students are to:

1. Define nonfiction film by introducing students to the **similarities and differences between fiction films and documentaries**. (page 3)

2. Teach students about the three main elements in documentaries: **visual, sound, and text tracks**. (page 17)

3. Present the role of **editing** in nonfiction film. (page 25)

4. Introduce students to the various **modes** found in documentaries. (page 32)

5. Address the **ethical considerations** of nonfiction film. (page 40)

Each of these sections includes suggestions of film clips and questions to consider. You can share these aditional questions with your students, or they could be just for your own thinking.

The following are additional topics to which you might want to expose your students:

6. Introduce the **history and background of nonfiction film** with your students and show clips from some of the films identified. (page 46)

7. Present students with samples of other nonfiction film texts, such as **reality television, propaganda,** and **blended genres,** to see how they employ the elements of documentary film. (page 52)

Defining Nonfiction Film

I tend to use the terms *nonfiction films* and *documentaries* interchangeably, but the first thing we ought to try to do is to determine exactly what a documentary is. Ostensibly, documentaries are true stories, starring real people, produced to inform an audience about an issue. But even as I write this, I keep thinking: is this any different from a fiction film? Plenty of fiction films are based on real events and try to inform an audience about an issue, and some even use real people to do this, not actors. This leads us to a crucial question: *What is the difference between a fiction film and a documentary?*

This is a much harder question to answer than you might at first think. When you're flipping TV stations and come across PBS, you can immediately distinguish between a Ken Burns documentary about the Civil War and a Masterpiece Theatre production of *Othello*. Certain stylistic features of documentaries allow us to recognize them at a glance, such as interviews, still pictures, and voice-over narration. But what about fiction films like *This Is Spinal Tap* or *Series 7* that appropriate the look of documentaries by using interviews and handheld cameras, though they are clearly fictional? Or what about a nonfiction film like *The Thin Blue Line*, which uses a variety of reenactments and stylistically looks a lot like a fiction film with its framing, lighting, and acting choices (see Figure 1.1)?

Throughout the writing of this book, I kept asking myself about the difference between the two kinds of film, hoping that by the time I finished it, I'd have a good answer about the differences between fiction and nonfiction film, but the more I write, read, and watch, the harder time I have answering it. So what to do? The same thing I do when I can't figure something out in my classroom: let the students try it out. First I ask them to make a Venn diagram comparing fiction films and documentaries. They write things like "are true stories" and "don't use scripts" for documentaries and "are not real" and "use actors" for fiction films (see Figure 1.2 for a typical result of discussion on this question). I do not interfere or make suggestions; I just write down what they say.

Then I give students a survey (see Figure 1.3) that asks them to try to distinguish between the two types of films. Students may want to mark both genre boxes for some items, but I force them to identify which one best describes a particular aspect of film. In the spaces beneath, I ask them to write down reasons or examples from films that would support their choice. As you and your students will quickly discover, all answers could be *both* nonfiction and fiction films. Then we spend some time going over each of the answers, trying to determine *why* the descriptors might apply to both types of films. The following discussions are my attempt to explain why each group of questions applies to both fiction and nonfiction film. The goal of your discussion after students take the survey is to provide them with reasons and examples of why the descriptors apply to both. In other words, you should try to blur the line between fiction and nonfiction film so that students can see how a documentary film is just as constructed as any fiction film.

To help promote discussion after students take the survey, let's look at each of the questions a bit more closely.

- *Question 1: Real people play themselves, not characters on film?*
- *Question 2: Uses actors to play characters in the film?*

Figure 1.1. If you saw only these shots from the documentary *The Thin Blue Line*, you could not be blamed for assuming they were from a fiction film.

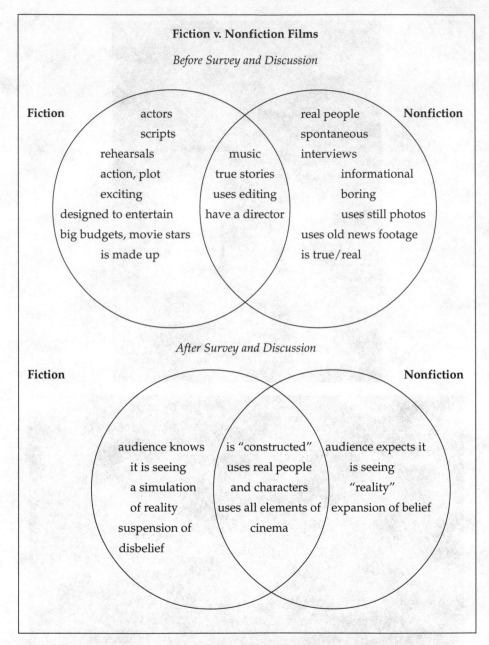

Fiction v. Nonfiction Films

Before Survey and Discussion

Fiction   Nonfiction

Fiction	music	real people
actors	true stories	spontaneous
scripts	uses editing	interviews
rehearsals	have a director	informational
action, plot		boring
exciting		uses still photos
designed to entertain		uses old news footage
big budgets, movie stars		is true/real
is made up		

actors — real people
scripts — spontaneous
rehearsals — interviews
action, plot — informational
exciting — boring
designed to entertain — uses still photos
big budgets, movie stars — uses old news footage
is made up — is true/real

music
true stories
uses editing
have a director

After Survey and Discussion

Fiction   Nonfiction

audience knows   is "constructed"   audience expects it
it is seeing   uses real people   is seeing
a simulation   and characters   "reality"
of reality   uses all elements of   expansion of belief
suspension of   cinema
disbelief

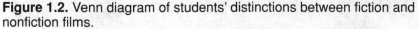

Figure 1.2. Venn diagram of students' distinctions between fiction and nonfiction films.

Fiction or Nonfiction Films: An Introductory Survey		
Put a check in whichever box you think best identifies the attribute described. In the space beneath, write the titles of fiction films or documentaries you have seen that might fit the description or reasons why the description fits.		
Which type of film—fiction or nonfiction (documentaries)—could be described with the following features:	Fiction Films	Non-fiction
1 Uses real people who play themselves?		
2 Uses actors to play characters in the film?		
3 Is intended to inform an audience about a particular topic issue?		
4 Uses the structure of conflict, climax, and resolution to entertain an audience?		
5 Focuses on historical, political, social, and/or scientific issues?		
6 Is true?		
7 Merely captures events on film as they happen without prior knowledge of how the events will turn out?		
8 The events in the film would not occur if the filmmaker had not set them in motion?		
9 Uses a script, and the director rehearses before filming?		
10 Uses cinematic elements, such as lighting, music, camera angles, and specific framing choices?		
11 Uses only natural sound recorded at the time of filming?		

Figure 1.3. An introductory survey about the differences between fiction and nonfiction films.

Figure 1.4. In case you are in doubt about how documentaries can be just as constructed as fiction films, look at this photo of the production of the nonfiction film *The Thin Blue Line* as the cast and crew prepare one of their numerous reenactments.

Typically, in a documentary you will see real people talking as themselves. As an audience watching a documentary about the Holocaust, for instance, we assume that the woman interviewed about being taken to Auschwitz is, in fact, a concentration camp survivor, whereas we know that Liam Neeson in *Schindler's List* is an actor portraying someone affected by the Holocaust. But there are any number of fiction films in which real people play themselves as cameos, such as Bob Barker in *Happy Gilmore*, which is certainly not a documentary, or John Malkovich in *Being John Malkovich*.

And though we think that documentaries use only real people, actors often play a major role in nonfiction films. Ken Burns's documentaries, for instance, have actors reading historical documents and letters. The recent nonfiction film *Touching the Void*, about a mountain climbing accident, uses actors to re-create the climbers' real-life actions. So the line between real people and actors is not nearly as wide as we might think (see Figure 1.4). And the line can continue to blur, as in another recent nonfiction film, *Assisted Living*, about the nursing home industry. This film uses real people in their real nursing homes, delivering "realistic" dialogue that was actually written by the film's director.

- *Question 3: Is intended to inform an audience about a particular topic/issue?*
- *Question 4: Uses the structure of conflict, climax, and resolution to entertain an audience?*
- *Question 5: Focuses on historical, political, social and/or scientific issues?*

When I teach genre in class, I try to help students distinguish genres by focusing on the purpose or topic of the piece. "Expository" is expected to inform, "narrative" to recount a story, and so on, but purpose and topic help us very little to distinguish between fiction and nonfiction film. While the purpose of a majority of documentaries is to inform an audience about a real-life issue, this certainly can apply to any number of fiction films. *The China Syndrome*, for instance, raises concerns of nuclear safety, and *Hotel Rwanda* questions the world's inaction in the face of genocide. In fact, it is possible to claim that with their wider releases, fiction films are potentially more effective at influencing an audience's understanding of real-life issues—historical, political, social, and scientific—than are documentaries.

As for the idea of being "entertaining," I don't imagine that any documentary filmmaker ever intends to create a boring film (sex ed films excluded, perhaps; some things we don't want to be too exciting), and most documentaries are quite entertaining through their use of humor, drama, and conflict. Many nonfiction films purposely adopt the structure of fiction films and are often intentionally constructed to follow the pattern of exposition, rising action, conflicts, climax, and resolution. Think about the built-in drama of *Hoop Dreams*, in which two boys make a run at the state championship: we meet the boys in middle school, see their conflicts along the way, and reach the climax of the film in their senior years. In fact, many documentary filmmakers deliberately rearrange the chronology of real-life events to make their film more dramatic. For example, an interview with one of the spellers in *Spellbound* in which she talks about her strategy to spell might have been conducted long after the tournament, but in the finished film it appears before the tournament begins. Audiences expect narrative, and documentaries will often construct reality to fit within a narrative the film itself has created. So, as with actors versus real people, looking at purpose and form does little to help us distinguish between the two types of film.

- *Question 6: Is true?*
- *Question 7: Merely captures events on film as they happen without prior knowledge of how the events will turn out?*
- *Question 8: The events in the film would not occur if the filmmaker had not set them in motion?*
- *Question 9: Uses a script, and the director rehearses before filming?*

These questions from the survey all get at the idea of how reality is filmed, constructed, and presented in nonfiction film. They are also at the core of this book, because most students are unaware of the ways in which documentary filmmakers can manipulate "reality." Obviously, both fiction and nonfiction films can present real-life events, as the earlier examples demonstrate, but which ones are more "real"? Our initial feeling is that of course documentaries are more real, because we have been conditioned to think so without considering the ways we are being manipulated to keep thinking this way. Is it ever possible for a fiction film to be "more true" than a documentary? Consider again the film *Schindler's List*; even though the movie is based on real events, there is no doubt that it has been fictionalized, and it uses actors, not real people, to tell its story. Now consider a documentary that uses dubious research and falsified documents to present the filmmaker's claim that the Holocaust never happened. Are you really willing to argue that the documentary is somehow more "true" than the fiction film in this example?

What about rehearsals? Obviously, fiction filmmakers often rehearse their actors before filming a scene, though some prefer to capture spontaneity with no rehearsal; improvised dialogue and actions are present in many fiction films. Nonfiction filmmakers who employ actors, as in *Touching the Void* or *The Civil War*, most likely will have to conduct some type of rehearsal. But even documentaries that do not use actors will often preview questions for their interview subjects, letting them know the topics for discussion. The filmmaker can certainly stop filming at any time and ask his or her subject to repeat or rephrase what was said. Many documentaries have voice-over narration, which of course is scripted and rehearsed before recording. Depending on the film, there can be as many retakes, edits, and reshoots in a documentary as in a standard fiction film.

We often think of documentarians as being like journalists, who collect facts and evidence in order to present them objectively to an audience. But sometimes the nonfiction filmmaker becomes a part of the story and is not a neutral observer; instead, the events in the film would not have occurred had the filmmaker not set them in motion. Think about *Super Size Me*, in which the filmmaker engaged in the experiment of eating nothing but McDonald's food for a month; while the effects on the subject's body are certainly (and frighteningly) real, the whole story is created, manufactured, and would not have occurred if the film itself had not initiated the events. The classic documentary *Nanook of the North* seemingly captures the daily life of the Inuit, until you learn that the director told the subjects of his film what events he would like to see: walrus hunting and igloo building with traditional tools, even though the people he was filming had access to more modern conveniences. Is what was presented in *Nanook* real? Is it any more real than if I hired an actor to portray an Inuit and build an igloo? The point of these examples is to show that nonfiction film can be very similar to fiction film in that the action/events/characters seen on-screen can be the result of careful construction and manipulation; what we see is still "real," but there are many more layers to what is real. This is important because our students certainly know that fiction films are not real, but they assume that nonfiction films are automatically true without realizing the layers of construction and manipulation that define their "reality"; nor are students aware of the ethical considerations that go into the making of nonfiction films, which is addressed later in this chapter.

Recently, I have been involved in the creation of three nonfiction film projects that might further illustrate these issues of the construction of reality in documentaries:

1. For a class I took last year, I made a film about the role of religion in politics. I wanted to include a scene of children in a classroom setting saying the Pledge of Allegiance (see Figure 1.5). This is not something my students normally do, but I brought in a camera and asked them to say it anyway as I filmed. Is this scene real? Yes, they were real students actually reciting the Pledge of Allegiance, but I was the one who initiated the event. I literally said "Action" to start them and said "Cut" when I was done filming. One kid started laughing during filming, so I even did a second take. In what way is this scene setting any different from what a director of a fiction film does? In what ways are my students different from actors (other than the fact that I didn't pay them)? And even more important, if you were ever to see this film, would you know that this scene had been created? Why would it matter? Would you be likely to conclude that this is a typical action in the classroom?

2. My wife and I are currently making a documentary about a production of *Romeo and Juliet*. When I interview the actors, I tell them to restate my question in complete sentences, and whenever I think they have

Figure 1.5. This shot from a documentary I made for a class that I took looks like a real group of students saying the Pledge of Allegiance, but I staged this entire scene. Does the staging make this scene any less real? Should I have failed the class?

not answered fully or even correctly, I ask them the same question again and again until I get the answer I had in mind from the beginning. Sometimes the interview subjects ask to say something again after they have thought of another way to say it. Now, on the final product, the audience will not hear my questions or see the subjects' retries, so the audience will assume that the subject got that eloquent answer the very first time. The subjects of the interviews are real people and they are giving their real answers, but these are also responses that have been carefully constructed and edited for our purposes. This doesn't make my wife or me evil or unethical, but, again, it is essential for the audience to understand how documentaries present versions of reality.

3. I was watching my wife Laura film a short nonfiction piece about a young woman who was once our babysitter. Laura had previously interviewed her about the difficulty of growing up and the changes one faces in life. Laura then wanted to have some scenes of the subject in-

teracting with our daughter Eleanor to illustrate the contrast of the innocence of childhood and the responsibilities of adulthood. On the final version of the film, there is a great shot of the young woman playing with Eleanor at the park when Eleanor runs out of the shot, leaving the young woman alone. Beautiful, sure, but real? Off screen and unbeknownst to any viewer (except you all now), I was pleading with my daughter to run to me, away from her babysitter, to create that image. I was begging her with toys, candy, anything that would make the shot work. The point of this and all of these confessions is that while documentaries are "real," that line between fiction and nonfiction is not as wide as we think.

- *Question 10: Uses cinematic elements, such as lighting, camera angles, and specific framing choices?*
- *Question 11: Uses only natural sound recorded at the time of filming?*

These questions get at the style and form we normally ascribe to fiction and to nonfiction films. If I were to ask you to picture a "typical" scene from a documentary, you would probably describe someone sitting in front of the camera being interviewed and maybe cuts to charts, diagrams, and so on. We don't normally think of documentaries as being particularly "cinematic" in their use of music, sound, and camera position, but again, there is considerable overlap between the two forms (see Figure 1.1 again). When we look more specifically at the parts that make up a documentary in the next chapter, we will see that documentary filmmakers use many of the same cinematic elements that fiction filmmakers use. A well-placed close-up is just as effective in a documentary as it is in a fiction film. A widow talking about her late husband, with a close-up on her wedding ring, would be appropriate in either film type. Documentaries also use editing techniques such as crosscutting, fades, wipes, and dissolves for reasons similar to those in fiction films. The documentary *Spellbound* crosscuts between the various spelling bee competitors in the same way that the end of *The Godfather* cuts to the various threats to the family being violently eliminated. I know, kind of odd to connect a spelling bee with a Mafia hit, but I lost my bee big time; I'm bitter.

As for sound, both types of films can use natural sound recorded during filming, but both can add additional sound and music in postproduction. We wrongly assume that only fiction films have sound tracks, but documentaries employ composers and musicians and use prerecorded music effectively. Philip Glass's haunting score for Errol

Morris's *The Thin Blue Line* is a key to expressing the film's tone and mood, and Michael Moore uses a few seconds of the Eric Clapton song "Cocaine" in *Fahrenheit 9/11* to make a claim about President Bush's military record without having to say anything himself about the drug accusations. While there certainly are documentary styles and conventions that often distinguish documentaries from fiction films, they are certainly not exclusive, and neither film type is bound to any particular restrictions.

Once my students complete the survey, we discuss how and why these attributes can be applied to both types of films. Then we create a new Venn diagram; this second one is *very* crowded in that middle section, so tell them to leave a large space (look at Figure 1.2 again for a sample postdiscussion Venn). Finally, I like to show students a few clips from fiction films and documentaries that illustrate the blurring of the lines between fiction and nonfiction film and ask some questions about the reasons for the choices the directors made; if you first show the clips without sound, you'll get better results because students won't be able to hear the voice-overs or interviews that may signal a documentary. Films that work well for exploring the lines between the two types of films are:

1. *Touching the Void* (Kevin Macdonald, 2003): a documentary that uses actors to reenact two mountain climbers' accident. How is this any different from a fiction film?

2. *The Thin Blue Line* (Errol Morris, 1988): another documentary that uses extremely cinematic framing and lighting choices in reenactments of what the subjects of the interviews describe about a police officer being shot. What is the purpose of these reenactments?

3. *The Blair Witch Project* (Daniel Myrick and Eduardo Sánchez, 1999): a fictional horror film that adopts the look of a home movie, thus giving the audience a sense that what we are seeing is really happening. What is the effect of this stylistic choice? How would the film have been different with a more typical fiction film look?

4. *This Is Spinal Tap* (Rob Reiner, 1984): the classic "mockumentary" that adopts many of the documentary features (narrator, text track, interviews, handheld camera, etc.) of a fiction film. How does the documentary form itself generate the humor? Other films of this type include *Waiting for Guffman* (see Figure 1.6), *A Mighty Wind*, and *Best in Show*.

5. *The Company* (Robert Altman, 2003): a fiction film that could very

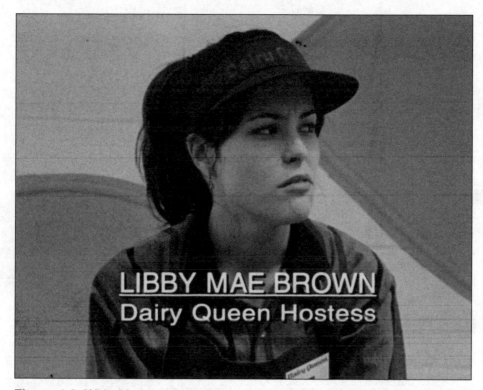

Figure 1.6. With this framing and the text track, this shot looks like it's from a documentary, but it is an image from the mockumentary *Waiting for Guffman*.

easily pass for a documentary about a ballet company, except that some of the characters in the film are recognizable actors. The dialogue looks improvised and the action does not appear to be constructed for the film, and yet we sometimes see intimate scenes that would probably not be captured in a documentary. When presenting a clip from this film, I like to ask my students to try to find the constructions of a fiction film. How do you know it's a fiction film?

In college, in a ridiculously misguided attempt to impress a girl, I took a calculus course (I lasted almost four weeks in the class; two weeks longer than it took the girl to realize I was an idiot). Before I dropped the course, the professor, in a futile attempt to get me to stay, told me that the reason I was failing was that he had to break down all my previous knowledge about math before he could build it back up again. I didn't have the heart to tell him that I had absolutely no math knowledge to break down in the first place, but I tell my students this story as we deal with documentaries in class. We need to break down our assumptions about nonfiction film; we need to reconsider what we do *not* know before we can start building up what we *do* know.

As stated earlier, I intentionally blur the line between fiction and nonfiction film so that my students can begin to recognize the ways in which documentaries are constructed and viewers can be manipulated. If all of this ambiguity has confused you as much as I was in calculus and made you want to forget the idea of using documentaries in the classroom altogether, as we move through the next chapters you'll find more specific information about what students need in order to "read" nonfiction film.

The close reader gets bonus points for recognizing that I still have not answered the question I started this chapter with about the differences between the two types of films. Even though there are a tremendous number of similarities, consider some of these differences:

1. Fiction films tend to ask us to *suspend our disbelief* about the situation presented (yeah right, thirty-year-old Catherine Zeta-Jones really is in love with seventy-year-old Sean Connery), but nonfiction film *expands our belief* in what is possible. The best nonfiction films cause us to say, "Wow, I had no idea that that could really happen."

2. I also think there is a difference in the audience's expectation of truth. No matter how much a viewer knows about the ways in which filmmakers can construct reality, he or she still has an expectation of veracity for a documentary that changes how we view the film. We don't expect accuracy in a fiction film to the degree that we do in a documentary. The factual errors in Oliver Stone's fictional *JFK* can be dismissed more easily than the time rearrangements in Michael Moore's *Roger & Me*. If you don't believe me, think about the uproar in 2006 over James Frey's *A Million Little Pieces*, a memoir about the author's battle with substance abuse. An Oprah-selected title, it quickly became a bestseller, but allegations were made, later admitted to by the author, that many of the key events in the book were fabricated. Oprah, who had first dismissed the furor as "much ado about nothing," quickly reversed herself and gave Frey and his publisher a public tongue lashing, telling them, "You conned us all." If *A Million Little Pieces* were a novel, no one would care whether the author actually went through the horrors of drug addiction, but because the book was marketed as a memoir, the audience expected reality and felt cheated when they didn't get it.

3. From watching my wife, who has worked on both fiction and non-fiction films, it's clear there is a difference in how these two types of films are conceived and produced. Even a fiction film that aspires to spontaneity usually begins with some kind of outline or script, and the film's development proceeds accordingly. Nonfiction films tend to be a lot messier. Documentary filmmakers tend to shoot a lot of footage and shape their story in the editing room afterward. This observation, like the others, is a generalization, but maybe they are helpful ones.

Additional Question to Consider about Fiction v. Nonfiction Film

1. Would you be upset if you found out that some of the scenes from your favorite documentary were scripted, reenacted, or manipulated like some of the examples previously described? Why? What does this reaction say about our expectations of documentaries?

2. What is the literary equivalent of a documentary film? What happens when an author of a nonfiction print text blurs the line between nonfiction and fiction?

3. How does the following excerpt from Tim O'Brien's *The Things They Carried* apply to the difference between fiction and non-fiction film?

You can tell a true war story by the questions you ask. Somebody tells a story, let's say, and afterward you ask, "Is it true?" and if the answer matters, you've got your answer.

For example, we've all heard this one. Four guys go down a trail. A grenade sails out. One guy jumps on it and takes the blast and saves his three buddies.

Is it true?

The answer matters.

You'd feel cheated if it never happened. Without the grounding reality, it's just a trite bit of puffery, pure Hollywood, untrue in the way all such stories are untrue. Yet even if it did happen— and maybe it did, anything's possible—even then you know it can't be true, because a true war story does not depend upon that kind of truth. Absolute occurrence is irrelevant. A thing may happen and be a total lie; another thing may not happen and be truer than the truth. (83)

Parts of a Nonfiction Film

Before we start examining nonfiction film more closely, we need to learn what makes up a documentary, and to do that, we need to help our students know what to look for and listen to. Typically, so much information comes at us in a documentary that we need a way to organize and

categorize the details. Most elements in a nonfiction film can be classified by the following three terms: the *visual track*, the *audio track*, and
the *text track* (sometimes called the "graphics track").

To help us think about these different tracks, imagine a documentary about a famous guitarist and look at Figure 1.7, a collage of images
that try to represent the following elements of this imaginary documentary.

The **visual track** is the one we generally respond to first and includes all the images we see on-screen. This can include *primary footage*, which is shot by the documentarian him- or herself, such as interviews of subjects, scenes of the surroundings, reenactments, or action
as it occurs. As presented in our example film, the footage of the interview of the musician himself is called *A-roll*. If the filmmaker moves in
to show a close-up of the subject's fingers on the guitar or a close-up on
his face, this is called a *cut-in*. But if the filmmaker then uses a *cutaway*
to a scene outside of the interview (to the subject playing at a concert,
say), or to a reaction shot of the interviewer, this footage is called *B-roll*.
When the subject is discussing his childhood, for instance, the B-roll
could be images of his old house, grade school, a street sign of the town
in which he was raised, and so on. In addition to this primary footage
created by the filmmaker, the visual track includes *archival* or *found footage* shot or created by someone else, often for an entirely different purpose, that the filmmaker uses in his or her film. Imagine that our guitarist mentions in the interview that he was influenced by Led Zeppelin; the filmmaker might then cut to a Led Zeppelin concert film made
in the 1970s or a home movie of the subject playing guitar, trying to look
like Jimmy Page. Found or archival footage can include news broadcasts, home movies, other films, and so on. *Still images*, such as photos,
maps, charts, and newspaper headlines, are a part of this track. For our
example, these might include yearbook pictures of the guitarist as a boy,
album covers, and magazine articles. Still images could be found or archival images, or they might have been created solely for the film.

It is always interesting to consider which visuals were shot for
the film and which images have been recontextualized and for what
purposes. A film titled *The Atomic Cafe*, for instance, uses government
news releases from the 1950s to illustrate how naive we were about the
dangers of atomic weapons. The power of this film comes from looking at the archival footage through modern eyes. It is essential to remember what we discovered in the last section about the use of cinematic
elements in nonfiction film. This visual track needs to be analyzed for
shot type, angles, editing, lighting, etc. When the filmmaker shows the

Figure 1.7. The text track of a documentary consists of the text and graphics that are added to the film in postproduction. Shots A, E, and H include a text track. Notice that, as in shot H, the text can appear by itself in a shot. Questions to consider about a text track are, what is included and for what intended effect. Shot C, though it includes words, does not contain a text track; students often make this mistake. For the visual track, shot B is an example of a cut-in, while shots C and E are examples of cutaways (often called B-roll), in which the director goes from the interview, in this case, to some other scene. Shot C is an example of archival footage that the filmmaker probably did not film him- or herself but instead found and used for different purposes. It is essential to pay close attention to the B-roll to see what other information a director is trying to convey. When examining the visual track, we should also consider questions such as, why a close-up in shot D, why the low angle in shot G, and why would the interviewer be included in shot F. The answers to these questions will give us much greater insight into the film's perspective and purpose.

subject in a close-up or from a low angle, he or she is doing so for a purpose, and we need to figure out why. In Appendix A, you will find a list of film terminology that identifies key cinematic elements and their effects. For additional information on these terms, my book *Reading in the Dark* (2001) includes a full chapter on these elements with examples and film clips.

Sound in film can influence us in subtle yet powerful ways, and if we're not paying close attention to the **audio track**, we might miss a filmmaker's intended meaning. As we did with the visual track, it is helpful to break down the audio track of a nonfiction film into its parts. The first and most prominent are *voices*, which consist of *dialogue* and *narration*. In our documentary of a musician, the dialogue would obviously include the guitarist talking, and perhaps we also hear the filmmaker asking questions. Dialogue, though, is not restricted to interviews; the film might capture the musician talking and working with his band or with his family and so on.

Narration, too, can take many different forms. The filmmaker could be narrating *on-screen*, saying something like, "Let's go now to see our musician at work," or the narrator could be *off-screen*, recorded at a later time but inserted at a particular place: "I was very nervous that day when I went to his studio." Both of these examples use an "I" narrator, someone we know is a real person in the movie, often the filmmaker him- or herself. Some films, though, employ a disembodied narrator (sometimes referred to as a *"Voice of God" narration*, similar to the third-person omniscient in literature); we see this type of narration most often in history and science films that present a complex issue to an audience unfamiliar with the topic. We might hear this type of narration as: "He was born on . . ." And though the voice may belong to a famous person, like Morgan Freeman in *March of the Penguins*, this narrator does not interact with the action on-screen.

In addition to voices, the sound track also includes *music*, which can be classified as *diegetic* or *nondiegetic*. Diegetic music is what could logically be heard by anyone at the time of filming. What we hear as our guitarist plays and sings as the filmmaker records is considered diegetic; a radio playing during an interview would also be diegetic. Nondiegetic sound, on the other hand, would be music that is added after filming and intended solely for audience reaction; it could not logically be heard by the people in the film itself. Imagine that our guitarist says that Bob Dylan was his biggest influence, and immediately we hear Dylan's "Like a Rolling Stone." The guitarist during the interview wouldn't suddenly turn around to look for where the song is coming from; he cannot hear it. This song has been added so that the audience can make a connection between the guitarist and Dylan. Other examples of nondiegetic music in our imaginary documentary would be the music playing during the opening titles or between scenes, or dramatic music during an emotional scene, as when the guitarist cries thinking about his wife's death.

A final element of the audio track is *sound effects*, which like music can be either diegetic or nondiegetic. Diegetic sound effects might include any ambient sounds at the time of recording that might be significant enough for the filmmaker to include or even highlight in his or her finished film. If our guitarist has a family, the filmmaker might want to be sure we can hear the sound of a baby crying in the background during the interview; this sound might reveal something about the guitarist that we might not have learned otherwise: maybe he is completely indifferent to the crying baby, for instance. Nondiegetic effects include any sound added or deliberately manipulated after filming for a particular purpose. Imagine our guitarist reminiscing about the time he was shot at by an angry fan; the filmmaker might choose to include the sound of a gun going off. Obviously, the guitarist could not hear the nondiegetic gunshot at the time of the interview, but the filmmaker wanted to connect the audience to the story as much as possible. Understanding the different types, uses, and purposes for sound allows students to see even more of the ways in which the filmmaker is influencing them.

The third aspect we need to examine in documentaries is the **text track**, or graphics track, which is made up of all the writing and graphics that are added to the film and which often overlays the visual track. These can include charts, drawings, or other graphics. Most commonly in documentaries, this track takes the form of *subtitles* that identify the person who is speaking ("Jim Thompson, Childhood Friend," for example), the location of the scene, or the source of stock footage, or that translate dialogue spoken in a foreign language. (Note: Sometimes students make the mistake of thinking that any words found on-screen are a part of the text track. If a subject is wearing a T-shirt sporting text or if there is graffiti on a wall behind the subject, these are still elements of the visual, not the text, track.) The text track in our example of the musician might include the lyrics to a song he is singing or identify the year of one of his concerts. Some interesting questions to consider about the text track are what is included and identified, what is not, and why.

Some documentaries intentionally do not translate foreign languages so that the audience experiences the culture in the same way as the film-maker. The text track can also provide viewers with information that could influence their feelings about a subject. For instance, if an inter-view subject is identified as a member of the ACLU, this can arouse sympathy or antagonism, depending on a viewer's political perspec-tive. If the subject's political affiliation is not identified, the viewer's reaction will be dependent more on what the subject says than on his or her association. How the filmmaker chooses to identify a subject can be revealing. Michael Jackson, for instance, could be identified as "pop star" or as "acquitted child molester." Both are truthful, but depending on the text track, we get entirely different impressions of him. Some documentary films employ a significant amount of material on the text track, sometimes avoiding voice-over narration altogether. We have a great tendency to believe automatically what we see on-screen and take it as fact, but we have to remember that the text track is just another tool, like sound and visuals, that documentary filmmakers can use to construct the meaning they want.

While just about any random documentary you have or you can borrow from a history or science teacher would work well for helping students to practice identifying the three tracks of a nonfiction film, the following are clips I have used successfully for this purpose. Be sure to try out a note-taking form like that in Figure 1.8 (you'll find a blank one in Appendix B). Because it is a lot of information for students to handle all at once, I generally assign one track to each student for the first two minutes and then add another track every two minutes after that. They grow comfortable with the note taking pretty quickly.

As always, all of this leads to the question my students dread to hear: Why? Why does the director use a specific lighting choice on the visual track? Why did he or she use that particular song on the audio track? Why did he or she *not* identify the newspaper from which the article was taken on the text track? When your students can answer these questions, they will be able to explain the specific effect of these choices, and most important, they will be able to understand and communicate the ways in which nonfiction filmmakers construct their films for their particular purposes. The overall goal, of course, is that students prac-tice these analytic skills with nonfiction films before applying them to nonfiction print texts. Specific opportunities for this are presented in Chapters 2 and 3.

Parts of a Documentary		
Title: *Outfoxed* Year: 2004 Director: Robert Greenwald		
Visual Track	*Primary/archival footage, still pictures, etc.* Found footage: Repeated images of FOX motto: Fair and Balanced. Close-up of dirty phone.	
Audio Track	*Voices, music, sound effects, etc.* Song "Dirty Laundry." Stalinist. Garbled anonymous employees' voices. "Kick 'em when they're down." People say they are scared.	
Text Track	*Identifications, subtitles, information, etc.* Graphics of Murdoch taking over the world. People identified as "former" employees. Ailes is identified as Reagan and Bush strategist, just as he said he'll be objective.	
On the back, in a topic sentence, identify the key visual, sound, and/or textual elements used, and in a paragraph explain the *effect* of these elements on the viewer.		

Figure 1.8. Parts of a documentary form.

Outfoxed (Robert Greenwald, 2004)

0:02:41–0:08:38

This film is an analysis of FOX News and its owner, Robert Murdoch. The film accuses the network of having a right-wing bias and of using deceptive and manipulative techniques in presenting the news. While both charges are probably true, this clip shows that director Greenwald is himself deceptive and manipulative. The best way to see Greenwald's own liberal bias is to closely examine the three tracks of a documentary film. The clip starts with an illustration of Murdoch's media reach: graphics of the newspapers and TV and radio stations Murdoch owns fill up the entire screen, and ominous music plays on the sound track. This dissolves into a picture of the Earth, half in shadow, with the numbers "4.7 billion" and "3/4 of population" on top of the image. Notice that all of the people interviewed are identified on the text track as *former* FOX News personnel; no current employees are given an opportunity to respond. During these interviews, listen closely to some of the charged word choices on the audio track, such as "apparatchik," "the flu" (referring to Murdoch's growing influence), "propaganda," and "Stalinist system." During a press conference with Roger Ailes, CEO of FOX Broadcasting, the text track identifies him as a "former media strategist for Nixon, Reagan, and Bush Sr. campaigns," which, though undoubtedly true, is clearly intended to paint him as biased. When Ailes says that he wants to do balanced journalism, we hear the song "Dirty Laundry" on the audio track, with the chorus "kick 'em when they're up, kick 'em when they're down."

Questions to Consider

1. What is the overall feeling about FOX News that has been created in this clip?

2. What information included in the visual, audio, and text tracks helps to create this feeling or attitude?

3. What is the effect of so many *former* FOX employees being interviewed? How did the director film the anonymous sources, and what is the effect of these choices? How could they have been included more objectively?

Super Size Me (Morgan Spurlock, 2004)

0:00:00–0:05:04

This is the opening sequence of a documentary that explores the role of fast food in the United States by filming a man (the director) who decides to eat nothing but McDonald's food for a month. The film begins with a group of young kids (most of whom are overweight) singing a song about how much they love Kentucky Fried Chicken, Pizza Hut, and McDonald's. Next, we hear the disembodied (for now) voice of the narrator list a series of facts—over a visual of the American flag—about the obesity problem in the United States, a problem the visual track displays through images of overweight people and that the text track further illustrates with various charts about the growing (pun, why not?) problem in this country. As this sequence continues, we see how the director is effectively using the three tracks of his documentary to establish the dominant role that fast food, McDonald's in particular, has in our lives. Before the opening titles, the narrator appears on-screen and announces himself as a subject of the film. As the opening titles run, we hear the song "Fat Bottomed Girls" and see more pictures of overweight people eating fast food. This establishes a tone that is both serious and mocking; Spurlock is not above using sophomoric humor to make a serious point.

Additional Questions to Consider about Parts of Nonfiction Films

1. Which one of the three tracks influences viewers the most? Why?
2. As a viewer, what is the difference between a film that employs a narrator and one that does not? As a filmmaker, why would you choose to use a narrator or not?
3. Does the presence of nondiegetic sound and music make a film feel less real? Why or why not?

Editing in Nonfiction Film

After students have become familiar with the three different tracks in documentaries, they need to begin learning how editing, the assembling of these three tracks, creates meaning. To truly understand nonfiction films, we have to understand the role that editing plays—and the power it has—in the creation and presentation of these films. And the editing actually starts the moment the filmmakers turn on the camera and when they turn it off.

Picture a documentary in which a filmmaker who wanted to make a film about an English class chose to film my second-period class. When I see the final version, my first question that editing addresses is why the filmmakers didn't choose my sixth period?! It's a much better class, and it doesn't have Jason in it! The fact that they chose to film second period instead of sixth made a huge difference in the final product. When the filmmakers caught me rolling my eyes when Jason asked for the third time to go to the bathroom, the moment might be "real," but it's not really "typical" of me—really. Another immediate question comes up as soon as the filmmakers stop filming: why did they miss the great point that came up a little later in the classroom? It would've made me look like Teacher of the Year. So, simply identifying the potential consequences of when the camera goes on and off is an essential step in understanding the power of editing and leads to some of the most important questions to ask when watching documentaries: *I know what I'm seeing, but what am I **not** seeing? What was left out of the final version, and why?*

A classroom activity to further explore editing is to have four students keep a list of everything that happens in a class period the day *before* you want to do this activity. They should try to keep track of what students and you say, what actions occur, and other details from around the room (clock ticking, papers rustling, phone calls, etc.). Collect these lists from the students, make copies, and, the following day, distribute them to everyone in class. Then ask students to imagine certain points of view that someone might have about your class: you are the best/ worst teacher ever, the class is made up of brilliant/stupid students, the class is exciting/boring, and so on. After generating a list of various points of view on the board, divide students into small groups and assign a different point of view to each small group. Each group then highlights which events, actions, descriptions, and dialogue from the lists created by students the previous day would support their point of view. When students share the items that support their position, the class can easily recognize that even though everything on those lists "happened," it's the way the events are presented that creates meaning.

Typically, when we speak of editing, we think less about what is chosen to be included in a film or not and more about what happens after the filming: the process of putting the sound and the images together into a particular order for a particular effect. In fiction films, this might mean cutting back and forth between the good guy and the bad guy in a chase in order to create suspense, but in nonfiction films, this process can take on an even greater significance because the filmmakers are editing what is supposed to be "real." Imagine two documentaries about the same presidential candidate; one filmmaker is a supporter and the other is critical of the candidate. Both filmmakers record the same speech about the economy at a rally in Ohio, in which the candidate said, "Yes, unemployment right now is high, but I feel that America is moving forward again." In their final versions, the supporter edited the speech to include only the line "America is moving forward again" and shots of smiling and approving faces in the crowd, while the song "What a Wonderful World" plays on the sound track. The other filmmaker used only the line "Unemployment right now is high," after which we see a graph that shows unemployment going up and the song "A Downbound Train" can be heard on the sound track. Now, both of these films are "true," and neither inaccurately represents the events, but clearly the point that each of the filmmakers wanted to make is much different, which they communicated through their editing choices.

This leads me to the only mathematical formula I know. When I discuss editing in nonfiction films with my students, I tell them that:

Image + Image + Audio + Text = Possible Meanings

While I wish I could take credit for inventing this concept, Sergei Eisenstein, the Soviet filmmaker and theorist, beat me to it by about a hundred years. His theories on "intellectual montage" propose that meaning results from the "collision" of images (and for us in the twenty-first century, we can add sound and text to this collision). When Michael Moore, for example, uses the song "What a Wonderful World" with images of U.S. bombs dropping all over the world, the meaning (and irony) comes from the juxtaposition of the information presented.

To figure out what the filmmaker is trying to say (**possible meanings**), we have to look closely at the pictures (**images**) he or she presents in combination with other pictures and what is heard (**audio**) or seen on the screen (**text**). The true essence of the example of the two documentaries on the political rally comes out only when you examine the way in which the songs and images are edited together. The line "America moving forward" added to smiling faces with an upbeat song obviously creates a positive feeling in the audience.

There is nothing necessarily untruthful or unethical about this editing, but once students can look critically at how a nonfiction film is constructed, they will better understand how to analyze texts for theme, tone, and point of view, all of which are explored in Chapter 3.

Once students have a good feel for how editing creates meaning, let them practice with a clip or two by using the full note-taking form (see Appendix B), which asks them to focus on the three tracks of a nonfiction film (defined in the previous section). Once they know what to look for and have a good grasp of the terminology, they will be well prepared to discuss these types of films effectively.

The following film clips work well to introduce students to the power of editing and to give them an opportunity to practice their math skills.

Fahrenheit 9/11 **(Michael Moore, 2004)**

1:18:11–1:22:09; Chapter 20 on DVD; Rated R

No one wants to like Michael Moore anymore. His arrogance and self-righteousness inflame many, but his filmmaking ability and especially his editing are on full display in this film. Even if you disagree with his politics, you should admire his skills. You could pick out almost any section of this film to examine its editing—shots of the Bush administration grooming themselves for interviews, the song "Cocaine" played over a visual of Bush's military record, and so on—but this scene about the media and their cheerleading of the war effort is an excellent place to illustrate how editing creates meaning.

The clip begins with Moore narrating, "Well, at least we have an independent media," and then cuts to a series of prominent newscasters and reporters revealing—oftentimes proudly—their bias in support of the war and the troops, with Katie Couric notably quipping, "Navy SEALs rock!" It is the clash of Moore's audio with these images and voices that creates the meaning. The irony of Moore's opening statement becomes even clearer when the strains of "America, the Beautiful" can be heard beneath the images of bombs going off and soldiers shooting.

The juxtaposition of images and sounds becomes even more affecting as Moore cuts immediately from the soldiers' coffins that the media were unable to show to what he calls Bush's "party on a boat," when the president landed on the aircraft carrier to declare an end to major combat operations. Again, the real meaning—Bush is indifferent to the pain of the war—comes through the collision of images, text, and sound. Shots of Bush glad-handing the sailors are shown as the theme song to "The Greatest American Hero" ("Believe it or not, I'm walking on air. . . . Flying away on a wing and a prayer. Who could it be? Believe it or not it's just me") plays on the sound track. The meaning of this ironic statement is clear through the editing: the media have falsely dubbed Bush a hero while missing the opportunity to identify real heroes.

But the most devastating cut comes at the 1:20:03 mark, when Bush says that the United States and our allies have prevailed. If you are teaching a group of younger students, you might want to stop here because Moore cuts right from Bush's words to a violent explosion in Iraq right in front of a pair of soldiers; on the sound track for a few seconds is an unearthly silence and then comes a series of shots of wounded American soldiers and the diegetic sound of screaming and chaotic orders. The final key editing sequence is when President Bush at a press conference, overlaying slightly ominous nondiegetic sound, exhorts the terrorists in Iraq with the line, "Bring 'em on." Moore cuts from this line to horrific images of the American contract workers in Fallujah who were tortured, burned, and hanged. (Again, be careful about using this section with younger students; you can easily stop at the 1:20 mark and present enough information to be successful in this activity.)

Questions to Consider

1. This section of the film is highly critical of President Bush. How would you describe the filmmaker's feelings toward the president, and how does the editing reveal this?

2. How do the music and other sound elements in this scene reveal the point that the filmmaker is trying to make?

3. If this film were going to praise the president, how would it have been edited differently? What would have been left out and what would have been added? Why?

4. How does the filmmaker use music, his narration, or the images as irony?

Powaqqatsi: Life in Transformation (Godfrey Reggio, 1988)

0:50:52–0:54:50

While I'm not a huge fan of this very popular series of mostly wordless films about the perils of modern life that also includes *Koyaanisqatsi* and *Naqoyqatsi* (maybe I don't like them because I don't know how to pronounce them), just about any sequence from any of the films will demonstrate the effect that juxtaposition plays in editing. The filmmaker's overall point is communicated through the collision of images. This sequence starts off with a long pan (there are a lot of long pans in these films) of a nondescript apartment building, and then we see the following images: young African girls marching, more apartment buildings, soldiers with sharpened bayonets marching just like the girls, crowds in China walking in slow motion, crowds in India sitting and waiting, more marching, an empty office building, police in riot gear, cars in slow motion in a tunnel, and last, a spot of sun on an office building. In each image, the people are portrayed as either lifeless or automatons; the connections between the indoctrination of children and the military/police is made clear by the closeness of the images to one another. Nor is there any escape: homes, offices, and public places are all represented in this sequence. Even though I don't know how to pronounce it, I did learn what the title *Powaqqatsi* in the Hopi language means: "An entity, a way of life, that consumes the life forces of other beings in order to further its own life." I usually tell my students the meaning of the title before we see the clip so that they can try to relate what they see to this concept; besides, it makes me look real smart.

Questions to Consider

1. What images are most closely related? What is the filmmaker's intention in mirroring them in this way?

2. What images are most dissimilar? What is the filmmaker's intention in juxtaposing them in this way?

3. How does the music enhance the point being made?

Born into Brothels (Ross Kauffman and Zana Briski, 2004)

0:00:05–0:02:17; Chapter 1 on DVD; Rated R

This film is a portrait of children who live in the red-light district of Calcutta, India (see Figure 1.9). One of the directors, Zana Briski, lived in the area and taught a group of kids how to take photographs. She felt compelled to help these children out of the fate that is in store for them, especially the girls, by getting them into good schools outside of their troubled neighborhoods. This scene is from the very beginning of the film. Ominous music, which plays during a shot of moths fluttering around a lightbulb, dissolves into nondiegetic voices, low and indistinct murmurings, which then lead into an up-tempo, driving, Indian-sounding song using a high-pitched flute, drums, and a plaintive-sounding vocal. The visual track, meanwhile, cuts quickly between images of brothels and close-ups of children's eyes. The images we see of the brothels, often blurred and dark, are of women standing in lines, often in bright-colored saris; men counting money; alcohol being poured and consumed; and children playing amidst it all. Every five or six shots, the director cuts back to the eyes of the children. Obviously, the children are not watching these street scenes at this time (and were probably not filmed at the same time), but the images are edited together to give us the impression that this is what the children have to see each day. The images of the streets around the brothels are shot from a very low camera angle, suggesting a child's view (though on the commentary, one of the directors says he had to film the brothels surreptitiously with the camera down by his side to avoid being caught filming). In just over two minutes, with powerful juxtaposition and effective sound layering, this clip establishes the central premise of the film: these children need to get away from this life.

Questions to Consider

1. Where are the images in contrast to one another? When do they seem to complement one another? What is the effect?

2. Describe the tone created through the editing. What role does the music play in establishing this tone?

3. Why does this scene make an effective opening to the film?

Figure 1.9. The opening of *Born into Brothels* is perfect for examining editing. Notice how the cuts between close-ups of the girls' eyes and images of scenes from the brothels create a sense of horror at the girls' surroundings. When you listen to the scene, you'll notice how the sound track adds to these feelings.

Additional Questions to Consider about Editing in Nonfiction Films

    1. What are the ethical concerns about editing? As soon as a film-maker cuts from one image to another, he or she has made an editorial choice that may not necessarily follow exactly what happened in real life. Think, for example, about that movie being made about my second-period class and me. Would it

be ethical for a filmmaker to insert a shot from my fourth-period class without clearly informing the audience of the change?

2. Does a film with fewer cuts feel more real to us? Why? Is it necessarily more real? Why or why not?

3. How is editing in documentaries similar to or different from editing in fiction films? Does editing play the same role and have the same purposes in both types of films?

Styles and Modes of Nonfiction Film

Just as there are different genres of fiction films—horror, comedy, action, etc.—there are multiple types of documentaries. While perhaps the majority of documentaries that students see are informational, fact-based films, it would be a mistake for us to try to lump all nonfiction film together into a single classification. The following sections discuss the main forms, or *modes*, of documentaries, each of which has its own style and conventions. These classifications are derived from Bill Nichols's *Introduction to Documentary* and *Representing Reality*, which are amazingly dense texts that I wish I could claim to fully understand. Luckily, Bushra Azzouz, a gifted filmmaker and instructor at the Northwest Film Center in Portland, helped me make sense of these definitions.

It's important to note that these modes are not exclusive. The clips I suggest using in the classroom and the examples I describe below do not always restrict themselves to a single mode; there is plenty of overlap, sometimes even within these short clips. The following is, however, still a worthwhile exercise for helping students to begin questioning why a film utilizes a particular mode and how all nonfiction films, regardless of how they appear, are constructions of reality and an expression of the filmmakers' points of view.

Typically, I give each of my students a description of one of the following modes and ask them to become "experts" on that mode, perhaps thinking of films they have seen that fit the definition. Then I show them the clips identified on pages 35–39 and ask them to try to determine which mode most closely describes the film.

Expository Mode

In the *expository mode*, which is the most familiar form to our students, the filmmaker explains a topic to an audience. An expository film on nuclear power, for instance, might provide history and background on the issue as well as interviews with various people knowledgeable or concerned about the topic. The goal of this documentary might be to give the audience a deeper insight into the dangers (or benefits) of nuclear power and to convince them to do something about it. Within this mode are two different types:

- *Direct address*: in which the audience is directly addressed through an on-screen narrator, through an off-screen narrative voice ("the Voice of God"), or through a purposeful text track that serves as narrator. In the nuclear power example, the audience might hear (or read) things like: "Nuclear power has its origins in the Manhattan Project during World War II." This narrative voice—either the filmmaker's voice, a disembodied narrator, or a text track—acts as a guide for the viewer throughout the film, providing context, background, and information the filmmaker deems significant.

- *Indirect address*: (also referred to as "Poetic/Impressionistic") in which the audience is not spoken to directly by a narrator or the filmmaker. This does not mean there is no talking in the film, only that no singular voice guides the viewer, though the viewer is still expected to draw conclusions about the issue through analogy, pattern, and inference. In an indirect address film on nuclear power, the audience might hear various people talking to one another about the dangers of nuclear power while the visual track shows pictures of Three Mile Island and Chernobyl. The point is not clearly stated by a narrator, but the audience gets the meaning ("Move far away from a nuclear plant.") just the same.

Observational Mode

A filmmaker working in the *observational mode* tries to be "a fly on the wall" in order to make the audience feel as if they are there. The filmmaker tries to "disappear," and he or she attempts to capture the reality of the situation by not interacting with the subjects at all. No questions are asked of the subjects, no interviews are conducted, and oftentimes there is a minimum of editing or cutting away to other elements on the visual track. For instance, an observational film on the nuclear power issue might capture a town meeting at which community members discuss the threats posed, but the filmmaker would probably not layer the Chernobyl pictures over the townspeople's concerns; the visual track would probably remain on the meeting itself. Typically, observational filmmakers use a minimum of B-roll and nondiegetic sound, preferring to include only the sound that is captured at the time of recording. Films in this mode are sometimes referred to as *direct cinema*, and students who watch MTV's *The Real World* or *Big Brother* have experience with this style. I've heard that C-SPAN is also an example of this style, though I have to confess I've never been able to sit through more than a minute of it. Because of the look of observational mode films, there might be a tendency to think of them as more "real" than films in other documentary modes, but you should remind your students about the ways in which nonfiction films—even these types—construct reality. (Speaking of *The Real World*, anyone who thinks of seven beautiful twenty-somethings who live in spacious, trendy Manhattan lofts as "real" needs to read this book—badly.) Observational mode films can be, and often are, expository as well, but they differ from that mode in the ways they present the issue through their stylistic choices and ethical philosophy of documentary filmmaking, which we explore in more detail later in this chapter.

Interactive Mode

Rejecting the intentional detachment of the observational mode, filmmakers who use the *interactive mode* of nonfiction film are actively involved in the issue and in the lives of their subjects. Not only do we often hear the questions asked of the interview subjects, but it also becomes obvious that the film and the filmmaker are affecting the action seen on-screen. The subjects of the film are acting differently than they would had they not been involved in the making of this film. The interactive mode can take on many different styles and forms, including what has been called cinema verité (cinema truth), which is oftentimes confused with direct cinema and is discussed further in the section on the history of nonfiction film.

Most reality TV falls into the interactive mode: do you think that person would really eat a rat if he were not on the show *Fear Factor*? The classic TV show *Candid Camera* is a perfect example of the interactive mode because the camera is capturing people's reactions that the show's producers themselves have created. The situations—and the humor—would not have existed were it not for the show and the show's producers. Think of Nick Broomfield, a filmmaker in the Michael Moore school of confrontation, whose films often become about his difficulty in getting the story he wants. In his *Biggie and Tupac*, he interrogates the imprisoned Suge Knight, whom he suspects of Tupac's death, and in his *Kurt & Courtney*, he has himself filmed railing about Courtney Love, though there has been no evidence linking her to Kurt Cobain's death. Or, consider a film titled *Stranger with a Camera*, in which the filmmaker interviews a woman whose father died when she was a young girl. It becomes clear that the process of talking about her father for this film is helping the woman to grieve and to come to terms with her father's death. In our fictitious nuclear power example, an interactive mode documentary might have the filmmaker actively involved in the fight against a nuclear power plant. In fact, it's possible that his or her camera's presence actually creates a larger town hall meeting and protests. The film cannot be removed from the events it documents.

Reflexive Mode

The term *reflexive* is also used in fiction films to describe a film that is aware of itself as a film. In other words, the filmmaker working in this mode knows and presents the constructions of reality or ethical considerations that are a natural part of documentary filmmaking but which are rarely acknowledged. This type of film, for example, might lead the viewer to question the film's own veracity by presenting multiple versions of a scene, edited in different ways. Often, reflexive documentaries raise questions, problems, and dilemmas about the very act of creating a documentary in the first place. Our nuclear power example, created in this mode, might show an interview with a plant official but then cut jarringly, midsentence, to an environmental activist who responds to the official's comments. Obviously, all films cut from subject to subject, but the suddenness of this cut and the obvious manipulation make the audience highly aware of the editing, which is a part of documentary filmmaking that often goes unnoticed. In short, a reflexive documentary will often pull back the curtain of documentary filmmaking and give the audience a glimpse of the inherent difficulties in trying to capture a universal truth. In the reflexive mode, documentary filmmakers remind us that we are seeing a construction, an approximation, of reality.

Since many films are a mixture of these modes, the previous sections are not intended to be hard-and-fast definitions but instead to give our students a way of talking about the choices a nonfiction filmmaker makes. After you have introduced these modes to your students, use the chart in Figure 1.10 (or a blank chart, which can be found in Appendix B) and the following clips to help them practice identifying the modes and the stylistic choices that often go along with the particular modes.

Super Size Me **(Morgan Spurlock, 2004)**
0:44:10–0:47:14; Chapter 18 on DVD

This clip quickly demonstrates the **expository direct address mode**. Spurlock includes facts, data, interviews, and even animated sequences

Modes of Nonfiction Film

As you watch each of the following clips, try to determine which documentary mode is most prevalent; the modes certainly overlap, but which one seems dominant? Then provide a reason for your choice of mode and describe some of the stylistic choices (shot type, editing style, use of sound, etc.) that this film demonstrates.

Title	Dominant Mode	Stylistic Elements of the Mode
Super Size Me	Expository: direct address	Statistics, charts, graphs, on-screen narrator giving us facts and conducting interviews, nondiegetic music
Baraka	Expository: indirect address	Images: still and moving. Nondiegetic sound, no narrator, no text track
The War Room	Observational	Camera moves a lot. Only diegetic sound, no interviews, no text track
Fahrenheit 9/11	Interactive	Interviews, confronts subjects, voice-over, on-screen narrator
Six o'Clock News	Reflexive	Voice-over, discusses documentaries, footage from many sources

To consider: What are the stylistic elements for each mode? In other words, how could you recognize each mode by examining how the information is communicated to the audience? Why do some modes use elements that others do not? Do any of the modes feel more "real" to you? Why is this?

Figure 1.10. Modes of nonfiction film chart.

to make a specific point about the negative effect of junk food advertising on children. We hear his voice leading us to the conclusions he wants us to draw. While there certainly are elements of the interactive mode here (every interview is, in a sense, an interaction), the film is more appropriately described as expository because of its intention to explain a topic to the audience. If you compare it to Michael Moore's *Fahrenheit 9/11*, you'll see that through the interactive mode Moore is using, he is documenting the *reaction* to his questions, whereas here Spurlock is trying to gain insight into his topic by documenting the *information* that his subjects are presenting. This mode is by far the most typical of documentaries that are widely available, so any other clip that demonstrates these characteristics will work just as well as this one.

Baraka (Ron Fricke, 1992)

6:29–10:55; Chapter 3 of DVD

This scene, an example of the **expository indirect address mode**, is without dialogue or narration and comprises a series of shots of various religious people from around the world saying their prayers. The point the film is clearly trying to make is that despite differences in geography and culture, the world's religions are quite similar, evidenced by the transitions between scenes that make a link between various religious icons and practices. No narrator leads us to this point, but the imagery and the audio track leave little doubt in the viewer's mind. Ask students why there is no information provided on the text track and how the sound track serves to link the cultures. Other widely available indirect address documentaries you might consider are those in the Qatsi Trilogy (*Koyaanisqatsi*, *Powaqqatsi*, and *Naqoyqatsi*) directed by Godfrey Reggio.

The War Room (Chris Hegedus and D. A. Pennebacker, 1993)

0:00:00–0:04:25; Chapter 1 on DVD

This opening sequence from a film about Bill Clinton's presidential campaign is a great example of the **observational mode** of documentary. We do not hear any narration, and no one speaks directly to the filmmakers for interviews. While we certainly feel the presence of the filmmakers as they decide what to focus on, the camera seems to merely capture and record the action as it occurs. This does not mean that the people on screen are not at some level reacting to the camera's presence, but the filmmakers do not involve themselves in the action as they would in an interactive mode documentary, nor directly addressing the audience through voice-over or other overt means as they would in the expository mode. Other filmmakers who work in this mode that you might consider instead include Frederick Wiseman (*High School, Titicut Follies*), Albert Maysles and David Maysles (*Salesman, Gimme Shelter*), D.A. Pennebaker (*Don't Look Back*), and Chris Hegedus and Jehane Noujaim (*Startup.com*).

Fahrenheit 9/11 (Michael Moore, 2004)

1:54:50–1:56:58; Chapter 28 on DVD

The **interactive mode** requires that the filmmaker be actively involved in the action we see on screen, and *involved* is always a good word for Michael Moore. In this scene (Figure 1.11), Moore wonders why so few children of Congress members are serving in Iraq. Moore then decides to confront members of Congress as they approach the Capitol building and record their reactions. He is trying to capture some kind of truth by documenting the congressmen's unguarded reactions to his questions. But questions to consider about this scene and other interactive films include: How does Moore's presence affect how the subjects react? Are we seeing their "true" reactions? Would they have responded differently if they had not been ambushed by Moore's camera? All of these are key questions for this mode of documentary. Another effective scene to illustrate the interactive mode is Moore's interview with Charlton Heston at the very end of *Bowling for Columbine*. Other filmmakers who like to work in the interactive mode are Nick Broomfield (*Biggie and Tupac, Kurt & Courtney*), Ross McElwee (*Sherman's March*), and sometimes Barbara Kopple, especially with *Harlan County USA*, in which the striking union workers protect her and her crew from the strikebreakers.

Six o'Clock News (Ross McElwee, 1996)

0:23:32–0:29:00

This is as clear an example of the **reflexive mode** of documentary as I can present to students. Ross McElwee is a documentary filmmaker who obsessively films his own life. In this sequence, a film crew comes to film McElwee as he films them filming him. McElwee captures the reporter and film crew entering his apartment three times as they try to get a "spontaneous" feel. Reflecting on the film crew's third entrance, he says that he never asks people to reenact moments for his films, so he wonders if his films are more "real" than theirs. But he also comments that both he and they will edit this sequence for their own pur-

Figure 1.11. No one illustrates the interactive mode of documentaries as well as Michael Moore. In this shot from *Fahrenheit 9/11*, he is inserting himself into the action he is filming. Is he getting the natural responses of the congressmen he is confronting, or is he creating an unfair and unreal situation?

poses. McElwee, if fact, incorporates a shot of himself holding his camera that could only have come from their footage of his own film. As they interview him, McElwee blocks out his own diegetic voice in favor of his nondiegetic voice-over, which comments on his inability to articulate the points he would like to have made at the time. The sequence ends with shots of the final show as it aired on TV. All of McElwee's comments, editing, and visuals are designed to reveal the construction of reality that goes on, both in TV news and in his own film. Though the concept of reflexivity is challenging, through this clip students are usually able to see how the film seems to be commenting on itself as a film. Other reflexive documentaries that are discussed in detail in Chapter 4 are Errol Morris's *The Thin Blue Line* and Jennifer Baichwal's *The True Meaning of Pictures*.

Additional Questions to Consider about Nonfiction Modes

1. Why does the observational mode somehow feel more "real" to us? Is it? Is the filmmaker working in the observational mode able to capture a reality that a filmmaker working in another

mode might not? What are the ethics binding an observational filmmaker that might not restrict another filmmaker?

2. Is it possible that the ambush techniques of an interactive filmmaker capture a truer sense of reality? Consider two films about a politician, one interactive and the other observational. The observational film often will capture the politician with his "public face" on, while the interactive filmmaker may surprise the politician into sharing something that has not been filtered through his speechwriters, lawyers, handlers, etc. Could this be more "real" than the whitewashed public face?

3. Does a reflexive documentary treat its audience more ethically than other modes since it reveals its own "self" to the viewer?

Ethical Issues in Nonfiction Film

Sometimes people complain about racial or cultural stereotypes that are presented in fiction films or point out historical inaccuracies in fiction films depicting real-life events, but when they discuss these types of films, the topic of ethics rarely comes up. And yet, Bill Nichols in *Introduction to Documentary* titles his first chapter "Why Are Ethical Issues Central to Documentary Filmmaking?" One answer, and a key element to explore with your students, is that documentaries use real people to tell stories that purport to be from real life. Therefore, documentary filmmakers and their audiences need to be aware of the ethical issues that can arise in the creation and the viewing of nonfiction films.

The issues, though varied, mainly focus on a filmmaker's ethical treatment of the people he or she presents in the film (the *subjects*) and the filmmaker's treatment of his or her *audience*. With my students, I use the term *ethics* not in any moral capacity, but rather to mean the rules of conduct that a group of professionals might agree to follow. Doctors, lawyers, and teachers have laws they must follow, but they also have a code of professional ethics that help guide their decisions. To help students think about the ethics of documentary filmmaking, I first present my students with a series of often competing "rights" that everyone— the filmmaker, the subject, and the audience—has when participating in a nonfiction film experience. I write these on the board:

1. The filmmaker has a right to tell his or her story in the manner best suited to the material and in the style, form, and tone that best fits the filmmaker's purpose.

2. The subjects in a documentary have the right of "informed consent," meaning prior knowledge of the purpose of the film and how the filmmaker intends for them to be represented.

3. The audience has a right to know when material presented in the film has been constructed and has a right to be free from intentional deception.

I am sure we could identify rights other than these, including those of the producers to make a profit, a corporate sponsor to have its company presented in a positive light, or a viewer to be entertained or educated. My use of the word *rights*, though, makes it appear that there might be some kind of documentary board that dictates the ethics and levies penalties on offenders, but there is none; nor are the guidelines for ethical consideration formalized or agreed to by all filmmakers.

Then I provide students with a series of "ethical dilemmas" (see Figure 1.12) that a documentary filmmaker might face. I typically assign two to three scenarios to each small group and ask them to discuss what they would do in the situation and to identify the ethical considerations of each. In other words, whose "rights" (as identified above) are paramount, and why? I tell my student that if they arrive at an answer too quickly, they have not fully explored all of the ethical considerations of the scenario. After they have had a chance to discuss in their small groups, they present their scenarios to the class and justify why they chose to act in the way they did.

It is important to stress that there are no right or wrong answers to these dilemmas; they are jumping off points for a discussion of the factors that go into creating, participating in, and watching nonfiction films. As noted earlier, there is no governing board of ethical behavior in documentary film. One documentarian may feel that all reenactments are unethical, while another incorporates them regularly; one may think that using a single, off-the-cuff remark by an interview subject is fair game, while another might choose not to use it because it is not representative of the entire interview. The ethical line changes over time and varies with the filmmaker's own personal beliefs.

A few of the scenarios described come from real situations that I have either witnessed or read about. Some also have been adapted from a great text titled *Documentary Filmmakers Speak* by Liz Stubbs, in which she interviews various filmmakers about all aspects of making a documentary, including the ethical boundaries they do or do not cross. Situation 4 comes from the fiction film *Broadcast News*, in which a news reporter does re-create tears for an interview, but it illustrates how the line can be easily crossed in nonfiction filmmaking. Michael Moore's theatrics with Charlton Heston at the end of *Bowling for Columbine* come to mind. Filmmaker Liz Garbus faced a situation similar to dilemma 5 and decided that she could not ethically give the family money because then

Ethics and Dilemmas in Nonfiction Film

Imagine that you are a documentary filmmaker facing the following situations. What would you do, and why? What are the ethical considerations in each scenario? Keep the following "rights" in mind as you consider each:

- The filmmaker has a right to tell his or her story in the manner best suited to the material and in the style, form, and tone that best fits the filmmaker's purpose.

- The subjects in a documentary have the right of "informed consent," meaning prior knowledge of the purpose of the film and how the filmmaker intends for them to be represented.

- The audience has a right to know when material presented in the film has been constructed and has a right to be free from intentional deception.

1. While making a film about the newspaper business, you have learned over several months of filming that journalists regularly lie in order to do their jobs. On one day of filming, you capture one of the journalists, who is aware you are filming and had given consent, making a date with a woman who is not his wife. Do you include this footage in your final film, knowing that his wife will most likely see it?

2. In the course of an interview, your subject uses a racist term. In several other opportunities, you have never heard her use it again. When she sees your footage, she asks you to remove the racist term. Do you take it out?

3. In a film about the coal industry's polluting effect on the environment, you manage to secure an interview with the president of the country's largest coal company. But before you film the interview, he asks that you sign a document giving him approval of the final version of the interview portion on the film. Do you agree to the conditions or do you make your film without the interview?

4. In the course of a very emotional interview with a subject, you begin to cry, but you only have a single camera, which is currently filming the subject. After the interview is over, you think it might be a powerful addition to the film to show that her story made you cry, so you have your cameraperson switch positions and film you crying. It takes you a moment to work the tears back up, but you do so, and the final film will make it seem as though you cried during the interview. Considering that you really did cry the first time, do you reenact the tears in this manner?

5. You are doing a film about the effects of poverty and homelessness in the United States. One family that you have been filming for several months has had its lights cut off and is close to being evicted from their home. While you are not rich, you certainly have enough money to get their power turned on. Do you give them the money? What if they ask you for it?

continued on next page

Figure 1.12. Ethical dilemmas in nonfiction film.

Figure 1.12. continued

6. In a film about drug use by teenagers, one of your subjects offers to shoot up heroin as you film him. Knowing that drug use is both illegal and dangerous, would you do this, knowing that he will shoot up anyway? Then, imagine that he says he has no money to pay his rent. Do you give him money knowing that he might use it for drugs?

7. You are a lifelong Republican and you are making a film about a Democrat running for president. In a speech caught on tape, the candidate says, "If my opponent's behavior is typical of a Christian, then I want nothing to do with Christianity." You could very easily edit this line to read "I want nothing to do with Christianity." Would you do so?

8. In a film about the effects of clear-cutting in old-growth forests, you interview a timber executive who says that the forests they clear are still healthy, even though you know this is not entirely true. You do not have the funds to travel to one of his forests to prove he is lying. As you edit your film, you consider cutting to footage of a devastated forest, but it is not one that his company cleared. Do you include it? Do you let your audience know it is not his site?

9. You have been filming a boy for several years as he pursues his dream of making it to the NBA. One day when the boy is playing basketball in the park, his father shows up to buy drugs. You did not mean to capture this on film, but it happens right behind the boy, who turns to watch. The father is not the subject of your documentary, but he is a part of the boy's life. A year later the father is off drugs. Do you still include the scene? What if the father or the boy objects?

10. You are a cameraperson for a reality TV show that presents families in crisis and how a professional nanny can come in and fix the family. As you film, one child attacks another child physically and starts to smother him with a pillow. Do you put down your camera and stop this? What might prevent you from stopping the child?

11. You are interviewing a rather paranoid person, who offers to show you a gun he keeps under his bed at night. When he shows you, he suddenly begins waving the gun around, acting very unstable, and at one point even putting the gun to his own head. Do you continue to film him? Do you try to stop him? Why or why not?

12. You are an American making a film in Cambodia about the devastating effects of the unexploded bombs that were dropped in the 1970s. A farmer finds a bomb, still loaded with TNT and a detonator. The farmer wipes away the dirt to reveal an American flag. He turns to you and says, "Do you want your bomb back?" It's a powerful line and an effective image, but unfortunately you were not filming at the time. Do you ask him to re-create the moment for you?

she and her actions would have influenced the story she was trying to capture. Once filming ended, however, she regularly sent food and school supplies to the family. The director of *Hoop Dreams*, Steve James, had to deal with dilemma 9 and decided to include the footage only because the father wanted it included as a testament to the dangers of drug use (see Figure 1.13). I am ashamed to admit that I was watching the reality show *Nanny 911* when I saw dilemma 10. There was no doubt that the child being attacked was genuinely struggling for air, and once he was released he was visibly shaken and hurt. Now, maybe a producer was off-screen yelling at the other child to stop and we did not hear that, but that cameraperson never stopped filming. I haven't watched the show since. Michael Moore faced dilemma 11 when he was interviewing James Nichols, the mentally unstable brother of Oklahoma City bomber Terry Nichols. Moore kept on filming, of course. Dilemma 12 happened to Skye Fitzgerald while making *Bombhunters*. Much to his own regret, his ethics got in the way of a great shot: he did not have the farmer re-create the scene.

A final ethical concern I discuss with my students is the issue of who has ownership of the stories that are made into films and the right to present them. Does the documentary filmmaker really have the ability to tell someone else's story accurately? Let's say I decided that I wanted to make a film about the Japanese education system in order to draw some kind of parallels to our own. No matter how long I stay in Japan, I will always be an outsider, even if I could miraculously learn the language. Mine would always be the perspective of a westerner. Would my film look anything like one made by a Japanese teacher? Is it ethical for me to present my film as the reality of the Japanese school system? Oftentimes filmmakers address this ethical concern head-on. In the wonderful film *Born into Brothels*, about children growing up in and around poverty in India, one of the directors points out several times that she lived there herself long before beginning this film. The directors also find a unique way to be sure that the children get to present their views directly by presenting the photographs the kids took of one another and their surroundings.

But this issue of who owns a story can also lead to charges of exploitation. Documentary filmmakers make money on other people's stories, and sometimes these are stories of poverty, pain, or disaster. Sometimes directors will enter into financial arrangements to pay their subjects during filming and perhaps even a percentage of the profits, but often the subjects receive no compensation. Not all exploitation is monetary. The documentary *The True Meaning of Pictures*, which centers

Figure 1.13. Is it fair to include in the documentary *Hoop Dreams* these shots of Arthur's father buying drugs while his son looks on? The director decided to include them, but not without wrestling with the ethics of the situation.

on Shelby Lee Adams, who regularly photographs the poverty in Appalachia, raises the question of whether the subjects of his pictures are being used and even ridiculed. Adams counters these accusations mainly by saying that since he is from the area, he is only showing a truth that he is ethically justified in presenting.

Additional Questions to Consider about Ethics in Nonfiction Films

1. Why is addressing ethical concerns essential to documentary filmmaking? Why are ethics not as important in fiction films?

2. Should a film be excluded from consideration as a documentary for the Academy Awards if it contains scenes that have been staged, reenacted, or scripted? Should there be a limit to the number of reenactments? At what point does a documentary with a lot of reenactments become a fiction film? Should the audience be made aware of which scenes have been reenacted? Why or why not?

3. Is the potential exploitation of a subject worth the potential benefit that could be gained with the exposure of the issue the film raises? For example, is it okay to film mental patients suffering the most degrading treatment if it brings about essential reforms in mental heath care, as Fred Wiseman's *Titicut Follies* did?

4. Can someone outside of a culture accurately and ethically depict that culture? What will the filmmaker have to do in order to accomplish this?

History of Nonfiction Film

Just as we blanch a bit when we see the CliffsNotes in the hands of our should-be-loving-*The Great Gatsby* students, I am a little concerned about including a section here that tries to compress over one hundred years of filmmaking into 2,000 words or less. But while a number of books provide an excellent overview of the history of the major movements in nonfiction filmmaking (especially *Documentary: A History of the Non-Fiction Film* by Erik Barnouw, from which I drew heavily), I have yet to find one that is much of a page-turner. So even though my summary will be no Grisham, it will at least be short.

The history of documentaries is also the history of film technology; as the means to make films and the access to cheaper and easy-to-transport equipment increased, documentary forms and styles changed. Documentaries also respond to history itself, changing and adapting as wars break out, social problems arise, and cultural standards fluctuate. The documentary, as you will see, is far from a static form.

The following headings are my attempt to classify sometimes as many as fifty years into a single section. Sometimes they are designated by a person, sometimes a specific film, a movement, or some phrase that I invented solely for this purpose. I like to provide my students with a brief overview of the form's history, and I often show a few short clips from some of the films listed below so students can see the changing nature of nonfiction film.

The Lumière Brothers (1890s)

The earliest period of documentary film history is actually also the earliest period of filmmaking in general. The first films of any kind shot and exhibited were by the French inventors Louis and Auguste Lumière, who filmed daily occurrences throughout Paris and marketed them with such riveting titles as *Arrival of a Train*, *Workers Leaving the Lumière Factory*, and *Feeding the Baby* (I don't know, maybe they sound better in French). The brothers' company quickly expanded operations and filming, presenting local documentaries like these in countries all across Europe. Unless we can imagine a world without moving pictures, we cannot conceive of how amazing this experience must have been for these early audiences. Even a train pulling into a station seemed like a miracle. The first thirst for film was not to see the comedies or dramas of the theater and stage that would soon dominate the motion picture industry; instead, the audience wanted to see the world. Barnouw reprints a schedule from an exhibition in 1897 New York that includes a gondola scene in Venice, a fish market in Paris, and German dragoons leaping hurdles. Documentary filmmakers in this earliest period also learned the power of editing and constructing "reality," such as using tabletop miniatures to re-create battle scenes to fill out or manipulate what they had captured on film. During this period, it became clear there was money to be made on this new medium, and the shift to the fixed sets, casts, and scripts of the Hollywood studio system had already begun to make documentary film less profitable; audiences were hungry for entertainment.

Nanook of the North (1922)

Nonfiction filmmakers had long been visiting remote locales, but until director Robert J. Flaherty made *Nanook of the North*, few went beyond the novelty film stage, something akin to watching someone else's home movies of a family trip. *Nanook*, a feature-length film about the traditional life of an Eskimo (Inuit) family, was considered a box office blockbuster. It is significant in the history of nonfiction film because it used many of the elements that would later be considered the defining traits of the documentary form. Flaherty employed many techniques of fiction film (close-ups, establishing shots, parallel editing) to present a reality that had as much drama, conflict, and emotion as any scripted fiction film (see Figure 1.14). He effectively uses subtitles and lighting to create specific effects for his audiences, which were apparently impressed with his results, though he was never able to match the financial success of *Nanook*. The film clearly tapped into a human desire to know and learn about a world outside of mainstream experiences that continues in much of the nature and travel documentaries produced today. I just got back from *March of the Penguins*, which took us deep into Antarctica, where, judging from how cold even those penguins are, I will not be visiting.

John Grierson (1930s)

An admirer of Flaherty's work, John Grierson saw a way out of the funding difficulties Flaherty faced by working with government agencies and corporations who shared his political views. Praising Flaherty's technique but ultimately rejecting his interest in remote and primitive countries, Grierson thought that documentaries should focus on the social issues and concerns of his native England. Film, Grierson argued, should be a pulpit, a "hammer, not a mirror" (Barnouw 90). Documentaries at this time began to look a lot like the expository mode described in the previous section; films such as *Housing Problems* and *Night Mail* identified key social problems and, through extensive and politicized narrative commentary, argued for particular solutions; there is no claim of objectivity or neutrality in these films. Grierson's influence spread to other countries, including the establishment of the short-lived U.S. Film Service, which produced "issue" documentaries like *The River*, about problems along the Mississippi. His influence as a muckraker (in its most flattering meaning) can still be seen today in films such as *Super Size Me*, *The Corporation*, and *Enron: The Smartest Guys in the Room*.

World War II (1930s–1940s)

The need of all countries involved in World War II to persuade their citizens to fight and die in the struggle led to extensive use of documentary film. Films such as *Triumph des Willens* (*Triumph of the Will*) and the Why We Fight series (both discussed below in the section on propaganda) built on Grierson's idea of film as a hammer and were extremely effective tools in the war effort. The March of Time newsreels became

Figure 1.14. A classic image from a classic documentary, *Nanook of the North*. Does it diminish the effect of the knowledge we gain from the film to learn that director Flaherty told Nanook to use spears in the hunting scenes even though more modern weapons were available?

important sources of information before and during this period, though these mini-documentaries always contained a lot of reenactments that often used paid actors to portray real people, a feature that would later become ubiquitous in TV shows like *America's Most Wanted*.

Direct Cinema (1950s–1970s)

Until this time, documentary filmmaking had been burdened by the size of the equipment and the inability to capture sound and images simultaneously. But as 16mm cameras became available and developments were made in synchronous sound technology, documentarians were able to minimize their own presence and become the proverbial "fly on the wall," recording the world with little intrusion on reality. Filmmakers working in this observational style—Richard Leacock, D. A. Pennebaker, Fred Wiseman, and others—rejected Grierson's thesis approach, which forced viewers to participate in a particular position. Rather, in attempting to remain as objective as possible, they avoided the traditional use of voice-overs, archival images, and nondiegetic sound, all of which can act as the filmmaker's editorialized statements. Instead, they followed and recorded action wherever they found it: schools, rock concerts, the workplace, people's daily lives, political campaigns, and so on. One of the most celebrated films from this era is *Salesman*, by Albert and David Maysles, in which the filmmakers follow a group of door-to-door Bible salesmen for over two months. Proponents of direct cinema knew that true objectivity is impossible because the filmmaker still determines what to record and the way a film is edited, but they felt that through the minimization of their role, they could present reality with fewer filters, allowing the viewer to draw conclusions. Sometimes viewers, critics, and even filmmakers call this style *cinema verité*, but see the distinction discussed in the following section. We still see the influence of the direct cinema approach today in TV shows like *Big Brother* and in work by filmmakers such as Barbara Kopple (*American Dream*; *The Hamptons*; *Wild Man Blues*) and Chris Hegedus and Jehane Noujaim (*Startup.com*).

Jean Rouch (1960s–1970s):

Like Flaherty and Grierson, Rouch is a key figure in the development of the documentary, and he is probably best known today for coining the term *cinema verité*, literally, "cinema truth." Rouch shared the practitioners of direct cinema's dislike for seemingly objective voice-over narration and for added music or titles on the text track. He felt, however, that a filmmaker should not be a mere observer, but instead needs to become actively involved in his or her subjects, and the final film should reveal this interaction. Rouch felt not only that the presence alone of the camera affected the subject, but that this relationship was the point of documentary film, because the camera itself can cause the subjects to be more truthful. The terms *cinema verité* and *direct cinema* are often incorrectly thought of as synonyms, but Barnouw (254–55) and Bill Nichols (citing Barnouw) summarize the differences as follows. In each type, the filmmaker is

Direct Cinema	Cinema Verité
invisible	participant
an uninvolved bystander	a provocateur
waiting for a conflict	creating a conflict

Early cinema verité films are Rouch's own *Chronicle of a Summer* and *The Sorrow and the Pity* by Marcel Ophüls. Instead of simply observing and recording people talking, filmmakers associated with cinema verité began to give prominence to the interview, in which the filmmaker directly questions his or her subjects. It is difficult to believe that the interview, a staple of contemporary documentary work, is such a recent addition. Interviews, especially the dialogue between subject and filmmaker, can be particularly revealing, and you can see this at work today in films by Errol Morris (*Gates of Heaven*, *The Fog of War*), Michael Moore, and Nick Broomfield. Though Rouch might be disgusted, we can also see his influence on reality TV, discussed later in this chapter, with its obvious manipulations of the subjects, who clearly are behaving differently than they normally would because there is a camera pointed at them. Cinema verité also has influenced fiction filmmaking; movies and TV shows that employ a handheld camera and use gritty, realistic dialogue are often characterized, inaccurately perhaps, as using a cinema verité style.

Video and First-Person Documentaries (1980s)

Once again, technology created new opportunities for documentary filmmakers, this time with the development of inexpensive and easy-to-use video production equipment. The costs of film production no longer had to include film, processing, or transfers to video for broadcast. The result was a leap in TV-produced documentaries, including locally created films for public access cable stations around the country. This was also a time when some documentarians stopped looking outside for subjects and began looking inward. A classic example is Ross McElwee's *Sherman's March*, which begins as a traditional documentary about the Civil War general's devastating march to the sea, but then quickly turns into an exploration of McElwee's difficulty in finding a woman to love. Personal documentaries like this one and the work of Peter Adair, Ralph Arlyck, and others are sometimes referred to as film essays, and in telling their own personal stories, documentary filmmakers force viewers to reflect on their own.

Ken Burns, PBS, and Cable Television (1990s–present)

Ken Burns's five-part, eleven-hour Civil War film of 1990 was a huge success on PBS, giving the network one of the largest audiences for a documentary ever and spawning similar films on baseball, jazz, and the American Revolution that use what quickly became identified as the

PBS style: still photos and actors reading letters and historical documents. PBS, also the producer of the Frontline series and the exhibitor of the POV series of documentary films, has in many ways created the audience for these alternative programs, which provide viewers with information on an extremely diverse range of topics. HBO, Sundance, and the Independent Film Channel also either provide essential funding for documentary work or give filmmakers an opportunity to share their work. Considering the vast reach of these stations, it is safe to assume that people have more access to nonfiction film than at any time in history.

Digital Video and the Web (today and the future)

Since technology has always been a prime mover in the history of nonfiction film, we cannot ignore the power that digital video will have on the form, but I don't think we have really begun to feel its effects. Not only have mini-DV cameras allowed for even more portability with extraordinary picture and audio quality, but also now anyone with a computer, a basic editing program, and a connection to the World Wide Web can become his or her own documentary editor and distributor. The ability to gather, edit, and share digital images is now so easy and inexpensive that we're bound to see a movement toward more personal, local, and independent films that can be shared with an online community. Already there are film festivals that take place entirely online. In 2005 we saw the rise of the Web log (or "blog"), in which people can share their thoughts on a range of issues with anyone who logs on to their site. Podcasts, too, allow people to share audio and video images with anyone who has a computer and an MP3 player. Once further technology brings down the cost of bandwidth and the speed for downloading, I predict that we will see personal documentary blogs and podcasts, giving audiences further insight into the world, which has been the ultimate goal of nonfiction film throughout its history.

Other Nonfiction Film Experiences

In addition to documentaries, a number of other nonfiction film texts that students encounter have importance in the classroom. Each of the following—propaganda, reality TV, and blended genres—have immediate connections with the real world that our students need to be able to decode in order to see the manipulation and construction at work.

Propaganda

I put off writing this section for a long time. It's not that propaganda isn't an important element of nonfiction studies that we need to help our students recognize. Nor did I delay because the subject does not belong in a book about documentaries, since propaganda, even the most outrageous government lie (Men landing on the moon?! Yeah, right.), is intended to be received by its audience as truthful. No, I put it off because I knew it was going to be really, really hard to write. Have you ever tried to define *propaganda* for your students? Maybe it's just me, but I always struggle with it. A typical dictionary definition reads something like "an effort to persuade a group of people to adopt a particular position." So, when my students deliver their persuasive speeches in class, are they spreading propaganda?

There are, of course, other associations with the word, such as "systematic," "deceptive," "distortion," and "indoctrination," that may keep my students from reaching this threshold in their speeches, but why is it that whenever we discuss propaganda, we tend to look to the past or to those who think differently than we do? For instance, a quick Web search of the word *propaganda* usually brings up hundreds of sites about Nazi and Soviet propaganda. Further searches might reveal a few examples of U.S. propaganda during World War II, usually in the form of posters urging citizens to buy war bonds. We can look at our history and quickly identify the propaganda going on and maybe even chuckle a little bit at people's naiveté in believing such obvious manipulation.

But does propaganda go on today in this country? Ask Democrats why they can't win an election and they'll blame it on right-wing propaganda. If you ask conservatives what's wrong in this country, they might say the propagandistic techniques of the left trying to influence America's social values on, say, homosexuality, welfare, and the war. Just as those on the left don't really see the liberal bias of PBS and the *New York Times*, those on the right can't see some of the same propaganda techniques used on different subjects over at FOX News. Just as fish do not really recognize the water all around them, we are not aware of propaganda because its very nature is designed to fit seamlessly into the fabric of our lives, nudging us in a few key areas.

That said, however, I think it is dangerous to use the word *propaganda* to describe the opinions of those who propose counterarguments, because it diminishes the true power of the word; it cheapens it to say that Michael Moore, for instance, uses propaganda in *Fahrenheit 9/11*.

He resorts to a lot of editing techniques that might be considered deceptive, but like my students reading their speeches, Moore would love to be powerful enough to be considered a spreader of propaganda to the masses. Every film has a point of view, but not every film (even one designed to be persuasive) is propaganda.

A definition that feels right to me comes from "A Habit of Lies—How Scientists Cheat," an online article by John A. Hewitt:

> [Propaganda is] a way of presenting a belief that seeks to generate acceptance without regard to facts or the right of others to be heard. Propaganda often presents the same argument repeatedly, in the simplest terms and ignores all rebuttal or counter argument. It is essentially self-interested and often associated with authoritarian regimes. Propaganda is often used to convey official descriptions of reality, when it may be allied with bureaucratic control of media, censorship of opposing opinions and deliberate misinformation.

So, before turning your fish/students loose to start hunting for the water/propaganda in our own fishbowl/time period, my colleagues Dave Lickey and Cindy Lucia recommend that you first try out this definition on your students by associating it with the most prevalent form of propaganda today: advertising. An ad, like propaganda, targets our most primitive motives: fear, safety, sex, power, aggression, and so on. Good propaganda, like a good ad, is impenetrable to reason and logic. Have students look for and bring in athletic shoe, automobile, or cosmetics ads (for older students, consider showing them beer and liquor ads). Look at the slogans and graphics to see how many parts of Hewitt's definition can be identified in these ads. All the typical advertising and persuasive techniques we teach students—e.g., bandwagon, weasel words, snake oil—are readily apparent and have immediate applications to political propaganda.

Next, ask students to look over the list of characteristics associated with propaganda in Figure 1.15, titled "Propaganda? You Decide." Some of these qualities come from Hewitt's definition and some are unique to what Susan Sontag calls the "Fascist Aesthetic." Then, using Figure 1.16, let students read an excerpt from George Orwell's *1984* and then watch sections of two films from World War II—Leni Riefenstahl's *Triumph of the Will* and any of Frank Capra's Why We Fight films, which are generally considered to be propaganda—in order to practice and clarify their sense of the term (see the following sections for discussions of suitable film clips).

Propaganda? You Decide

After you read or watch the following texts, answer *yes* or *no* to the following questions:

Text #1: Orwell's *1984* Text #2: Riefenstahl's *Triumph of the Will*
Text #3: Capra's *Why We Fight* film Text #4: _____

	1	2	3	4
Is the message created and disseminated by the state or an organization of similar power and reach?				
Does it seek acceptance of a particular idea or position?				
Is it intended to appeal more to emotion than to logic and reason?				
Does it eliminate others' positions or rights to be heard?				
Does it make the same point repeatedly?				
Does it ignore or summarily dismiss opposing arguments?				
Does it present an "official description of reality"?				
Does it appear to be self-interested?				
Does it use sleight of hand or deception to make its point?				
Does it present a sense of historical inevitability and infallibility?				
Does it seem or strive to be "invisible" or deliberately difficult to recognize as persuasion?				
Does it ignore the complexities of reality?				
Does it seem to deify a leader or a political party?				
Does it appear to offer simple readings of the complexities of history?				

Compare two of the pieces you examined by writing an explanation of how they manipulate their viewers in similar and different ways based on the answers to the questions above. Use specific examples from the texts to support your points.

Figure 1.15. Check sheet for determining whether text is propaganda.

Excerpt from *1984* by George Orwell

[*The following excerpt describes the end of a film that the citizens watch every day:*]

The Hate rose to its climax. The voice of Goldstein had become an actual sheep's bleat, and for an instant the face changed into that of a sheep. Then the sheep-face melted into the figure of a Eurasian soldier who seemed to be advancing, huge and terrible, his sub-machine gun roaring, and seeming to spring out of the surface of the screen, so that some of the people in the front row actually flinched backwards in their seats. But in the same moment, drawing a deep sigh of relief from everybody, the hostile figure melted into the face of Big Brother, black-haired, black-moustachio'd, full of power and mysterious calm, and so vast that it almost filled up the screen. Nobody heard what Big Brother was saying. It was merely a few words of encouragement, the sort of words that are uttered in the din of battle, not distinguishable individually but restoring confidence by the fact of being spoken. Then the face of Big Brother faded away again, and instead the three slogans of the Party stood out in bold capitals:

WAR IS PEACE

FREEDOM IS SLAVERY

IGNORANCE IS STRENGTH

But the face of Big Brother seemed to persist for several seconds on the screen, as though the impact that it had made on everyone's eyeballs was too vivid to wear off immediately.

[*This excerpt is from a television broadcast the main character hears:*]

"Comrades!" cried an eager youthful voice. "Attention, comrades! We have glorious news for you. We have won the battle for production! Returns now completed of the output of all classes of consumption goods show that the standard of living has risen by no less than 20 per cent over the past year. All over Oceania this morning there were irrepressible spontaneous demonstrations when workers marched out of factories and offices and paraded through the streets with banners voicing their gratitude to Big Brother for the new, happy life which his wise leadership has bestowed upon us. Here are some of the completed figures. Foodstuffs—"

The phrase "our new, happy life" recurred several times. It had been a favourite of late with the Ministry of Plenty.

Figure 1.16. Excerpt from *1984* by George Orwell.

After students have had a chance to identify propagandistic techniques in advertising and examine and define propaganda from the past, they should have an opportunity to find and examine current propaganda. They can look at coverage of political conventions, inaugurations, government press releases and Web sites, FOX News or the *New York Times* (depending on your or their political views), election ads, and so on. In early 2005, there was considerable coverage (mainly liberal) accusing the Bush administration of using propagandistic techniques. Examples these critics cite include:

- Showing President Bush in a fighter pilot suit landing on an aircraft carrier, declaring an end to major combat operations in Iraq with a banner reading "Mission Accomplished." The aircraft carrier was just off the California coast but had been ordered to turn around so that only open sea would appear behind the president.

- Holding "town meetings" on issues, though the audience is made up entirely of Bush supporters.

- Manipulating the coverage of Jessica Lynch, the female soldier captured in Iraq at the beginning of the war.

- Paying newspaper and radio commentators to promote particular policies.

- Allowing partisan supporters to pose as reporters and ask questions during press conferences.

- Distributing government press releases that looked and sounded like actual TV news broadcasts to local news stations without identifying their source.

- Paying Iraqi newspapers to publish "good news" articles that were written by the U.S. government but published under Iraqi bylines.

Of course, every administration tries to control its message and to present its leader in the best possible light. I remember that a lot of time and effort went into the planning of the Camp David photo op with Yasir Arafat and Ehud Barak to make sure that then-President Clinton was situated perfectly between the two as they shook hands.

How do these recent examples hold up compared to the historical examples? Put them to the test questions and see. When you or your students find pieces they suspect of being propaganda, they should examine them using the same questions they used for the historical pieces (see Figure 1.15 again). My general feeling is that, yes, the U.S. government does practice propaganda on us, although without state-run media (FOX really does not count), it takes a lazy and complicit news media and a complacent audience to be successful. While we like to pride ourselves on being much more sophisticated than the audiences who bought into the propaganda of the 1940s, the practitioners, too, have grown more sophisticated; without increased education and vigilance, we cannot hope to understand or counter the messages being sent our way.

1984 (George Orwell, 1948)

In these two short excerpts, the main character, Winston Smith, encounters a propagandistic film and radio broadcast. The film shows Goldstein, the country's enemy, as a bleating sheep dissolving into a ferocious soldier, until the calm, reassuring face and voice of Big Brother, the country's leader, takes over the screen. The three slogans of the Party are obvious examples of reductive logic and methods for controlling thought. The television broadcast triumphantly announces success after success, for which the Party is always responsible. Note: a film version directed by Michael Radford that accurately and effectively captures the first excerpt is widely available. It is the opening scene in the film.

Triumph of the Will (Leni Riefenstahl, 1935)

First, a little background on the film is necessary. Riefenstahl, a popular German dancer and actress before beginning to direct her own films, was commissioned and personally selected by Adolf Hitler to document a huge weeklong rally in Nuremberg in 1934. From the very beginning, the project was intended to present a powerful and united Germany in the midst of a cultural and political rebirth to a world already skittish about Nazi aspirations. Riefenstahl was not at the rally as a journalist or typical documentarian, catching what she could of the events; rather, the events were specifically constructed to best suit her film (see Figure 1.17). The schedules of speakers, parades, arrivals, and departures were timed to best take advantage of light and settings. She had a crew of over a hundred people and more than thirty cameras positioned at various points in systematic locations to present Hitler and the rally in the best possible light. The film is mostly wordless; there is no voice-over, only selected identifications on the text track and excerpts of key speeches delivered by Hitler and high-ranking Nazi members. Much has since been made of Riefenstahl's role as a propagandist for Nazi ideology, and she clearly succeeded in the stated mission of the piece: Hitler, the Nazi Party, and the German people certainly do seem overwhelmingly powerful. The effective documentary *The Wonderful, Horrible Life of Leni Riefenstahl* (Ray Müller, 1993) explores Reifenstahl's culpability in great depth. What we are left with is a problematic film to watch with our students, who have seen Hitler portrayed only as the embodiment of evil; rarely have they seen him speak or address the people for extended periods of time. Of course the film glorifies Hitler, but we need to examine exactly how Riefenstahl does this so that we

Figure 1.17. While the Nuremberg rally certainly did happen, the entire event was staged for Riefenstahl's camera in *Triumph of the Will*, in which, through the director's positioning, Hitler's army and the German people are always presented as unified and powerful.

can recognize the techniques closer to our own home and time period. Students find the entire film a bit slow, so I recommend looking at three short sequences that give students enough to get the idea of the larger piece.

Sequence One: 0:01:35–0:09:42; Chapters 2–3 on DVD

The first image after the black screen is the Nazi symbol of the eagle and swastika, immediately after which we learn that this film was commissioned by Hitler, which is true and is important to note since it cannot be acknowledged that there might be things out of his control. After the text track summarizes recent German history, which identifies the German "crucifixion" and "rebirth" dated backwards from this moment in Nuremberg, we see a plane (presumably Hitler's) in the

clouds, beginning to descend from the heavens to the medieval-look-
ing city below. I'm not overstating the symbolism that Riefenstahl creates here of a god coming down to earth. Hitler is greeted as a conquering hero by the adoring masses, and on the open-top car ride from the
airport, we see many low-angle shots of Hitler, a benevolent god who
is nice even to children, as evidenced by the series of close-ups of smiling kids. On the way to Hitler's hotel, we also see a number of low-angle
shots of German architecture, reflecting strength and unity. The only
sounds we hear are crowds cheering and the nondiegetic triumphant
march on the sound track.

Sequence Two: 0:34:16–0:41:21; Chapter 9 on DVD

In this scene, Hitler reviews the Reich Labor Corps, which presents its
shovels and marches to a drumbeat rhythm exactly like that of a military squadron. Riefenstahl's planning and coordination with the rally
organizers is apparent in the close-ups she gets here of the men as they
list the various regions of the country from which they come, thus pro-
jecting a unified German face to the rest of the country and the world.
"One people, one leader" is heard on the sound track, and she cuts to a
close-up of Hitler. Though we do see individual workers/soldiers in
close-up, they quickly become indistinguishable from one another in
the rows and rows of men in long shots, signifying the importance of
uniformity and conformity as Hitler praises them for their work and
service. The sequence ends with lines and lines of workers, armed with
their shovels, marching directly toward the cameras. If you let the film
run just a few minutes further, you'll see some amazingly beautiful shots
at the night rally—beautiful, but scary.

Sequence Three: 1:45:06–1:50:23; Chapters 17–18 on DVD

I suggest starting this clip at some point in the midst of Hitler's final
speech to the party faithful. I also suggest that you ask half of your class
to pay attention to what Hitler says and the other half to watch closely
for the cutaways that Riefenstahl inserts. Hitler's words are about uni-
fication and eternal domination, while the cutaways are of Nazi iconog-
raphy and reaction shots of attendees. After the speech, Rudolf Hess
asserts, "The Party is Hitler, but Hitler is Germany, as Germany is
Hitler," in a statement that could not have made it past Logic 101. Crowd
shots of arms raised in *Sieg Heil* salutes move into close-ups of the Nazi
swastika, which then dissolves into the final image of the film: a long
line of soldiers marching again toward the camera and us.

While they are not a part of the film, there are two quotes I like to share with my students from Joseph Goebbels, Nazi minister of propaganda: "The rank and file are usually much more primitive than we imagine. Propaganda must therefore always be essentially simple and repetitious." Also, "If you tell a lie big enough and keep repeating it, people will eventually come to believe it. The lie can be maintained only for such time as the State can shield the people from the political, economic and/or military consequences of the lie. It thus becomes vitally important for the State to use all of its powers to repress dissent, for the truth is the mortal enemy of the lie, and thus by extension, the truth is the greatest enemy of the State." The point of these quotes and of the film itself is that the Nazis were very much aware of the power and techniques of propaganda, especially when it is presented as reality.

Why We Fight (Produced by Frank Capra 1943–1945)

This series of seven short films was commissioned by the U.S. government to generate support for World War II. The series explains the background of all the various fronts in the war—Russia, China, England, the homeland, etc.—in clear, though not objective, terms by using newsreel footage, reenactments, and images provided by the U.S. Army, and utilizes the talents of the best of Hollywood at the time, including director/producer Frank Capra, composer Dimitri Tiomkin, and actor Walter Huston, who provides the dramatic narration. While this series is much different in aesthetics and structure from *The Triumph of Will*, they share a similar purpose: to persuade a nation and the world about its country's resolve to fight and win a war. You could use any segment from the series, which is widely distributed in an inexpensive, four-DVD box, but I particularly like to use either of the following segments.

Sequence One: 0:00:00–0:09:44 (Prelude to War)

The film starts with this proclamation: "The picture you are about to see is the first in a series produced by the War Department exclusively for members of the Armed Forces. The Office of War Information has arranged with the War Department to release it to the American public." Although the films were originally intended as part of the "political education" (Barnouw 162) of those soldiers preparing to fight (and were, based on surveys, extremely effective), the films did have wide releases, and *Prelude to War* won an Academy Award for Best Documentary in 1943. The next title card makes it clear that while the film includes reenactments, they have been approved by the War Department, which is also said to be in possession of "enemy films" included in this documentary (specifically *Triumph of the Will*, which had seen a wide release in the United States in the 1930s). The film itself starts with scenes of American soldiers marching in a parade, as a Voice of God narrator wonders aloud why we are fighting, showing us images of war around the world. He continues to wonder what has turned our country into a vast arsenal of weapons and one dedicated to fighting on every continent. Then the film shows us two earths as seen from space: one is the slave world and one is the free world. The rest of this sequence contrasts these two worlds. Notice how the images of peacefulness and religion, and the soft, patriotic music in the free world, are contrasted with images of war, violence, and strident music in the other world. Pay attention to the word choices the narrator uses to describe Mussolini, Hitler, and the emperor of Japan. You'll also recognize scenes from *Triumph of the Will* included here, though obviously they have been recontextualized for different purposes.

Sequence Two: 1:02:01–1:15:37 (War Comes to America; the last of the seven films)

After the same title card from the previous sequence identifies this as a product of the Department of the Army, we see children saying the Pledge of Allegiance and then a close-up on the American flag, which dissolves into soldiers, boats, planes, and so forth involved in fighting all over the world. These images then dissolve into places in the United States where these soldiers come from, with soft string music on the sound track and a low-angle shot of the Statue of Liberty. From there, we get a condensed and simplified version of American history from Jamestown to present day (mid-1940s). Included are a lot of American symbols: the Liberty Bell, flags, the Constitution, and so on. The final section of this sequence deals with how people from all over the world have come to America to make this country strong, all of which builds to a tremendous and stirring climax of music and images of hard work and success in industry, commerce, and architecture.

Reality Television

I put off writing this section for a long time too: I knew that as soon as I wrote about reality TV, I would lose my last excuse for watching these shows. It started innocently enough. Like an undercover cop infiltrating a drug ring, I watched *Survivor*, *American Idol*, *Fear Factor*, *The Apprentice*, and *The Bachelor*, pen in hand, notebook on the lap, trying to figure out why this genre is so appealing. Quickly, though, like that cop taking drugs first for cover and then for real, I was hooked, and I knew more about the daily happenings of Richard, Simon, those pig-intestine-eating contestants, Donald, and Trista than I did about my own students. It all came crashing down when I caught my own reflection in the screen, contorted with rage, yelling at the TV during one of those third-rate reality dating shows at 2:00 a.m., without a pen or paper anywhere around. The point of my confession is that reality TV is addictive and it should be banned, or at least include one of those government warning labels.

Actually, in this section, I would like not only to rationalize the hours I spent watching but also to examine the reasons for the genre's popularity, how it relates to documentary film, how it manipulates even its own tenuous grasp on reality, and what kinds of effects it has on its audiences and its participants. A fantastic book on this topic, with a title that got me funny looks from airline security personnel last month, is *Shooting People: Adventures in Reality TV* (the second part of the title is in small print) by Sam Brenton and Reuben Cohen.

First, reality TV (or "unscripted" TV or "human drama," as these shows are sometimes dressed up by the network marketing folks) is so prevalent today because the shows are so cheap to make. That huge $1 million prize on *Survivor* is a tiny portion of the collective salaries of the *Friends* cast for a single episode. It's also popular, at least to my addicted mind, because the actions of the participants are not limited in the way they are in a scripted drama. If a character on, say, *CSI* does or says something stupid, we chalk it up to bad writers, but any discussion afterward can exist only in the realm of analysis of characterization, plot, theme, etc. But when someone says or does something stupid on a reality show (most of the time), we know it is, on some level, a real action that we can critique in the same way we do with our own friends and family: "Do you believe what she said?" "What was he thinking when he did that?" Though a good deal of identification occurs with scripted shows, I don't tend to project myself into them as much as I do with reality TV. I may laugh at George and Jerry on *Seinfeld*, but I don't picture what I would do or say if I sat there in the coffee shop with them; but after every episode of *The Amazing Race*, I yell at my wife for hours about what I would have done differently if I'd been there. I know, I know, I need help.

Even though all documentaries can have this effect on viewers, Brenton and Cohen quote Charlie Parsons, the inventor of the *Survivor* format, who describes reality TV as documentaries in a "controlled environment" (44). The question, then, is what exactly is reality TV documenting? The authors say that because of the dictated format of the shows (people living on an island, young people living in a house together, people competing in tasks as a job interview), the only thing these shows can possibly document are the controlled environments themselves. *Survivor* does not really illustrate the dangers and difficulties of living on a deserted island as much as it illustrates the behavior of a group of people who have chosen to pretend that they are on a desert island with no cameras filming them or catering tables just out of view. This might be true, but don't scientists learn something by watching rats play in a maze that scientists have constructed for observation? Intellectually, I understand the question posed by historian Daniel Boorstin in *Shooting People*—"Why are we watching ourselves?"—but emotionally, the desire to connect and experience vicariously is pretty strong. The fact that they are trapped on the island obviously affects all of their actions, but we get to see "real" people existing under unusual circumstances and observe their reactions, comparing their reactions to those we imagine we would have.

Of course, the last thing these reality shows are is "real." The unreality starts with the initial idea for the controlled environment (an island, a job interview, handcuffing people together, etc.) and continues with the casting of the show, the most crucial element of the process, producers will tell you. The casts of reality shows are hardly a cross section of the American public. First, they are much better looking than the rest of us. They also have been subjected to a battery of psychological tests and interviews to determine how much drama they would be able to create on the show. Then, of course, the rules of the show affect the participants' reactions; we know that people put under stress do not act as they normally might. Think of how you react any time a camera is focused on you. Do you really think you act the same as you usually do? Don't you fix your hair, watch what you say, and so on? For example, when I am being observed teaching by my administrator, I act just like me, only a little bit better and with less swearing. My nonscientific adaptation of the ridiculously complex Heisenberg uncertainty principle says that the very act of watching, photographing, or filming a subject affects that subject, which means that when the producers intentionally cast exhibitionist people with an inclination toward conflict, put them in a figurative rat maze, and turn a camera on them, we cannot be seeing "reality." Also, there is a tremendous amount of pressure on these participants to play a "character": the good guy/girl, the dumb one, the jerk, etc. No one can really be quite as clueless as Jessica Simpson appears on *Newlyweds* or Paris Hilton on *The Simple Life* (well, maybe). I remember reading that when the second season of *Survivor* was filming, everyone on the island was trying to be this year's "Richard" (the first season's winner), and they talked about it so much that the producers had to ban them from discussing the previous year's show at all. By limiting references to the fact that this is merely a TV show, the producers are able to create their own reality in which this season of *Survivor* exists in a bubble, supposedly uninfluenced by the previous ones, even though the audience, of course, has seen them and will continually draw comparisons.

The unreality of these shows continues in the editing room after filming has ended. As we saw earlier, much of the meaning in nonfiction film is communicated through its editing. Many ex–reality show participants have complained that the way they came off on the show was not how they actually behaved when they were on the set. This only makes sense. Several days' worth of footage has to be cut down to less than an hour, and the editor's job is to create the most exciting show possible. Twenty wonderful things that someone says or does are left on the cutting room floor in favor of that one sarcastic comment he made when he thought no one could hear him. An editor, to create drama and conflict, can change the time, place, and context of anything that anyone says or does. A simple comment like "I hate that guy" can be directed to any male participant on the show. Real reality is messy, so reality shows have to wrap up the reality they present in neat, exciting one-hour packages. To miss the editing at work is to confuse these shows with something true.

If, as Brenton and Cohen say in *Shooting People*, reality shows can only document the controlled environment itself, and if these shows construct reality beyond anything recognizable, what then do we learn about ourselves and others as we watch these shows? It really depends on the show. Each reality show has its own subtext, and one of the activities I like to do with my students (see Figure 1.18) is to have them try to determine the "value system" of reality shows. Some seem to value competition and treachery (*Survivor* and other "elimination" shows), some value cooperation and teamwork (*The Amazing Race*) or avarice (*The Apprentice*), while others put a premium on self-loathing (*The Swan*, *The Biggest Loser*) and exhibitionism (*The Real World*).

To determine a show's value system, we look to see who is rewarded by the show's rules and who is punished or ridiculed. On *The Apprentice*, for instance, the team that wins a particular task gets to travel for a night in Donald Trump's shoes, playing golf, eating at expensive restaurants, meeting celebrities, etc., which illustrates that winning at

Reality TV Activities

1. *Identify the unreality.* Choose a reality show, watch an episode or two, and try to describe the methods and purposes of its construction. Look at its casting choices, the rules of the show, and the editing. What are your conclusions about its manipulations of reality? How does it do it and for what purposes?

2. *Guess the one eliminated.* Many shows, such as *Survivor*, *The Apprentice*, *The Amazing Race*, *Big Brother*, and others, have one contestant eliminated by the end of almost every episode. Because the elimination took place before the editor began working, he or she can construct the episode to make the ending as dramatic as possible. Look for the amount of screen time someone gets, identify conflicts that someone gets into, and pay attention to which contestant most people seem to be discussing. Make a guess based on your observations and evaluate the editing choices made once you learn the outcome.

3. *Determine its values.* Choose a reality show and watch an episode or two, paying attention to what the show seems to value in its contestants. What skills and abilities are praised and rewarded with prizes or the respect of the host and other contestants? Are these the same values that you, your family, and community hold? Would these values be rewarded in the real world? Why or why not?

4. *Ethical treatment of subjects.* It is too easy to say that the participants on these shows, because they agreed to do it and probably signed a waiver, are not entitled to ethical treatment. Select a reality show that appears to exploit its participants for the enjoyment of its audience (*The Swan*, *The Biggest Loser*, *Wife Swap*, and many others) and watch carefully to see how the show represents its contestants. Is the audience expected to laugh *at* them or *with* them? Are the producers being fair to them or taking advantage of their life situations? How do you think the participants of the show you selected might feel about their portrayal?

5. *The Sims.* One of the most popular video games, The Sims, is similar to but goes beyond reality TV by allowing players to control the controlled environments of the game. Why is The Sims so popular and how does it relate to reality TV and voyeurism?

6. *Parody.* Look at one of the shows or movies that mock the reality TV genre (*The Joe Schmo Show*; *My Big Fat Obnoxious Boss/Fiancé*; *The Truman Show*; *Edtv*; *Series 7*; *The Comeback*). What specific elements of the genre does the program hold up for criticism or ridicule? What is its underlying message about reality TV? What conventions of the genre does it employ as well?

Figure 1.18. A list of activities that revolve around reality TV.

all costs leads to material wealth. On *Survivor*, physically weaker players or those unable to conspire diabolically are cast off the island. A number of "makeover" reality shows (*Extreme Makeover: Home Edition*, *Queer Eye for the Straight Guy*, and others) imply that most emotional, social, or economic problems the participants face can be overcome through consumerism; if only they dressed better or had a new big-screen TV, they would be much better off—with product placements and tie-ins whenever possible, of course.

Before my addiction fully took hold, I could watch these shows with a sense of detachment that I'm only now reacquiring. With this analytical eye for a reality guy, I could see that the values these shows present can be dangerous if you are not able to see the construction of reality going on. Are corporate environments really as cutthroat as represented on *The Apprentice*? Can there be no room for collaboration and cooperation? Are the skills most needed in the business world the ability to escape blame by placing it on another? At Enron, sure, but is this really what the corporate world in general values? Worse, for our students, are the reality dating shows. In the *Sorority Life* and *Fraternity Life*, for instance, college is represented solely as competition to attract members of the opposite sex through alcohol and sexual exhibition. Even if this one might be more real than others, what about *Chains of Love*, which handcuffs men and women together for three days to see if they are well suited for each other, or *The Fifth Wheel*, in which two couples date, then switch, and then await the arrival of a fifth person whose job appears to be to break up the couples? With these, plus *The Bachelor*, *The Bachelorette*, *Joe Millionaire*, *For Love or Money*, and many others, what messages about dating and relationships are sent to teenagers trying to figure out the inscrutable rules of real dating?

I know from experience that part of the pleasure of watching reality shows is the sense of superiority the viewer gets in relation to "those fools" on the show, but even this detachment does not fully counter the values and messages these shows can perpetuate. Just as we've been doing with documentaries, it's important to look critically at reality TV with our students, who instinctively tell me "of course they're not real" but are unable to articulate exactly the source and purpose of the construction. The activities in Figure 1.18 are ones my students have enjoyed doing individually and then presenting their findings to the rest of the class. As I continue my withdrawal from reality TV, I can begin to see these things clearly again, and when I sneak a few peeks every once in a while, I feel appropriately guilty and take a shower immediately after.

Blended Genres

As we saw in the beginning of this chapter, the differences between fiction and nonfiction film are not so easily identified. But when we watch a film, we generally know ahead of time whether it will be a fiction film or a documentary. Even if we do not, within a few minutes, we can generally tell what type of film it is. And yet some filmmakers intentionally blur this line by adopting the conventions of the other. Some fiction films are made to look like documentaries and some documentaries use many of the elements normally associated with fiction films. The purpose of including this section is for us to help our students be able to identify the ways these genres can blend and be able to explain the reasons for the filmmaker's choice to blur this line. Sometimes we don't know what's real and what's not, which is often exactly what the director intended.

- *Documentaries with fiction film elements*: Certain documentaries employ cinematic qualities that would make them indistinguishable from fiction films if you were to look only at particular scenes. *The Thin Blue Line*, discussed in detail in Chapter 4, uses actors to reenact key scenes of a shooting and employs close-ups, lighting, and music choices that are much more common in fiction films. *Touching the Void*, a documentary about a mountain climbing disaster, reenacts the entire accident with actors, a script, costumes, and props; I estimate that nearly 90 percent of the footage is re-created in some way. The opening scenes of *The Kid Stays in the Picture* use a dolly or tracking shot, low-key lighting, and nondiegetic music to set the mood of a Hollywood mogul's private home and could easily be the establishing shots of any fiction film. There are a number of reasons why a documentary filmmaker might want to take on the look of a fiction film, including a desire to visualize what he or she was not able to film as it occurred (*Touching the Void*) or to represent the problematic nature of eyewitness accounts (*The Thin Blue Line*). Contemporary audiences have also come to expect to *see* rather just *hear about* events, so a filmmaker trying to reach a larger audience might be more inclined to use the conventions of the more popular fiction film genre.

- *Fiction films with documentary elements*: Oftentimes you will see fiction films that deliberately use the conventions of a nonfiction film—a handheld camera, interviews, a text track, even a voice-over narrator—but you know they are fiction films because you can recognize the actors from other films you've seen. "Mockumentaries" such as *This Is Spinal Tap*, *Waiting for Guffman*, and the British TV show *The Office* do not really mock the documentary form itself as much as poke fun at the characters, who "reveal" their true selves in these pretend "behind the scenes" films. Audiences of mockumentaries are rarely tricked into thinking that the films are really documentaries, though the fictitious band Spinal Tap released a real album and went on tour, and I did read one review of *A Mighty Wind*, a mockumentary about aging folk musicians, whose author apparently missed the joke and complained that the music and subjects were unworthy of a full-length film. The audience of some fiction films, however, might be a little unclear about the use of documentary elements. Oliver Stone's *JFK*, for instance, is clearly a fiction film, but it uses clips from the Zapruder film of Kennedy's assassination to bolster its claims, and Stone even filmed additional fictional scenes with film stock, filters, and costumes intended to look just like the Zapruder film. This appropriation of documentary images is also used in such films as *Forrest Gump*, *Zelig*, and *Medium Cool*. The result is that the audience sometimes has to work very hard to distinguish what is real from what is fiction. Other fiction films may adopt documentary film elements for stylistic or thematic reasons. A horror film like *The Blair Witch Project* derives much of its suspense from the fact that it pretends that the events are really happening and captured on film, and *Series 7* adopts the look of a reality show to point out the dangerous line that our TV- and violence-obsessed culture seems to be crossing.

- *Films without clear demarcation*: Though both types of films discussed above may employ the conventions of the other, audiences are rarely so confused by these elements that they do not know exactly what type of film they are watching. In some films, however, the line is so blurry that unless we could interview the filmmaker, we might never be certain what kind of film we're seeing, and even afterward, we still might not be able to distinguish fiction from nonfiction. *In This World*, directed by Michael Winterbottom, is a fiction film that uses not only the style of documentary film but also its methods; many scenes in it might as well be a documentary. The film, about two Afghani boys trying to emigrate, stars two Afghani boys who do indeed want to emigrate, and the film uses improvised dialogue and captures the reactions of real people to the boys. *The Story of the Weeping Camel* does this as well; many scenes have been re-created and scripted so that it is not always clear to the viewer whether this is a fiction film or a documentary. (The Academy Awards folks didn't seem as confused as I was: they nominated it for Best Documentary.) A documentary about the nursing home industry, *Assisted Living*, uses real nursing home residents reading lines from a script provided by the director. *Incident at Loch Ness*, a fiction film directed by Zak Penn, stars Werner Herzog, playing himself as a director hired by Zak Penn to make a documentary about the Loch Ness monster, with a producer who is intent on creating the monster if necessary to make a good film. As the movie progresses, it becomes increasingly difficult for Herzog and the audience to distinguish the fiction from the real, though the confusion is played mainly for laughs. A film listed as a documentary, *The Five Obstructions*, involves director Lars von Trier challenging another director, Jørgen Leth, to remake a twelve-minute fiction film five times, each with various rules, or obstructions, that von Trier comes up with. These are real situations that are then imposed onto a fiction film; the result is, I think, a documentary of fiction filmmaking.

What is the purpose of these films' intentional blurring of the line between fiction and nonfiction? It varies, of course, from film to film, but most of them force us to confront the thinness of that line in our own lives. Think about how often you begin telling a "true" story to a colleague but then add a few embellishments here and there to make the story more interesting. Whatever the purpose, the number of these types of films seems to be increasing. Documentary filmmaker D. A. Pennebaker agrees and says this blurring is good because "the imagination always gets tired of the obvious" (qtd. in Stubbs 64). For me as a teacher, I'm not so sure it's a good thing; students are not critical readers of nonfiction—print or visual—and this mixing of the modes can pose serious problems for students unable to see the construction and the manipulation.

Putting It All Together: What Next?

To summarize this first chapter, my suggestions for teaching documentaries to students are to:

1. Define nonfiction film (two class periods, p. 3)
2. Discuss visual, sound, and text tracks (one class period, p. 17)
3. Present the role of editing in nonfiction film (one class period, p. 25)
4. Introduce students to the various modes (two class periods, p. 32)
5. Address the ethical dilemmas of nonfiction film (one class period, p. 40)
6. Discuss the history/background of nonfiction film (optional one class period, p. 46)
7. Present other nonfiction film texts (optional two class periods, p. 52)

Note that without the optional activities, you can introduce your students to the key elements of nonfiction film in a little over a week. From here, you can have them:

1. Look at a complete documentary (see Chapter 4 for suggestions and teaching activities).
2. Use this knowledge to work on some of their nonfiction print reading skills (see Chapter 2 for activities on cause/effect, compare/contrast).
3. Use their skills and knowledge of nonfiction film to support other class activities, such as writing about theme or tone or

improving their narrative, expository, and persuasive writing (see Chapter 3).

4. Take a break; you've worked hard.

Wherever you go next, once you have introduced these elements, you have turned on a switch for students that is unlikely to be turned off. My students tell me that I have ruined them, because they are continually analyzing what they see, whether it's a science documentary, a news program, or a cereal box. I tend to laugh my Dr. Evil laugh and say, "Sorry," but I don't really mean it.

2 Nonfiction Reading Skills and Strategies

I don't know about your state tests, but well over half of my standardized reading test deals with nonfiction texts. This bugs me every year I give the test because I know that as an English teacher I went into this business for the money, the fame, and the chance to teach Keats any time I wanted. I mean, isn't teaching nonfiction texts the social studies and science teachers' job? And why is it that the English teachers always get the dirty looks at faculty meetings when student scores go down? Are the math teachers teaching their students to read those word problems? The critical reading skills that students need to demonstrate on standardized tests are, for the most part, the same ones that will help them to understand *Beowulf*, but we have to get at them a little differently. While the skills might be similar, the processes that students use to make sense of a nonfiction text are different from those for a fictional one.

But the real point of this chapter is that since the skills students use to understand a *nonfiction print text* are nearly identical to those they use to understand a *nonfiction visual text* (documentary), we should use the inherent interest students have in film by identifying and practicing these skills first with the visual texts and then transferring those skills to print texts. I've included here some activities that allow students to practice crucial skills—compare/contrast, problem/solution, and cause/effect—they need to employ as they read nonfiction texts, and I've also included some of my favorite nonfiction reading strategies—SOAPStone, Levels of Questioning, and Cornell Notes—so that students can practice with a few documentary clips and then transfer the skills effectively to print texts. These activities are most successful when you are able to use both the film clips suggested here and a nonfiction piece of your own choosing within the same class period. The clips I have suggested in this and the next section are ones I have used successfully in my own classes, and they are all widely available, but this is certainly not meant to be an exhaustive list of film clips; as you work with these activities, you'll find yourself thinking of other clips that should work as well and probably better.

Nonfiction Reading Skills

Compare and Contrast

Comparing and contrasting is an essential skill that students need to improve in any number of subject areas. The ability to see the similarities and differences between two subjects, genres, themes, and so on is crucial for understanding nonfiction. Venn diagrams (see Figure 2.1) continue to be one of the most effective graphic organizers, though it's important to note that the Venn should not be an end point, but rather a tool used to generate a topic or thesis statement about the subjects being compared. Following are descriptions of clips that I like to use for compare/contrast.

Spellbound (Jeffery Blitz, 2001)

0:25:36–0:37:49; Chapters 5–6 on DVD

This documentary follows eight young people as they prepare for and compete in the National Spelling Bee. To help the audience get to know each of these contestants, the director presents short vignettes of the spellers, their families, and schools. In this sequence, we meet Ashley, from Washington, D.C., and Neil, from San Clemente, California. Their lives could not be more different and yet they are both participating in the same competition. Ask your students to focus on the similarities and differences in the following areas: parental support, school facilities, preparation for the Bee, attitude toward spelling, their houses, and so on. The filmmaker spends a lot of time on the poor academic and social conditions of the D.C. environment—illustrated by the bent sign warning that drugs and weapons are not allowed on school property—that contrast clearly with Neil's affluent home overlooking the beach and a school where he has a Latin teacher and excellent facilities. Their preparations for the Bee are also quite different (see Figure 2.2): Neil has coaches, computer programs, and parents who drill him, while Ashley uses the dictionary and did not receive her spelling materials from her school district on time. There are similarities in their parents' support and expectations for their children, though it is clear that Neil has a tremendous advantage. The film does not make any overt political statement about the distribution of wealth or inequities in the system, but a viewer certainly might.

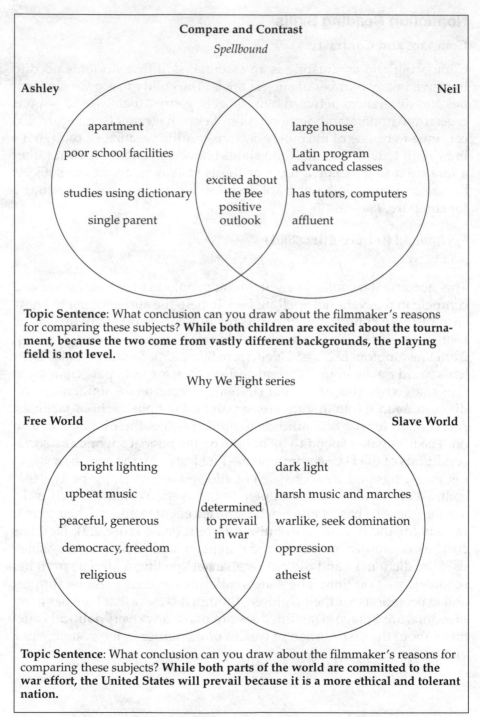

Compare and Contrast

Spellbound

Ashley   **Neil**

apartment   large house

poor school facilities   Latin program
                                                                           advanced classes

                                        excited about
studies using dictionary   the Bee   has tutors, computers
                                        positive
single parent   outlook   affluent

Topic Sentence: What conclusion can you draw about the filmmaker's reasons for comparing these subjects? **While both children are excited about the tournament, because the two come from vastly different backgrounds, the playing field is not level.**

Why We Fight series

Free World   **Slave World**

bright lighting   dark light

upbeat music   harsh music and marches

                                        determined
peaceful, generous   to prevail   warlike, seek domination
                                        in war
democracy, freedom   oppression

religious   atheist

Topic Sentence: What conclusion can you draw about the filmmaker's reasons for comparing these subjects? **While both parts of the world are committed to the war effort, the United States will prevail because it is a more ethical and tolerant nation.**

Figure 2.1. Venn diagram compare and contrast strategy.

Figure 2.2. Contrasting ways in which spellers prepare for the Bee. Ashley: uses Scrabble letters with her teacher in a classroom; Neil: at home with a private spelling tutor and several computers.

Why We Fight Series (Frank Capra)

Prelude to War *(1943); 0:04:40–0:09:40; Chapter 1 on first DVD in the series*

During World War II, Frank Capra produced a series of informative, persuasive films for American servicemen and the general public as part of the war effort. In this short sequence from the first in the series, the film compares the United States (the free world) with Germany, Italy, and Japan (the slave world). Ask your students to focus on the roles of religion, politicians, and government in both "worlds." If your students are somewhat sophisticated in documentary construction, you might want them to compare the representations of the two. In other words, how does the film choose to present the United States, Germany, and the other countries? They will probably notice the music and the images. They will probably also recognize the repeated references to tolerance of religion in the section on the United States and the name-calling of the leaders of the other countries (thugs, rabble-rousers, and so on). The reasons for the comparison ought to be obvious enough, though you might want to lead students into a discussion about the effectiveness of the comparison and why compare/contrast can be such an effective persuasion tool.

After your students have viewed a clip, it's important that you give them time to draw conclusions about why the filmmaker used a compare/contrast approach. What is the director suggesting with this structure? Once they have practiced with a clip or two, provide your students with a nonfiction print text (see the end of this chapter for models) to which students can apply their newfound skills.

Problem and Solution

Much of the nonfiction that students read requires them to be able to point out an identified problem and its proposed solution. Think of your typical newspaper editorial that raises the alarm of a serious problem (gang violence in schools) and proposes a solution (school uniforms) that the writer insists will address the problem he or she brought up. These activities are designed not only to help students identify these elements of nonfiction texts, but also to help them evaluate whether the solution really does address the problem. Too often, writers, filmmakers, and politicians propose a wonderful-sounding solution that has very little to do with the actual problem stated (how exactly do school uniforms fix violence?). These activities are intended to make students more critical and aware readers (see Figure 2.3). Following are descriptions of clips I have used to practice reading for problem/solution.

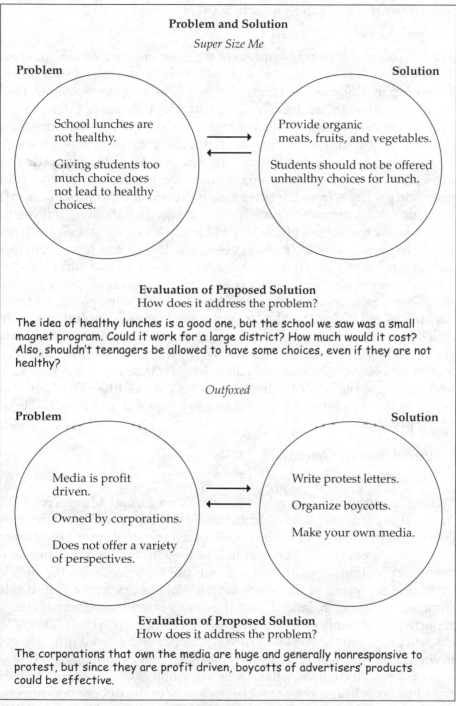

Figure 2.3. Problem and solution strategy.

Super Size Me (Morgan Spurlock, 2004)

51:13–57:50; Chapter 20 on DVD

This clip begins with a description of the problem with school lunches. The fat content is high, and the school official interviewed thinks that with proper education, students will make the proper choices and eat healthier, although, as the film demonstrates, they do not. Part of the problem is that the schools turn a blind eye to what are obviously bad student choices and to companies that make a lot of money on snack and sugared foods. An additional problem is that some schools do not even cook much of their own food anymore, but instead receive it in premade packages from the government. Notice how Spurlock presents these problems visually: dismal food and rowdy kids, with editing to clearly show that school officials do not really know what their students eat. The real solution, the film suggests, is to have a lunch program like that of Appleton Central Alternative High, a school that turned its attendance and behavior problems around through diet changes. The school serves only nonprocessed, organic foods with plenty of fresh vegetables and fruits. The film suggests that this is a real solution: school officials need to make the food choices for their students. If given a choice, kids will choose the fries; without a choice, they will be healthier and better behaved. Notice again the selected images: well-behaved kids and close-ups on beautiful fresh fruits and vegetables. The film also suggests that this alternative costs roughly the same as a typical school lunch program.

Outfoxed (Robert Greenwald, 2004)

1:06:09–1:13:03; Chapter 20 on DVD

While the entire film is a relentless attack on Rupert Murdoch's FOX News, this particular section deals mainly with the problem of the concentration of the media in the hands of a very small number of very powerful corporations. The first half of the clip lays out the problem: since corporations are driven by profit, not necessarily by the public good, the reporting of the news suffers. The media, according to this film, are no longer balanced, and they are geared more toward cheap reporting that requires less money for investigation. The solutions to this are proposed by a series of media activists and elected officials: get involved by protesting, writing to the FCC, and organizing with others. I ask my students whether these are viable solutions and whether the filmmaker thinks they are. Listen closely to the upbeat nondiegetic music for evidence of the answer. If you continue playing the film through the closing credits, you'll see clips of interviews with media activists who have had success confronting the power of media concentration.

As with compare/contrast, the real power of using these clips is in the students' ability to transfer the analytical skills they develop here to the evaluation of proposed solutions in the print texts they encounter, such as those found at the end of this chapter or editorials from the local newspaper.

Cause and Effect

Similar to problem/solution, this type of nonfiction reading skill asks students to identify and to evaluate logically what they read. If an author makes the claim that peanut butter sandwiches cause attention deficit disorder, a reader needs to be able to determine whether one element does in fact *cause* the other, or whether lots of kids just happen to both eat peanut butter and have ADD. As students develop their cause/effect reading skills, it is important for them to learn to evaluate the connection between the stated cause and the effect (which I often refer to as "outcome" for my students). Most important, students need to practice the ability to read nonfiction texts critically in order to identify exactly what the writer or filmmaker is trying to say about the underlying causes of a situation. The following are descriptions of clips I have used to help students practice this skill.

Cane Toads: An Unnatural History (Mark Lewis, 1988)
00:01:05–00:06:20 (Not available on DVD)

I first saw *Cane Toads*, probably one of the strangest nature documentaries ever produced, in a film class and thought it was an obscure relic my teacher had dug up from somewhere, until I started asking around and found that the film has a huge following among science teachers. An advertisement for the film proclaims that it is like a National Geographic special made by Monty Python, and it is very funny in places. I would wager that a science teacher in your building has either heard of it or, like biology teacher Carolyn Ames in mine, has a copy he or she can share with you. In this clip, from the beginning of the film, various causes and effects are identified about the cane toad that was introduced to Australia in order to deal with the cane grub that was destroying the sugar cane crops. The only problem was that the cane toad, through a series of biological misunderstandings, did not eat the grubs and reproduced at such an alarming rate that it caused an infestation of its own.

Students have no trouble identifying several outcomes and their causes from this clip, including how and why the cane toad reproduces the way it does. Some students even laugh.

Roger & Me **(Michael Moore, 1989)**
0:13:38–0:21:00; Chapter 6 on DVD

In his first documentary feature, Michael Moore investigates the causes and effects of the General Motors plant closings on his hometown of Flint, Michigan. This sequence begins with various news reports of the plant shutdowns and continues with an interview of a friend of Moore's who has had a breakdown as a result of the layoffs. Notice the ironic use of the Beach Boys' "Wouldn't It Be Nice" on the sound track, as well as his choice of headlines about layoffs, which are crosscut with shots of empty storefronts and news stories about the rat population in Flint. From there, Moore moves into a brief scene about Ronald Reagan and then to a "Great Gatsby Party" thrown by the most affluent in Flint. He then contrasts these people with the most devastating economic effect of the shutdowns: eviction from one's home. The clear juxtaposition is intended to illustrate that the greedy rich are the cause of the suffering poor. As they watch, students should observe how Moore tries to create effects that might not logically be connected to the causes he identifies. Visually, the closed-up storefronts are effective—but were they caused by the layoffs? Moore wants us to believe so.

As with each of the previous skills, the next step is to let students examine a few print texts so that they can evaluate the validity of the connection between cause and effect. Again, see the end of this chapter for sample texts.

Reading Strategies

I introduce my students to a number of strategies for reading nonfiction early in the fall so that they can employ them with a variety of texts throughout the year. I wish I could say that I invented any of these strategies, but in good teacher fashion, I stole or soaked them up from workshops over the years. Most of these are probably not new to you either, but what I've tried to do here is focus the strategies on the reading and analysis of nonfiction texts. In each case, I describe how I use the strategy in my class, and I suggest clips from documentaries that you might want to practice using the strategy with before you have students apply the strategy to a nonfiction print text. As with the previous reading skills activities, you can do these with students even if they do not have

Subject	How can you paraphrase the text in a sentence or two?
Occasion	What are the larger historical issues that inform this piece as well as the immediate need to speak at this particular time?
Audience	To whom is the piece directed? How do you know?
Purpose	What is the point or the message of this piece?
Speaker	Who is the speaker? What can you say about the speaker's age, situation, social class, etc.?
Tone	What is the attitude of the speaker to the subject? What words and phrases reveal this?
Analysis: Choose one or more of the elements above and explain them with supporting examples, and/or contrast them with another text or a similar subject.	

Figure 2.4. SOAPStone chart.

much of the background on documentaries provided in Chapter 1, but if they do, you will find that students can add another layer to their analysis because they can also comment on what the filmmaker might be saying through his or her use of various nonfiction film elements.

SOAPStone

This is one of my favorite strategies for nonfiction document analysis and it's a key strategy for many Advanced Placement classes. It asks students to analyze the significant elements of a text individually by using a simple acronym that refers to the Speaker, Occasion, Audience, Purpose, Subject, and Tone (see Figure 2.4 for questions you can use to guide your students through the strategy). The strategy can be applied just as easily to fiction texts, and I also use it sometimes as a prewriting strategy, in which students have to consider their purpose, audience, and tone before they begin writing.

To practice this strategy, I like to use clips from a film recommended by my friend and colleague Dave Lickey, *The Atomic Cafe*, which is a collection of newsreels, government archives, military training films, and newspaper headlines from the late 1940s and 1950s about the atomic bomb, the cold war, and atomic energy. The film works well for SOAPStone because it contains a series of stand-alone clips that allow students to recognize how *purpose, audience*, and, especially in this film, *occasion* can be effective ways to analyze a nonfiction text. Plus, when students become comfortable with the forms and styles of documentaries, they will also be able to analyze not just the tone of the speaker in the text but also the tone of the filmmakers toward the speaker and the occasion.

Atomic Cafe (Jayne Loader, Kevin Rafferty, and Pierce Rafferty, 1982)

Clip 1: 0:05:02–6:12:00; Chapter 2 on DVD

The first clip I show is a very short one that includes two excerpts from speeches that President Truman delivered in the days after the United States dropped the first atomic bomb on Hiroshima. I provide students with the S, O, A, and S portions of SOAPStone and then as practice ask them questions about the purpose and tone (see Figure 2.5). I ask students to key in on Truman's word choices about having "*found* the bomb," bearing the "awful responsibility which has *come to us*" (my emphasis), and invoking God to guide us to use it for "His purposes." Then I ask them to choose any one of the letters of the acronym and analyze its use. For instance, how does the fact that Truman was addressing the American public affect what he says and how he says it? How would his speech be different if he were addressing, say, the Japanese? Having identified purpose, *why* was this Truman's purpose at the time? How would it change after the war had been won?

Clip 2: 0:16:46–0:19:13; Chapter 4 on DVD

The second clip I like to use from this documentary is a newsreel titled "1947: The Year of Division" produced by Paramount Studios (whom I identify as the speaker for my students) about the dangers of the spread of communism. For this sequence, I ask students to complete a full SOAPStone, though I typically assign only two parts to each student at first for practice, and they share afterward with the rest of the class in order to fill in the whole chart. This particular section begins with historical information about the spread of communism and continues with coverage of one American town's enactment of what our country would be like under communism. It concludes with images of the Statue of Liberty exploding and cartoon images of marching armies and fists smashing our most trusted institutions. When discussing tone, students should refer to the images as well as the words. Students should also consider that tone here can also be used to examine the film's attitude toward the townspeople. Note: if you want to continue the clip for another minute or two, you'll see the narrator of the newsreel thanking his business sponsors and using the opportunity to contrast capitalism to communism even further; apparently it comes down to free parking!

Clip 3: 0:59:10–1:00:50

This very short clip, about the risks associated with nuclear weapons, is clearly designed to calm people's fears. It equates the risks of nuclear

Clip 1: The Atomic Cafe	
Subject	The acquisition and first use of the atomic bomb
Occasion	The dropping of the first atomic bomb in 1945
Audience	The American public
Purpose	What is Truman's purpose in this speech?
Speaker	President Harry S. Truman
Tone	What is Truman's attitude (tone) toward the subject?
Analysis: How do you know Truman's purpose? What words and phrases reveal his tone?	

Clip 2: The Atomic Cafe	
Subject	
Occasion	
Audience	
Purpose	
Speaker	
Tone	
Analysis	

Figure 2.5. Using SOAPStone.

war with slipping in the shower or losing your hair and includes a pie chart that compares America's worries with the "destroying potential" of a bomb, concluding that the fears are unfounded.

Clip 4: 1:01:28–1:05:25

The last clip I like to use for this activity includes the famous "duck and cover" defense against nuclear war and other recommended procedures for survival of a nuclear blast. It focuses on young people's preparation and includes a cartoon of Bert the Turtle and enactments of various people practicing the "duck and cover."

SOAPStone works especially well when students need to compare and contrast nonfiction texts. By seeing the various elements laid out for them this way, students can easily identify topics that would be suitable for a strong analysis. I usually ask students to compare the audiences or purposes for clips 3 and 4.

Students familiar with the documentary elements discussed in Chapter 1 should be able to consider the points that the filmmakers who assembled all of these clips are making about nuclear weapons. They ought to be able to point to specific visual, audio, and text information as well as editing choices that lead us to draw conclusions about the filmmakers' purposes. So these clips can be treated as nonfiction documents of a time period and then analyzed as contemporary films that look back at that time period. Once the SOAPStone strategy has helped students make sense of challenging texts, the discussions on these clips are wonderful.

As always, the next step after practicing with these clips is to let students try out a SOAPStone for a nonfiction print text. Speeches work well (see the Gettysburg Address in the next section), as do other historical documents and editorials.

Levels of Questioning

Another strategy that is a part of my regular tool box is to teach students about the levels of questioning. Students spend most of their days being asked questions, but they rarely get a chance to frame the discussion with questions of their own. This strategy gives students the knowledge and confidence to engage with a text independently by presenting them with the three types of questions that can be asked about a text. By teaching them how to write good and varied questions, all students have a way into any text, regardless of their own initial understanding. I use the questions they generate in a number of ways: reading quizzes, class discussions, Socratic seminars, journal entries, and so on.

I like to introduce the different levels of questions in a nonfiction text by presenting students with the Gettysburg Address, identifying one question at each level, and then soliciting others from the class (see Figure 2.6). In short, the three levels of questions are:

Level 1: Questions of Fact. These are questions that cannot be debated and the answers to which can be found within the text itself. For the story of "The Three Little Pigs," for example, a level 1 question might be: what did each of the pigs build their houses out of? At first glance, these types of questions might seem simplistic, but they are actually essential for identifying evidence to support a position.

Level 2: Questions of Interpretation. These are debatable questions that are answerable only after analyzing the text closely. The answers, though, should be found within the text itself. Often these questions begin with "why" or "how" and might relate to the tone, word choice, or theme of the text. For the pig story: what is the effect of the repeated refrain "I'll huff and I'll puff"? These are great classroom or small-group discussion questions, ones that can lead to topics for an analytical essay.

Level 3: Beyond the Text. These questions have their basis in the text, but the answers are found outside of it. The answers to level 3 questions are always debatable, but the evidence for the discussion is found out in the world, in other texts, or in one's own personal life. A level 3 for the pigs might be: The third pig displayed patience and advanced planning. Are these qualities we value in society today? These questions are perfect for Socratic seminars or for journal topics.

Once students have an understanding of the different levels of questions with the Gettysburg Address, I play a clip or two from the films described in the following sections, ask students to come up with their own questions, and then have them hold small-group discussions that revolve around their levels 2 and 3 questions. Their questions should not be solely on the information provided but also on the construction of the documentary itself; they should be able to write questions about any of the visual, sound, and text elements you may have introduced to them from Chapter 1. After they have practiced with the documentaries, it is important for them to have a chance to apply this skill to a nonfiction print text. Editorials or letters to the editor from your local or school newspaper could work well for this activity; the Practice Nonfiction Print Texts section at the end of the chapter contains short nonfiction pieces written by students of mine that you may want to use. Although the answers to the questions are certainly worth exploring, it is really the questions themselves that encourage students to look closely at the text, which will then generate deeper thinking and productive class discussions.

Tupac: Resurrection (Lauren Lazin, 2003)

These clips come from a fantastic documentary suggested by one of my students, Conor Jeans-Gail, about the late rapper Tupac Shakur, and it

Levels of Questioning

The Gettysburg Address (1863): Four score and seven years ago our fathers brought forth on this continent, a new nation, conceived in Liberty, and dedicated to the proposition that all men are created equal.

Now we are engaged in a great civil war, testing whether that nation, or any nation so conceived and so dedicated, can long endure. We are met on a great battle-field of that war. We have come to dedicate a portion of that field, as a final resting place for those who here gave their lives that that nation might live. It is altogether fitting and proper that we should do this.

But, in a larger sense, we can not dedicate—we can not consecrate—we can not hallow—this ground. The brave men, living and dead, who struggled here, have consecrated it, far above our poor power to add or detract. The world will little note, nor long remember what we say here, but it can never forget what they did here. It is for us the living, rather, to be dedicated here to the unfinished work which they who fought here have thus far so nobly advanced. It is rather for us to be here dedicated to the great task remaining before us—that from these honored dead we take increased devotion to that cause for which they gave the last full measure of devotion—that we here highly resolve that these dead shall not have died in vain—that this nation, under God, shall have a new birth of freedom—and that government of the people, by the people, for the people, shall not perish from the earth. . . .

Level 1: Questions of Fact
These are questions that cannot be debated and the answers to which can be found within the text itself. For the Gettysburg Address, level 1 questions might be, "During which war was the speech delivered?" or "What does Lincoln say is his purpose for coming to Gettysburg?" At first glance, these types of questions might seem simplistic, but they are actually essential for identifying evidence to support a position.

■ **Write another level 1 question:**

Level 2: Questions of Interpretation
These are debatable questions that are answerable only after analyzing the text closely. The answers, though, should be found within the text itself. Often these questions begin with "why" or "how" and might relate to the tone, word choice, or theme of the text. For the Gettysburg Address, level 2 questions might be, "Why does Lincoln begin his speech by dating back to the beginning of the country?" or "What is the effect of using the word *consecrate*?"

■ **Write another level 2 question:**

Level 3: Beyond the Text
These are questions that have their basis in the text, but the answers are found outside of it. The answers to level 3 questions are always debatable, but the evidence for the discussion is found out in the world, in other texts, or in one's own personal life. Examples of this level for the Gettysburg Address are, "Do soldiers really die in vain if their side does not win the war?" and "Why do people need to be persuaded to continue fighting in wars?"

■ **Write another level 3 question:**

Figure 2.6. Levels of Questioning exercise.

is always popular with high school students. The film traces his rise from poverty to fame and fortune, narrated, in a sense, by Tupac himself through various interviews over the years. The rapper is often quite articulate about social issues and, luckily for us, is most often not too vulgar in this film, except where noted.

Clip 1: 0:13:57–0:15:27; Chapter 2 on DVD

This first clip presents Tupac's views on poverty and racism, which the filmmaker reinforces through images of homeless people edited to juxtapose with the extravagance of the Reagan White House of the 1980s. See sample questions at each level in Figure 2.7.

Clip 2: 0:45:44–0:49:30; Chapter 8 on DVD

In this sequence, Tupac explains the philosophy called "thug life" that he popularized through his tattoos, clothing, and videos. The beginning of the section contains excerpts of a music video and Tupac talking about the pressure and the power he feels in being looked at as a role model. From there, he begins to define *thug life* by comparing it to other great American perspectives like "Give me liberty or give me death." He goes on to describe a code of conduct for regulating the violence in the ghettos, and we see a truce picnic for rival L.A. gangs. You might want to cut the clip slightly short if you are concerned about the profanity at the very end of the sequence. By the way, "OG" refers to "original gangsters." I always try to mention this off-the-cuff in class so students might accidentally think I'm cool. Possible questions for this clip are:

Level 1

1. How old is Tupac at this time?
2. What words best define *thug* according to Tupac?
3. What does Tupac say is the purpose of the "thug life code of ethics"?

Level 2

1. Why does Tupac feel pressured and scared at the beginning of this clip?
2. Why does "thug life" give Tupac pride?
3. Why does this outlook scare some people?
4. What is the filmmaker's attitude toward the thug life? How is this revealed through editing?

Level 3

1. What are the solutions to the problem of street violence that Tupac identifies?

Using Levels of Questioning	
Title: *Tupac: Resurrection*	Director: **Lauren Lazin, 2003**
Level 1	• What are Tupac's specific suggestions for addressing homelessness? • What does former President Reagan say about hunger in America?
Level 2	• What is the effect of using contrasting images of the White House and the homeless? • Describe Tupac's values. How are they revealed in this sequence?
Level 3	• Why do we have hungry people and homelessness in America? • How realistic are Tupac's suggestions? Why?
Discussion Notes	

Title: *They Give You a Dollar*	Writer: **Becca Carlson**
Article found at end of this chapter	
Level 1	• What is the current minimum wage? • Which president tried to raise it?
Level 2	• What are the benefits and disadvantages of raising the minimum wage? • What is the effect on the overall economy?
Level 3	• How does America treat its working poor? • Does every citizen have the right to a "living wage"?
Discussion Notes	

Figure 2.7. Using Levels of Questioning.

2. Does America's history really contain examples of thug life?

3. Do rap videos glamorize criminal behavior? What are the images and editing that reveal this glamorization?

4. Why do people join gangs? What positive experiences can gangs provide?

Mad Hot Ballroom (Marilyn Agrelo, 2005)

0:59:05–0:37:09; Chapter 6 on DVD

If you are working with younger children, this clip from a film about elementary school students taking ballroom dancing lessons (Figure 2.8)

Figure 2.8. From *Mad Hot Ballroom*.

might be more appropriate for introducing them to the Levels of Questioning. The clip opens with a montage of kids playing on the playgrounds at various schools. The music is a gentle, light tune. All kids, the film suggests, play and have fun, regardless of race and class. Then the film cuts between several of the kids all talking about what it means to be age ten or eleven. Some are confused by changes in their bodies and the difficulties of the schoolwork, and some are excited about getting older. The sequence ends with images of the children at home or at play with one of their parents: rollerblading, studying, riding on the back of a motorcycle. If these are single-parent homes, they're great ones for the kids. This sequence includes only positive images.

Level 1

1. How old are most of the kids at this time?

2. According to one of the girls, at what age are kids most likely to be targeted by kidnappers?

3. What are some of the things the kids like and don't like about being ten or eleven?

Level 2

1. Why are the children happy or unhappy about their ages?

2. Why are some of the children scared or confused at this age?

3. Why does the film include so many images of the kids playing?

4. What is the filmmaker's attitude toward being ten? How is this revealed through editing and music?

Level 3

1. Are kids allowed to just be kids these days?

2. What makes children happy?

3. What are the differences between being ten and [fill in blank with your students' age]?

Cornell Notes

The final strategy I like to use with students as they engage with nonfiction texts is the Cornell Notes process of note taking developed by Walter Pauk and presented in his *How to Study in College*; it is often given to students as a tool for taking notes during a class lecture or discussion, but it is also applicable to the reading of challenging nonfiction texts. Students, before taking notes on a difficult nonfiction text, divide their paper into three areas, each of which has a separate purpose. A full piece of paper should be divided to look like Figure 2.9.

Section 1 is the large space in which students write down the information they feel is important in the text. These might be facts, dates, names, chapter headings, etc. This material should not be in complete sentences, and students should have an opportunity to compare their notes in this section with those of their classmates, especially when you have just introduced this format to them. This is also a place for them to write down any significant visual, sound, and text elements (if you introduced them from the previous chapter). It is important to remember that documentaries are made up of more than just factual information; we want students to be able to pay attention to all of the elements that go into documentaries.

Section 2 is the place where students write a brief summary of all the information found in section 1. This summary should try to connect the information by describing how the various facts, names, dates, and so forth relate to one another. This section needs to be completed as soon as possible after students have taken the notes and must be in their own words. It can also include a brief analysis of the author's purpose and tone.

Section 3 is where students write questions or "cues" about the information that can be found in section 1. If, for instance, a student

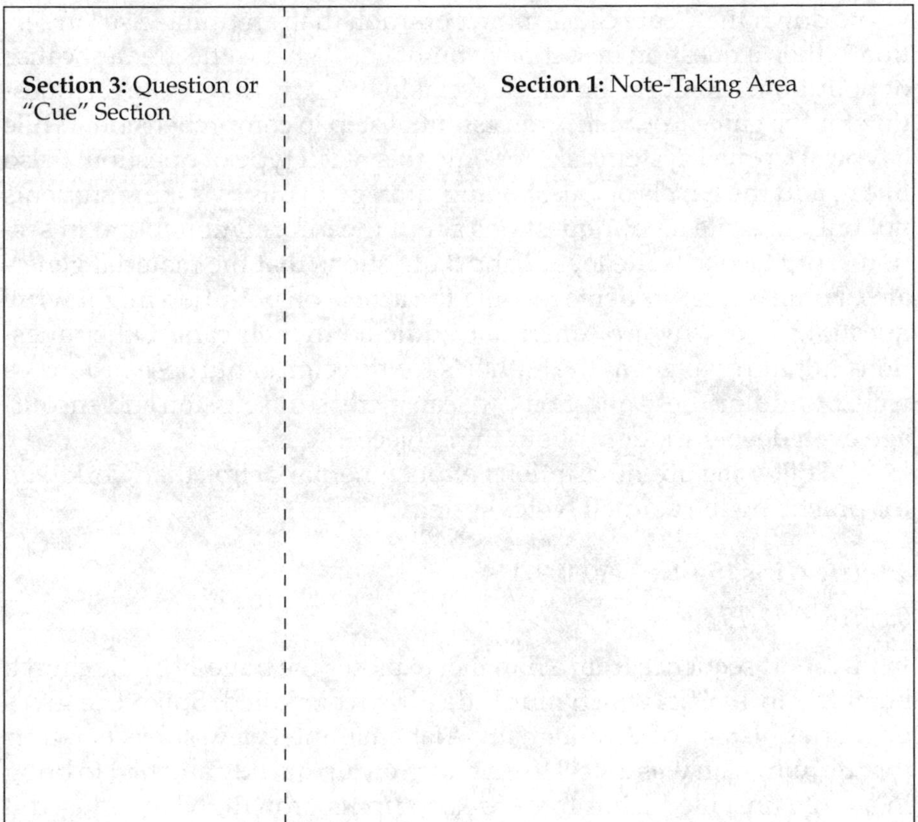

Section 3: Question or "Cue" Section

Section 1: Note-Taking Area

Section 2: Summary Section

Figure 2.9. Cornell Notes divisions.

wrote down that "cars cause more pollution than anything else" in section 1, then a question in section 3 might be: "What is the greatest cause of pollution?" Rephrasing the material in this way (like writing a question for the game *Jeopardy!*) is an essential step in comprehension. While a typical Cornell system asks for only this recall type of question, I also like to add the Levels of Questioning strategy to this by asking students not only to write level 1 questions about the information found in section 1, but also to write level 2 and 3 questions that the material generates. For instance, students reading the article on pollution might write questions like: why are Americans addicted to their cars? Other questions might try to get at the author's (or director's) purpose or tone as well. By adding these questions, we can increase discussion and encourage even deeper thought about the subjects.

Following are descriptions of documentary clips that work well for practicing the Cornell Notes system.

4 Little Girls (Spike Lee, 1997)

0:07:16–0:12:19

In this short sequence from a film that explores the tragedy of the church bombing in 1963 in which four little girls were killed, Spike Lee gives us a brief history of Birmingham, Alabama. Interview subjects tell us that Birmingham was a steel town that grew up quickly and had to bring in a large unskilled labor force to keep up its growth, which caused it to be a violent town. Even though no one mentions lynching, Lee cuts—with a bold and threatening drumroll on the sound track—to a series of graphic pictures of black men being lynched by smiling mobs. The images are rural looking and are not identified as being committed in or around Birmingham. While most people recall how violent Birmingham was at the time, Lee juxtaposes these with a white circuit court judge saying that Birmingham in the 1950s was a quiet, wonderful place to raise a family, from which Lee cuts to archive footage of a KKK group (complete with young kids in white robes) marching through the streets. The real power of this sequence comes from Lee's ability to make the concept of segregation felt in such a personal way. One family recounts a time when their child wanted to eat at a whites-only lunch counter and they had to tell her, a six-year-old girl, about racism (see Figure 2.10 for a sample Cornell Notes on this clip with multiple levels of questioning in the cue section).

| **Title**: *4 Little Girls* | **Author/Director**: Spike Lee | **Topic**: Birmingham, AL |

Section 3: Question or "Cue" Section	**Section 1**: Note-Taking Area
	1950s Birmingham
What made Birmingham so violent at that time?	Difficult to get work; a steel town then
	Built in late 1800s by Northerners
	History of labor violence, US Steel
	Rural people moving in to city
What does segregation mean?	Foreboding music
	Lynchings
	KKK
	Great place to raise a family
What was segregated at the time?	Segregated, separate bathrooms, water fountains
	Awful time for young people
	Man tells story about his daughter, wants to eat a sandwich at store
Have conditions improved since the 1950s?	Still pictures of daughter
	Father tells her that she can't b/c she's black
	CU on father at the end
Why does racism exist?	
What does Spike Lee think about Birmingham at the time?	

Section 2: Summary Section

This section is about how difficult it was to be black in Birmingham in the 1950s. Things were violent and everything was segregated. Only one person thought it was a great place to raise a family, and he was white. The most powerful part is when a father has to tell his little girl that she can't eat at the lunch counter because she's black.

Figure 2.10. Using Cornell Notes.

The Fog of War (Errol Morris, 2003)

0:06:45–0:12:30

This clip comes from an extended interview with Robert McNamara, the secretary of defense in the 1960s, in which he proposes a series of lessons of war. In this sequence, which focuses on the Cuban missile crisis, McNamara identifies lesson 1 as "Empathize with your enemy," and suggests that nuclear war was averted because Kennedy and some of his advisors were able to put themselves into Soviet leader Khrushchev's shoes. Students familiar with the elements discussed in Chapter 1 will find a tremendous amount of material to note on the director's editing and text track choices. The clip works well for practicing Cornell note taking because most information will be new to students and many of the issues raised will prompt good questions.

March of the Penguins (Luc Jacquet, 2005)

0:00:00–0:06:30

If you are planning to use this strategy with younger students, this clip about the mating rituals of the emperor penguins in Antarctica would be perfect (Figure 2.11). In this opening sequence, we learn a lot of facts about the location, the distance covered, the temperature, and the methods of travel as the penguins try to get to their mating ground.

The Cornell Notes system empowers students by giving them an easy tool for organization, summary, and reflection. Once students practice with it a few times, you'll see how quickly they catch on. Maybe they'll even start using it in other classes and subjects.

All of the skills and strategies presented in this chapter are designed to isolate a few areas on which students should concentrate as they encounter nonfiction texts. As with all of these activities, the goal is for students to practice the strategy with the film and then to transfer the skills to a nonfiction print text immediately afterward. Throughout the year, I collect newspaper editorials, short scientific articles, and even essays from educational journals, and I pull out copies whenever I want to practice a particular skill or strategy. Please don't think that the print text you select always needs to match the topic of the film clip you have just shown; it's great when that happens, but we are most interested in the transfer of skills. The following section consists of short nonfiction pieces written by some of my students that you might want to copy and use to practice this transfer of skills.

Figure 2.11. The opening of *March of the Penguins* presents a lot of information, so it's a great sequence for having students practice their Cornell Notes. My page of notes, however, would have a single word: COLD!

After students have practiced with the film and print texts, it is a good habit to ask students to reflect on which strategies seem to help them the most and to be able to explain why. The goal cannot be simply to help them do better on standardized tests, though they certainly will; we need to give students a way to make sense of the texts they will encounter once they leave our classrooms.

Practice Nonfiction Print Texts

As I noted earlier, this chapter has been about the skills and strategies that students need in order to read and understand nonfiction texts, and the clips I have recommended can serve as practice for students before they transfer these skills to challenging nonfiction print texts. What follows are a few pieces written by my students that you might want to copy and use to help this transfer process.

They Give You a Dollar, We Keep Your Jobs

By Becca Carlson

Our country is built upon the ideals of life, liberty, and prosperity. One of the many liberties that this country provides is great work opportunities. Yet, with our ever growing population the demand for living has increased. More jobs are needed, but there are not always enough opportunities for work. The liberal parties of this nation feel that the solution to ridding low-wage poverty in this country is to raise the Federal minimum wage. The reality is that raising minimum wage would cause a vast loss of jobs across the country. Companies cannot afford the hourly increase in workers' pay, and small privately owned businesses are not equipped for the salary increase. The result of this high demand on the United States' businesses would lead to nothing less than the destruction of our economy.

Susan Miller, life long resident of Spokane, Washington, has spent the past 7 years of her life raising three children in her one bedroom apartment. Up until last month she worked two jobs, barely bringing in enough money to put food on the table. Today she is left jobless. Her workplaces could not afford to pay the state's high minimum wage.

While in office, the Clinton Administration made many attempts to raise the Federal minimum wage to $7.00 an hour. The American national unemployment rate in 2002 was 5.1%. As of right now the current federal minimum wage is $5.15 an hour. As national salary increases, it is predicted that the unemployment rates will rise accordingly. In their feeble attempt to help the low-wage people of this nation, the Democratic party failed to realize that having a job is better than having no job at all.

The states in this country which have the highest minimum wages also have the highest unemployment rates. According to the U.S. Census Bureau, Washington and Oregon are in the top three in both categories. Both have a minimum wage of over $7.00, and have unemployment rates of 7.3 and 7.5%. On the other hand, South Dakota, which has the lowest unemployment rate in the nation of 3.1%, uses the federal minimum wage.

It is obvious that there is a correlation between how much workers are paid, and the number of jobs available. It is appalling to think that people are willing to make thousands of helpless families suffer in poverty, just to raise their pay to $7.00.

President Bush is willing to support raising the federal minimum wage by a dollar, as long as certain states are allowed to opt out of it. This would prevent any potential job loss in states with smaller budgets. While some may argue that that defeats the purpose of raising the wage in the first place, it is obvious that this allows states to focus on economical issues at hand, as well as to help out families.

During the Depression our national unemployment rate sky rocketed from 3.1% to 24.75% over the period of a few years. In this day and age we are steadily working to keep up the economy. Raising the minimum wage could have catastrophic effects on our country. In the time of our grandparents there were hungry unemployed people lining the streets. Here we are eighty-one years later doing everything in our power to keep that from happening again.

Reading in the Reel World: Teaching Documentaries and Other Nonfiction Texts by John Golden © 2006 NCTE.

It's Time to Feel the Heat

By Emma Dobbins

The United States alone accounts for over 25% of the world's emissions of greenhouses gases. And even as the largest producing country of greenhouse gases, our government is *still* refusing to take appropriate action. In February of 2002, the White House Council of Economic Advisors said, "We need to recognize that it makes sense to discuss slowing emissions growth before trying to stop and eventually reverse it." The fact is, it's made sense to talk about this issue for the past fifteen years and now it's time for serious action. The Bush administration needs to get out of their comfortable chair of ignorance and show some ecological responsibility.

As this problem has continued to go untreated, our planet has literally begun to suffocate. Harmful greenhouse gases are trapping excess heat in our atmosphere. Normally, this heat would radiate out of the atmosphere but now much of it is being radiated back towards the Earth's surface resulting in the unnatural warming of our planet.

In the past century, the average surface temperature of the Earth has increased a total of 1.1°F (0.6° Celsius). Although this may not sound like much, its ecological impact is huge. Ecosystems all throughout the world are extremely delicate and can be altered or destroyed with a temperature fluctuation as small as 2°F. The U.S. climate action report from May of 2002 stated that since the industrial revolution, there has been a 30% increase of carbon dioxide, a 15% increase in nitrous oxide concentration and methane concentrations have nearly doubled.

Global warming isn't just a casual change in temperature but a raging invitation for ecological disaster. Ocean levels will rise dramatically not only endangering the surrounding lands, but the ecosystems within. Droughts and heat waves will deepen the problem over water resources. Weather extremes will initiate floods causing heightened levels of property damage and destruction. Most importantly, the potential for heat related illnesses and deaths would soar as well as the level of infectious diseases. The Union of Concerned Scientists also reported that mountain glaciers all over the world are receding and the global sea level has risen 300% faster in the past century than in the past 3,000 years.

Despite all of these facts, the Bush administration has still been hesitant to take action. In 2001, Bush pulled the United States out of the world wide treaty called the Kyoto Protocol. The Kyoto Protocol was the first legally binding treaty aimed towards the reduction of the emissions of greenhouse gases all throughout the world. In the same year, Bush also rejected a campaign pledge to limit carbon dioxide in burning fossil fuels.

Awareness is not only lacking within our government, but within our country itself. Too many people are not fully aware or do not believe in the harsh realities of global warming. The impacts are beyond serious and we need to stand up and recognize this. Nationwide recognition is the first step towards prying open the eyes of our oblivious government.

Reading in the Reel World: Teaching Documentaries and Other Nonfiction Texts by John Golden © 2006 NCTE.

Government Sells Out to Vioxx

By Jon Coon

In recent months the story of the prescription drug Vioxx has sparked keen debate over the issue of FDA licensing. After all, how is it possible that a drug with so much potential for health damage was ever approved for the general public? With an estimated number of 27,785 heart attacks and sudden cardiac death between 1999 and 2003, Vioxx must be seen as a menace to society.

Marketed as a painkiller to relieve arthritis, Vioxx exemplifies the very problem with today's prescription drug market. A large company, in this case Merck & Co., produces a number of studies in a limited time to allow the drug to be approved faster. While there have been multiple drugs that help to ease the pain of those in need, the lasting effect is never truly known until years after the drug's release. In Vioxx's situation it is evident that during the four years of its sales many millions of people were exposed to a harmful treatment.

The problem here is that in an effort to make big profits, the drug companies campaign and push the FDA to approve of their drugs before enough information is known. Vioxx was one of Merck's biggest moneymakers with estimated sales of over $2.5 billion dollars worldwide.

Solemnly, all the blame cannot simply be given to the FDA. It is after all not the FDA who sets their own budget. Where do American Congressmen or even President Bush stand on the issue? Obviously neither thought that providing additional funding to the FDA was a necessity before the latest news of mismanagement was divulged. When compared to the amount of money drug companies spend purely on marketing, one can see the discrepancy in the process of approving drugs. Based on an article by Stephen Pomper the FDA has shot itself in the foot so to speak. With regulations passed during the late 90's that folded to corporate demand for advertising and cut the approval process from 30 months to 12 it is not surprising that a Vioxx would turn up sooner or later.

To fix this substantial dilemma of American healthcare the government would be thoughtful to give more funds to support the FDA, restrict the ability to advertise (a key component of sales) and finally enact a larger time frame for approval to ensure better safety. Without action the citizens of America will undoubtedly be the ill-advised guinea pigs to drug companies of the World.

Reading in the Reel World: Teaching Documentaries and Other Nonfiction Texts by John Golden © 2006 NCTE.

3 Nonfiction Writing and Analysis

This chapter includes classroom-tested activities that use documentaries to teach writing and analytical skills that are a regular part of the high school curriculum. Every classroom teacher, especially when working with nonfiction texts, should help students to identify the author's purpose, tone, and perspective. In the activities that follow, I suggest clips from documentaries that work well when you want students to practice these analytical skills that can then be applied to other print texts.

In the second half of this chapter, I offer ideas for how to use documentaries to help students improve their nonfiction writing skills in the main modes of communication: persuasive, narrative, and expository. While students will most certainly benefit from the information about nonfiction film in Chapter 1, they can still be successful with these activities without extensive knowledge about documentaries.

Analytical Writing Skills

Theme

Each of the skills presented in Chapter 2—compare/contrast, cause/effect, and problem/solution—leads students to the point where they should be able to interpret the message or theme of a text. This message can be clearly stated or it may only be implied, but students need to be able to synthesize what they have read or seen and create a statement with which the author of the text would probably agree. The next step, of course, is for them to support that statement with examples from the text. The ability to discern the point an author is trying to make is a valuable one for typical standardized tests, but it becomes even more important as students encounter texts in the media that have inherent messages about public and social policies that can greatly influence their lives. I like to use clips from Michael Moore films because they resonate so well with students and because his documentary techniques are so readily apparent and good for discussion. When working with theme, I like to use the following clips.

Bowling for Columbine (Michael Moore, 2002)

Clip 1: 0:26:00–0:28:26; Chapter 8 on DVD

During the course of this film, Michael Moore explores the roles of guns and violence and their effects on American society. This clip begins with an interview of a spokesperson for Lockheed Martin, one of the largest U.S. defense contractors, which is located in the Colorado town where the shootings at Columbine High School took place. After getting him to admit that Lockheed is closely involved in the life of the community, Moore asks him whether the fact that the United States uses weapons around the world might have had an effect on the boys who did the shooting. When the spokesperson denies any such connection, Moore makes the connection for him with a montage of various violent U.S. interventions accompanied by Louis Armstrong's "What a Wonderful World" playing on the sound track; the visual track displays extraordinarily brutal pictures of bombs dropping and dead bodies. The statements on the text track feel authoritative—like facts—but many of them are subject to interpretation, though they come too quickly to really process. By the fifteenth country or action listed and visualized (ending with September 11, 2001), Moore's point, regardless of historical accuracy, has been driven home. According to Michael Moore, the United States is a violent aggressor, which, when modeled by schoolchildren, causes even more violence.

Questions to Consider

1. Consider the following statements about the theme expressed in this clip. Why would Moore agree or disagree?
    a. American military intervention has been largely unsuccessful over the years.
    b. State-sanctioned violence, like war, is different from individual violence.
    c. It is a wonderful world.
2. In what ways do the song and the graphic images presented support Moore's theme?
3. Do you agree or disagree with the point Moore is trying to make in this clip?

Clip 2: 1:07:32–1:11:40; Chapter 22 on DVD

Another factor that Moore suggests might cause violence is the way our media tends to demonize minorities, which causes people to fear them.

As evidence, Moore shows clips from the reality TV show *Cops*, in which police officers regularly chase and roughly handcuff suspects, a majority of whom, the producer of the show admits, are minorities. During the interview with the producer, Moore suggests a different kind of show called "Corporate Cops," in which we see Moore chasing down white-collar criminals (see Figure 3.1). This clip ends with the producer agreeing that, as envisioned by Moore, the show would be a good one but probably not a realistic one. Note: the DVD of this film includes the full "Corporate Cops" episode that ran on Moore's TV show.

Questions to Consider

1. Consider the following statements about the theme expressed in this clip. Why would Moore agree or disagree?

   a. The media demonizes minorities, which causes people to fear them.

   b. The TV show *Cops* brings black people and white people together to reduce our fears and celebrate our diversity.

   c. Tolerance and understanding should be featured in the media.

   d. Corporate criminals and other criminals are treated about the same by police and the media.

2. Select one of the preceding statements with which you think Moore would agree. How did he express this through his editing and other cinematic choices?

3. How does Moore use humor to help make his point?

4. Do you personally agree or disagree with the preceding statements? Why?

Tone

My students always have difficulty with tone. They often confuse it with "mood" or know it only as "tone of voice." I can generally get them to a better definition by enacting a scene in which I pretend to be upset about the quality of their last papers, hurling the papers to the ground and cursing them out in PG-13 words. Students quickly learn that tone is the speaker's *attitude* toward the subject; in my case, it is angry and frustrated at their apparent lack of effort and ability to use semicolons properly. They are also usually able to support that statement of tone by referring to my actions and word choice, but when we turn to a print text, they often are not able to discern tone solely from the written word. If, however, they are given the opportunity to practice first with a documentary clip, using a note-taking form like that included in Appendix

Figure 3.1. Moore in *Bowling for Columbine* making his point satirically, dressed as a cop who busts white-collar criminals.

B, students have been more successful in applying their analysis to a print text.

Since tone is almost always expressed with an adjective, I usually provide students with a list of tone words from which they can select. It is then their job to identify the words and images in the film that express that tone. Finally, I try to get students to see a connection between tone and purpose because authors typically employ a specific tone to achieve a particular purpose. The following clips work well for students to examine the word choice and images that lead to a solid analysis of tone.

The Fog of War (Errol Morris, 2003)

0:33:43–0:38:23; Chapter 12 on DVD

This documentary is an in-depth interview with Robert McNamara, the controversial secretary of defense under Presidents Johnson and Kennedy during the early years of the conflict in Vietnam. In this section, Errol Morris, the filmmaker, is asking McNamara about the firebombing of Tokyo, the planning of which McNamara was involved in, at the end of World War II. Students will need only the brief background I have included here to understand the clip, though McNamara does refer to a man by the name of LeMay, who was an American Air Force general at the time.

The clip begins with World War II archival footage of the mechanisms of war: bombs being loaded, flight plans charted, bombing results tallied, bombers dropping their payloads, etc., underneath slow, ominous music that is a decided contrast to the images. Morris then adds McNamara's voice talking about the Air Force's insistence on target destruction, cutting to a close-up of McNamara saying, in a tone that could be interpreted as gleeful or proud, that the Air Force killed over 100,000 Japanese civilians in Tokyo in a single night; under this Morris adds archival black-and-white footage of a city in flames and sounds of fire. Only occasionally in this film do the viewers hear the questions Morris asks McNamara, but here Morris clearly asks him, "Were you aware that this was going to happen?," to which McNamara hems and haws for a bit until settling on the explanation that he was "part of a mechanism that, in a sense, recommended it." Not quite the "yes" Morris might have been looking for.

An interesting transition occurs next when Morris moves from a chart of bombing calculations to an animated sequence that he probably created in which numbers—not bombs—are falling from the sky, as McNamara tries to make the case that he was attempting to be more efficient, not in terms of killing more people, but in terms of weakening the enemy. Morris continues to let McNamara talk, and while McNamara rationalizes his own part in the decision to firebomb a civilian center, Morris cuts to a series of charts, diagrams, damage reports, and efficiency reports. After a brief discussion of a lost American pilot, we see the stark black-and-white footage of Tokyo as it burns: horrific images of a flattened and destroyed city, and then a hush and quiet breeze as the scene fades to black.

Questions to Consider

1. What is the filmmaker's attitude toward war? What images, sounds, words, or phrases reveal this tone?

2. What is the filmmaker's attitude toward McNamara? What images, sounds, words, or phrases reveal this tone? How do Morris's editing choices reveal this tone?

3. What do you think is Morris's purpose in this scene? What message does he want to deliver to his audience, and how does the tone reflect this purpose?

4. Choose a different tone that another filmmaker might have brought to this story of the Tokyo firebombing. What images, sounds, words, or phrases might he or she use to create this tone?

Baraka (Ron Fricke, 1992)

00:41:46–00:48:31; Chapter 12 on DVD

Baraka is a dialogue-free expression of the difficulties and ironies of modern life. This scene includes a series of time-lapse filmed images of people walking, driving, working, and commuting. The people are often shot from overhead, and they are indistinct from one another as they rush in and out of the frame. The locations are not identified on the text track, but it becomes clear that they are cities from around the world. On the sound track is a rhythmic, driving beat that seems to accelerate and add parts and other sound effects as the scene goes on. At the very end of the sequence, you'll see images of people going up and down an escalator, from which the director cuts to a scene of baby chickens spinning around on a conveyor belt until they are dropped down a hole. Can anyone say "metaphor"?

Questions to Consider

1. What is the filmmaker's attitude toward the modern world? What images reveal this tone?

2. What comparison is the director trying to make between people and the baby chickens? How does this support the filmmaker's tone or theme?

3. How do the music and sound effects contribute to the tone?

Born into Brothels (Zana Briski and Ross Kauffman, 2004)

0:39:40–0:43:53; Chapter 10 on DVD

This is a perfect clip to show how *contrasting* tones can express a point of view. The subjects of this Academy Award–winning film are eight children of women and men who live in the brothels of India. Zana Brinski, one of the directors, lived in the brothels, taught a photography class for the children, and would occasionally take them on field trips out of their poverty-ridden neighborhoods. In this short clip, we see the children arrive at the beach for what looks like the first time ever. We see them in bright light, running, jumping, and laughing and smiling a lot. The music is upbeat and filled with life and energy, just like the children. Stop at the 0:41:39 mark and ask students about the tone. They will probably say things like "joyful," "exuberant," "celebratory," etc., but be sure they offer some specific evidence from the audio and visual track as evidence. When you restart the clip and play to the end, you will see a sharply different tone as the children return to the brothels. Now the camera is jerky and the images are blurred. The music has become harsh and discordant. Next, we hear the diegetic sounds of the neighborhood: car horns, shouts, cries, and whisperings. The music that starts up sounds sinister, and the camera follows the children through the brothels, though we appear to be stalking them through the prying eyes of the people on the streets.

Questions to Consider

1. What is the filmmakers' tone toward the children? What about toward the brothels? How do you know?

2. Why do the filmmakers so rapidly switch tones in this clip? What point are they trying to make about the children and the brothels?

3. If the filmmakers had a more positive attitude about the brothels, how might they have filmed and edited this scene differently?

Bias/Perspective/Point of View

Any discussion of tone and theme, as in the preceding activities, will inevitably lead to an examination of the bias of the author. The point an author makes by using a particular tone is often the result of his or her point of view. When an author or filmmaker discusses the issue of global warming, for example, we need to be able to analyze exactly what his or her perspective is so that we can better understand the validity of the solution the piece presents. Since *bias* has negative connotations, I tend to use the word *perspective*, which also distinguishes this idea from the literary term *point of view*, though all three get at the same question: how do we determine the agenda of the piece? Unfortunately, a lot of the nonfiction texts students encounter these days present a partisan political perspective, so I usually begin these activities by introducing or reminding students about the "liberal" and "conservative" labels that may apply to the authors of nonfiction texts. As a class or in pairs, students complete the following chart:

	Liberal/"The Left"	**Conservative/"The Right"**
People	John Kerry	George W. Bush
Political Party	Democrat	Republican
Abortion	right to choose	right to life
Gun Control	more limitation	strict interpretation of the Second Amendment
Gay Marriage		
Education		
Death Penalty		
Assisted Suicide		

Luckily, not every nonfiction piece is political, but it still has a perspective that students need to be able to identify, so next we discuss the following four questions that I have found most useful in determining the perspective of just about any nonfiction piece. Imagine applying these questions to a scene from a documentary about global warming.

1. *WHAT information is included?* Statistics about rising carbon emissions, interviews with a climatologist who says that the temperature spikes are "unprecedented" and a doctor who says the temperature rises are causing a "severe health crisis" in developing countries.

2. *HOW is this information presented?* We see stark black-and-white images of billowing smokestacks, and then the film cuts to a school playground. The statistics are shown in a bar graph with the amount of emissions overlaying the playground in red, stretching all the way across the screen. A slow, mournful song by a single trumpet can be heard as images of malnourished children in Bangladesh dissolve into the original picture of the smokestacks.

3. *What information is NOT included?* There are no interviews with the owners of the factories or alternate theories about the rise in temperatures. No connection is made between global warming and the health of the Bangladeshi children.

4. *What can you assume about this piece's PERSPECTIVE? Why?* The filmmaker is an environmentalist who probably would like more restrictions on pollution, because he or she interviews only those who propose more regulations and he or she uses powerfully emotional images, music, and editing to give the viewer the clear impression that pollution is the direct cause of the world's health issues.

So, what should students be looking for as they try to detect bias in a nonfiction piece by using these four questions?

1. *WHAT information is included?* Students should look for facts and evidence presented but also pay attention to word choice and the topics presented. They also need to keep track of who is interviewed and to identify the subjects' backgrounds and affiliations, if known.

2. *HOW is this information presented?* Students should look at the text and visual tracks and listen closely to the audio track. These will include the images seen, music heard, and textual information overlaid on the screen; see Chapter 1 for more details.

3. *What information is NOT included?* Students should always be wondering: what am I not seeing, reading, or hearing?

4. *What can you assume about this piece's PERSPECTIVE? Why?* Students should make a statement of the author's or film-

maker's perspective followed by a "because" statement that uses evidence they collected from each of the other three questions.

When Michael Moore's *Fahrenheit 9/11* came out in the midst of the presidential election of 2004, people on all sides of the political spectrum went a little nuts. It aroused such passion and raised key questions about the purpose, role, and ethics of documentary filmmaking. And it was wonderful for a film teacher, because not one, but two "answer films" (*Celsius 41.11* and *Fahrenhype 9/11*) to Moore's were released, allowing us to demonstrate perspective very easily. While neither of these answer films is a particularly well-made film, almost any clip chosen at random from either one would work well for this activity. I have to thank my social studies colleague Don Gavitte for the idea of using the following pair of documentaries, which present two decidedly contrasting views on who is responsible for the United States being unprepared for the terrorist attacks of 9/11.

Fahrenheit 9/11 (Michael Moore, 2004)

0:17:53–0:19:19; Chapter 5 on DVD

This section begins with footage of President George W. Bush receiving the news that the second tower of the World Trade Center has been struck. As Moore dissolves to Bush remaining seated in the classroom, demonstrating the passage of time, he speculates on what Bush might have been thinking at that time. We then see a series of images, including Bush dressed in casual clothes at his ranch in August while receiving an intelligence briefing, and then Condoleezza Rice, Bush's security advisor, testifying before the 9/11 commission. Moore includes only the section in which she states the title of that August briefing: "Bin Laden Determined to Attack inside the United States." The final image of the sequence is that of Bush fishing.

Celsius 41.11 (Kevin Knoblock, 2004)

0:13:06–0:15:31; Chapter 2 on DVD

The clip from this film, which is subtitled "The temperature at which the brain begins to die," explores the same issue and time period of *Fahrenheit 9/11* and even uses a section from the same testimony by Rice. After a former Republican congressman says that there are some people who believe that Bush did not do enough to protect us before 9/11, we hear a stirring speech by Bush and see images of 9/11 intercut with images from the bombing of Pearl Harbor. Whereas Moore's film has

Figure 3.2. Contrasting images of President Bush from two different films that illustrate the perspective of each. The first shot is from *Fahrenheit 9/11* and the second is from the answer film *Celsius 41.11*.

Rice only stating the title of the daily briefing in August, here she says that the briefing was historical in nature and was not prompted by a specific warning. When a terrorism expert lays the blame on the former president's inaction, we see still pictures of Clinton, passive in the back of the frame, contrasted with those of Bush, animated, pointing, and clearly in charge. See Figure 3.2 for contrasting images of President Bush from these two films.

Questions to Consider

1. What impression does each film give of President Bush? What specific images, words, or sound effects give you that feeling?
2. How do the editing choices affect the perspective each film takes?
3. How does a viewer watching both of these films determine "the truth"?

After students have had an opportunity to examine paired texts for their particular perspectives, I show them another clip and, using a chart like the one titled "Perspective in Nonfiction Texts" in Appendix B, they imagine creating a piece on the same subject but with a different viewpoint. Still using the first three questions—what's included, how is it presented, and what is excluded?—they should think about what information they would present or not present in this new film and how they would present it to their audience. Students should be able to articulate this new perspective with another "because" statement; sometimes I have them work with a partner to analyze each other's statement.

After this activity, students should be in a position to read some nonfiction articles and apply these questions to determine the perspective offered by each. I especially like to use newspaper editorials and editorial cartoons, but every nonfiction text has a perspective, and these questions will help students be better able to determine what it is.

Writing Skills

Documentaries can be used in a number of ways to improve students' writing abilities. Already the activities described in this book have provided many opportunities for students to write in a variety of forms, including compare/contrast, explaining editing choices, and others, but this section focuses on the specific skills students need for the types of writing that are most typical in high school classrooms: the persuasive, expository, and narrative modes.

Persuasive Writing

One of the most successful activities I have done with my students comes by way of my friend Kenyatta Graves, who wrote and delivered workshops on argumentation for the College Board. He made it easy for me, and ultimately for my students, to recognize the key elements of a strong persuasive piece: pathos, logos, and ethos. To introduce these concepts to my students, I give them the material in Figure 3.3, which asks them to write a series of short persuasive pieces using a scenario

---

Introducing Pathos, Ethos, and Logos

Scenario: You arrive home one hour after your curfew and your parent or guardian has decided that you should be grounded for a week as punishment. Try to persuade your parent or guardian to change his or her mind by using the three types of arguments.

- **Argument 1:** Appeal to your parent or guardian by showing that you are trustworthy and that you care deeply about the situation and its effect on him or her. You should use "I."
- **Argument 2:** Appeal to your parent or guardian by telling a story with lots of details in order to create pity for yourself and your situation. You can use "I," though you may refer to other people as well.
- **Argument 3:** Appeal to your parent or guardian by citing statistics and commonly held beliefs. Refer to experts and facts that can be supported and explained. You should not use "I."

Now, look over the following descriptions of each of the persuasive appeals. How did you use each in the pieces that you wrote?

- **Logos** (Logical): This type of appeal uses inductive or deductive reasoning by citing statistics, facts, experts, and evidence. When using this type of argument, you offer your audience examples that are similar to this subject and convince them to draw the conclusion you want. (Argument 3)
- **Ethos** (Ethical): This type of argument requires that you establish yourself (the author) as trustworthy and respectful of your audience. You do this by demonstrating that you have taken the time to research your topic, which establishes your credibility on the subject. (Argument 1)
- **Pathos** (Emotional): This is when you appeal to the emotions of your audience by describing in detail the effect of a particular situation. You should try to arouse a sense of pity, anger, fear, or other emotion in your audience. (Argument 2)

Figure 3.3. Introducing pathos, ethos, and logos.

they may have themselves faced. To further confirm their knowledge of these concepts, I ask students to imagine they are going to write a persuasive essay that explores both sides of a controversial topic—say, capital punishment—and to think about what logos, pathos, and ethos information they might include in their pieces. Their charts might look something like this:

Type	Pro-Capital Punishment	Anti-Capital Punishment
Logos	Facts and evidence on how the penalty reduces crime rates	Statistics on numbers of minorities and poor people on death row
Pathos	Recount the details of a story of a brutal crime for which the offender was sentenced to death	Recount the story of a condemned mentally retarded man who confessed to a crime after the police had beaten him
Ethos	Include interviews with death penalty opponents and even condemned prisoners	Acknowledge the human nature of an "eye for an eye" approach

The next step I take with my students is to show them a few clips from documentaries (see the following recommendations) and ask them to try to identify these appeals by using a chart like the one titled "Persuasive Appeals" in Appendix B. Usually I assign students only a single type of appeal to identify for the first clip and then add more as we go on. After they watch the clips, students evaluate how persuasive the section is and which appeal was most effective for them. Before moving on to the next clip, I ask them to think about what other information the filmmaker might have included, using each of the three types of appeals. The following clips work well.

War Comes to America (final film of the Why We Fight series, Frank Capra, 1945)

1:36:00–1:40:30

Before showing this clip, you might want to tell (or remind) your students about who the United States was fighting in World War II and that before the bombing of Pearl Harbor, we had a policy of neutrality that evolved into greater support for the Allied nations. This clip, from a series of films intended to attract support for U.S. involvement in World War II, begins with a newspaper headline announcing Germany's invasion of Poland. From there, we hear an ethical appeal from the British prime minister about how German leaders cannot be trusted, and we see emotional images of preparations for war, including an infant being fitted with a gas mask. The narrator uses a logical appeal by referring to a Gallup poll stating that most Americans feel Germany is responsible for the war, and some congressmen use logic to try to change the official neutrality policy of our country. The sequence ends with another Gallup poll about America's changing feelings toward Japan.

Fahrenheit 9/11 (Michael Moore, 2004)

1:23:08–1:30:16

This scene about military recruiters begins with interviews with soldiers in Iraq who are unhappy about the way the war is going. Images of wounded soldiers (pathos) are added to the charts and statistics (logos) about declining military enlistments. Moore uses ethical appeals by casting himself as the champion of the poor and disenfranchised. Pictures of people in poverty support Moore's central point that the military preys on the poor; a group of young black men who say they are constantly targeted by recruiters also supports this point. Moore also includes a military TV ad that itself includes each type of appeal. The last section of this clip shows a pair of Marine recruiters on the prowl to the sounds of a *Saturday Night Fever*-ish song on the audio track. After showing the two recruiters make promises, cajole, and gather information, Moore cuts back to the group of young males, one of whom says that he would love to experience college life without the risk: a statement that uses both logos and pathos appeals.

Fahrenhype 9/11 (Alan Peterson, 2004)

0:51:20–0:54:59

This is an answer film to Michael Moore's that is determined to "unravel the truth" about *Fahrenheit 9/11*. In this sequence, three people—conservative columnist Ann Coulter, former Democratic Senator Zell Miller, and actor Ron Silver—offer reasons why Americans should support Bush's Iraqi and homeland policies. Each one offers readily identifiable pathos, ethos, and logos appeals in each of their persuasive statements.

After viewing some of these clips and identifying the various appeals used or that could be added, students should now begin to select a topic for their own persuasive essay. As they conduct their research, they should identify what kind of information they might need to locate to make their piece as convincing as possible. Still working with the template (the Persuasive Appeals chart in Appendix B), students should consider how to use all three of the appeals in their piece. I usually require that students include examples of all three types of appeals in their final drafts.

Narrative Writing

Maybe it's just me, but every time I read something, I picture it as a movie. If it's a fictional story, I try to imagine who would act in it, what kind of lighting or framing the director would use, and what music would be playing. If it's a nonfiction story, I imagine it as a documentary with a voice-over, visuals, and a text track. When working with fiction print texts, I often ask students to storyboard literary texts to help them visualize the key details. In my storyboarding activities, students are asked to draw how a print text would be filmed (shot type, editing, sound, lighting, etc.) as a way to begin analyzing the text. If a student draws the scene using low-key lighting, for instance, this probably says something about the mood of the story.

As I was doing this storyboarding activity with my students one year, I realized that this kind of visualization could help them with their own narrative writing. I have always found that my students neglect the use of visual and aural details in their writing, so I have begun asking them to insert storyboarding as a prewriting step, which is described below.

Once students have brainstormed a list of possible narrative topics to write about, I show them a series of first-person documentaries in which the narrator reflects on a significant event while the visual, text, and sound tracks give us additional details and information. After one of the clips, I show them what a *film treatment* for that scene might look like (see Figure 3.4 for an example from *The Kid Stays in the Picture*; blank forms are available in Appendix B). A nonfiction film treatment includes all the visual and audio information that is seen on screen, in addition to commentary about what the director might have expected the audience to be thinking or feeling. Then, as we watch another clip, I ask students to imagine themselves as the filmmaker and to write their own treatment for that scene in the manner prescribed. They may need to see the clip more than once, though they do not need to have all the dialogue, just the key moments. You can show as many clips as you think necessary for your students to get the idea; I usually show two or three. The best clips I have found for this activity tend to be quite short and have a lot of visual details to go along with the narration. Following are descriptions of the clips I have used and that I recommend.

The Kid Stays in the Picture (Nanette Burstein and Brett Morgan, 2002)

0:03:00-0:04:23

This is a brief sequence in which legendary Hollywood producer Robert Evans describes the time when he was "discovered" as an actor one afternoon at the Beverly Hills Hotel. This scene, like most of the film, is told through Evans's voice-over and still photos that have been enhanced and animated. It's a great clip for recognizing the visual details in a narrative piece.

Touching the Void (Kevin Macdonald, 2003)

Clip 1: 0:33:13–0:35:03; Chapter 6 on DVD

This documentary features extensive reenactments of a mountain climbing accident, and this clip presents a moment in which one of the climbers has slid off of a high ridge and is hanging on only by the rope being held by his climbing partner. Because it is snowing and he is far from

Nonfiction Film Treatment *The Kid Stays in the Picture* (The Pool Scene)		
Visual: *What will the audience see?*	**Audio**: *What will the audience hear? Key dialogue?*	**Commentary**: *What do you want the audience to feel?*
Blue sky, palm trees, the Beverly Hills Hotel, perfectly blue water, cabanas and deck chairs lined carefully alongside	Evans: I decided to play hooky, sit by the pool, and get some sun at the Beverly Hills Hotel. Music: Soft, light strings Sounds: no other sounds	That it is an ideal day in Evans's memory
Evans in pool, hair slicked back, skin tanned. A pretty woman in a bathing suit extends both hands towards Evans.	Evans: Suddenly, a woman approached. "Excuse me, young man, are you an actor?" Music: same, but pace is quickening for the next shots	That Evans is a pretty good- looking and cool guy
Norma, dressed in pearls, holding an Oscar, a small smile	Evans: Norma Shearer, one of the few remaining icons of Hollywood aristocracy	That Norma comes from money and has a lot of power
Rows and rows of deck chairs	Shearer (as told by Evans): Would you like to play my deceased husband, Irving Thalberg, in film?	That Evans is at first overwhelmed by the idea
Close-up of Evans smiling, streaks of sun radiating out of his head	Evans: I'm thinking to myself, wow, this can't be happening to me.	That Evans is very excited
Evans, shirtless and very serious, shaking hands with Shearer, who is in a blue-and-white-striped robe, smiling with bright red lipstick	Evans: Miss Shearer, it would be an honor. Why not? Music: slowly fades out	That his sex appeal has a lot to do with his success

Figure 3.4. Nonfiction film treatment.

his friend, the climber holding the rope does not realize that his friend is dangling off the side of the mountain. When using this scene as well as clip 2, I usually split the class in half, asking each to watch from one climber's perspective (see Figure 3.5).

Figure 3.5. This powerful scene from one of the many reenactments of
Touching the Void provides students with a great prompt for narrative writing.

Clip 2: 39:30–0:41:21; Chapter 7 on DVD

Just a little further on in the film, the climber holding the rope has a
decision to make: should he cut the rope or not? Each climber gives his
own perspective on what should be done, and we see great visual details and sound effects of the moment when he cuts the rope and the
other climber falls. We see the reaction of the climber who cut the line
and then the scene fades to black. Your students are going to scream at
you when you stop the film here, but tell them it all turns out okay in
the end: remind them that the one who fell is still alive, at least enough
to narrate the film.

When students return to the list of ideas for a narrative they have
brainstormed, they should select one that includes a scene for which
they can write a treatment like that in Figure 3.4. This treatment, it's
important to note, is not a final product; it has been most successful for
me when it is used as a prewriting stage, a step before students begin
drafting. I am not entirely sure why it works, but the process of visual-
izing their scenes and having to write commentary alongside the scene
descriptions encourages students to produce a tremendous amount of
detail they might not otherwise include.

Expository Writing

This book provides numerous opportunities for expository writi[ng,] as analytical essays on the modes of documentaries, the cons[truction] of reality in nonfiction film, the manipulation of audience thr[ough ed]iting, and so on; you will have no shortage of expository essa[y assign]ments for your students while using documentaries. In addit[ion to the] two expository assignments that follow, I also want to pass [on my] favorite strategy for helping students, particularly ninth and t[enth grad]ers, to understand the key factors they should consider *befor[e they start]* to write. To get at this, I introduce students to RAFT, an a[cronym for] Role, Audience, Format, and Topic. The main purpose of [RAFT is for] students to understand how their audience, purpose, and mode of expression affect their word choice, sentence structure, organization, etc. This strategy gives students an awareness of the different voices they need to use for different situations and the tools to use their voices effectively.

RAFT

When first introducing RAFT, I tell students to imagine that they witnessed a fight in the hallway during lunch and to write a letter to a friend describing the fight in detail. Next I ask them to revise their letter by imagining they are writing it to the principal of the school. They should then highlight or underline the changes they had to make in their letters because of the change in audience and discuss why they made these changes. Then I draw a chart on the board like the one below that identifies the components of RAFT:

Role	This is the persona you take on as you compose or deliver your piece: *student, historian, parent, movie star, inanimate object*, and so on.
Audience	This is who will receive your piece: *a child, a celebrity, a lawyer, teacher*, and so on.
Format	This is the form you have chosen to use to communicate your ideas:*letter, job application, pamphlet, poem, diary entry*, and so on.
Topic	This is the topic or the purpose of your piece: *to inform, to sell, to convince, to protest, to warn*, and so on.

After I have introduced them to the components of RAFT, I ask students to return to that same letter and change it by changing its format. Their letters could be turned into diary entries, poems, newspaper articles, and so forth.

Looking back at their original letters, we can see that the main topic or purpose of the letters was **to inform** their audience about the fight. Then I ask students to change the topic or purpose of their letters: **to warn** others from fighting, **to demand** a change in school safety, **to praise** the fighters, etc.

Once students have an understanding of the strategy and can see how the text changes when the elements of RAFT change, I let them practice by responding to scenes from the following documentaries.

Night and Fog (Alain Resnais, 1955)

0:04:27–0:09:12

This film is an extremely powerful and graphic documentation of the Holocaust. In this sequence, we see and hear about people being rounded up, loaded on to trains, and transported to concentration camps; we also learn about their first days at the camps. After showing the clip, I ask students to identify RAFT elements of the piece as presented and then to reimagine this section of the documentary as it would be if it were made for young children. What images would be shown or not shown? What would the narration include or not include? How would the music be different? Then I ask them to change the text one more time by imagining themselves as one of the prisoners writing a diary entry about their experiences. Whenever you are working with RAFT, it's important to spend a little time reflecting on what changes in the text when RAFT elements change: word choice, organization, text features, etc. When TBD (to be decided) appears in the following charts, it means that students can choose to do whatever they want with that part of RAFT.

Night and Fog	Original	New Text 1	New Text 2
Role	Poetic expository mode	Poetic expository mode	**Prisoner leaving on train to camp**
Audience	Adults familiar with the Holocaust	**Elementary children unfamiliar with the Holocaust**	Elementary children unfamiliar with the Holocaust
Format	Documentary film	Documentary film	**Diary entry**
Topic	To remind us never to forget	To remind us never to forget	To remind us never to forget

Jackass (Jeff Tremaine, 2002, rated R)

0:39:23–0:40:29

Depending on your age, gender, and tolerance for stupidity, you m
view the *Jackass* movie and the MTV show that preceded it as either
funny or very stupid. This film is a compilation of humiliating and
gerous stunts that the participants willingly do to themselves or
ers. Me? I laugh a lot, but at least I feel a little guilty about it. Mo
the scenes in the movie are extremely gross and contain nudity
profanity, but this one, relatively free of those (though be sure to
off at the identified counter), focuses on one of the participants, Jo
Knoxville, trying out what he calls his "Rocket Skates," in which he
straps fireworks to his Rollerblades in an effort to move at super speeds.
Afterward, students should take on the role of a concerned parent who
wants to get this movie removed from theaters by writing a petition to
the producers of the film. Or they can write a review of the film from
the perspective of someone who liked or did not like the film. Again, I
try to end a RAFT activity by discussing what has changed and why.

Jackass	Original	New Text 1	New Text 2
Role	Interactive mode	**A parent**	**Someone who likes/does not like the film**
Audience	Teenage boys?	**Producers of film**	**TBD**
Format	Documentary	**A petition**	**A review**
Topic	To show how ridiculous . . .	**To demand the movie be removed from theaters**	**To persuade someone to see or not see the movie**

Koyaanisqatsi (Godfrey Reggio, 1983)

0:16:26–0:20:30

This sequence from a wordless documentary about the state of the
modern world illustrates the conflicts between nature and industrial-
ization. Beautiful images of open, pristine landscape are contrasted with
heavy machinery and destruction. The music changes as the pipelines
and electrical towers scar the otherwise beautiful surroundings. The
students' first task is to write a letter to the editor about the problems
associated with development and the effects on our natural resources.
Then, even though poetry is not expository, I like to have students construct a poem from what they have seen in this clip in which they take
on the role of Nature itself speaking to one of the industries highlighted
in the film.

Koyaanisqatsi	Original	New Text 1	New Text 2
Role	Poetic expository	**Concerned citizen**	Nature
Audience	General audience	General audience	A company that is represented in the clip
Format	Documentary film	**Letter to the editor**	A poem
Topic	To inform about the destructiveness of industrialization	To inform about the destructiveness of industrialization	To inform about the destructiveness of industrialization

This Is Spinal Tap (Rob Reiner, 1984, rated R)

0:18:43–21.37

This clip from a comedy about a group of aging heavy metal musicians has the look and feel of a documentary and is usually referred to as a "mockumentary." In this sequence, one of the musicians is complaining to his manager about the "catastrophe" of the backstage catering, with the little bread not matching up to the larger-sized meat slices. Then, when we see the band on stage, the guitarist is unable to get back up while playing the guitar lying on his back. I like to ask students to picture these two scenes as if they were from a real documentary about the problems that celebrities face. Last, I let students take on the role of one of the musicians (Nigel Tufnel) and to construct a piece for whatever audience, topic, and form they choose; they might choose a letter, a song, a poster, an e-mail, a comic book, and so on.

Spinal Tap	Original	New Text 1	New Text 2
Role	Expository mode	Expository mode	**The musician**
Audience	Adults familiar with heavy metal music	Adults familiar with heavy metal music	TBD
Format	Mockumentary	**Real documentary**	TBD
Topic	To make fun of the proclivities of celebrities	**To inform about difficulties of rock-and-roll star**	TBD

The War Room (Chris Hegedus and D. A. Pennebaker, 1993)

I recommend this RAFT activity only if students have been exposed to the various modes of documentary style discussed in Chapter 1, because this activity asks students to imagine a scene from this observational documentary that is largely favorable to candidate Bill Clinton as though it were from an interactive documentary that mocks him, and then to imagine it as part of a reflective film. Students will need to know each of the stylistic and ethical considerations of each mode in order to be successful with the activity. Just about any five-minute clip from this film will work well.

War Room	Original	New Text 1	New Text 2
Role	Observational	**Interactive**	**Reflexive**
Audience	Political enthusiasts	Political enthusiasts	**TBD**
Format	Documentary film	Documentary film	**Documentary film**
Topic	To emphasize the need to control the political message	**To mock Bill Clinton and his supporters**	TBD

By the end of the year, my students are more than a little sick of hearing me say "Let's make a RAFT" before they start writing an expository piece (an anonymous student made a raft out of popsicle sticks labeled "USS Golden" and sunk it in the sink in the back of my classroom), but it is an easy exercise that empowers students to think about how and why they write.

Expository Writing Activity: Home Movies

Another expository assignment that I enjoy doing with my students came about, like most of my best ideas, by accident. For a narrative writing assignment one year, I asked some students to bring in a home movie from a vacation or a holiday and to narrate the action to the class. My hope was that the film would trigger those key visual and aural details that are so essential to good narratives. What I forgot was how deadly *boring* most home movies are. After the fifth one, the class and I were either nodding off or trying to poke our eyes out; the only thing that made them bearable were some funny, offhand comments students were making about the films. One student, for instance, showed a scene with his brother and sisters in front of the Grand Canyon, but the camera suddenly veered off to follow a young guy with his shirt off, and the student who was narrating in class said, "Oh, yeah, my mother had just gotten divorced, so I guess she was looking." More seriously, another student brought in a Christmas video and seemed to realize for the first time that she was rarely in the film when it was shot by her stepmother.

Students' off-the-cuff analyses of their own films were much more engaging than the stories they were telling, and this led me to an interesting assignment in which I ask students to examine their own home movies in the same way they would any other documentary. To generate the analysis, I ask them the following questions:

1. Who usually films your home movies? Why do you think *this* person does?

2. Identify the mode of the home movie (see Chapter 1 for definitions). Is it merely observational, or is there a sense of interaction? Do you get any sense of reflexivity? Why do you think the "filmmaker" chose this mode?

3. Home movies are rarely edited (unfortunate for anyone forced to sit through them), but what can you say about what the "filmmaker" chooses to film or not film? Why? What seems to be missing from the film? Why? What is framed in close-ups? Why?

4. Observe the behavior of the people being filmed. How are they acting compared to how you know they behave when the camera is not on?

5. If you were to add music and/or sound effects to this film, what would you include and why? How would it change the feelings of the audience? If you were to add to the text track of the movie, what information would you want to communicate and how would this affect the audience?

Students' final projects include a summary of a key five- to ten-minute scene from one of their home movies, an analysis that considers some of the points generated by the previous questions, and a conclusion in which they come to some kind of understanding about themselves, their families, or the nature of home movie–making. Some students who are technically savvy and have their home movies shot digitally have incorporated still images from their films into a PowerPoint presentation as evidence of the conclusions they draw.

Expository Writing Activity: Transformation

Another type of expository writing I like to do with my students is to transform a nonfiction print text into a documentary. Through this activity, they begin to really understand the ways that "truth" can be constructed and different meanings can be represented through the documentary form.

Select a story from the local paper. It can be the same story for the entire class, or students can select their own. Certain stories work best, of course. Look for stories with a number of people involved, with a variety of perspectives; human interest pieces or crime stories have been successful for me. One I have used that works well is about a police shooting in which various eyewitnesses saw things differently from the official reports.

Once they have selected their piece, students need to consider how this story would look if it were filmed as a documentary. The elements they need to consider are:

Interviews: Who would be interviewed and why? If one person on your list could not be interviewed, how might that affect the story?

Archival or found footage: What visual images would you try to locate and what effect might they have on the story?

Sound track: What music and sound effects would you include? Where and why?

Visual track: Besides the interviews and archival footage, what other visuals would appear in your film? Where and why? What types of cinematic elements (lighting, framing, angles, etc.) would you use and why?

Purpose and tone: What is your overall purpose in presenting this story: What do you hope your audience will learn from your story? What tone would be appropriate for this film? Why? How will you go about creating this tone?

Next, students create a storyboard of a key scene from their documentary that illustrates these documentary elements. A storyboard is a representation of what the final product of the film will look and sound like on screen. The visual track can be drawn or described, and the audio track should include dialogue from interviews, music, sound effects, etc.

Last, students should examine one another's storyboards. This is especially interesting when they have done the same story in an effort to explore the variety of ways that filmmakers can present the same story.

Note: This assignment can be modified extensively depending on student knowledge of documentary form and style:

- If they have studied the different forms of documentaries from Chapter 1, you could ask students to identify which mode their piece might be in and why that mode is appropriate for this story.

- If they have studied more than one filmmaker, they could be asked to mimic a specific director's style and explain how the story is different depending on the filmmaker's choices.

- If they have access to a video camera and editing equipment, students can film their stories in a style and mode that appeals to them.

- They could also transform the nonfiction story into a fiction film. What actors would play the roles, what action and dialogue would need to be added or eliminated, what music or other cinematic elements would be appropriate, etc.?

Just as with the nonfiction reading skills and strategies discussed in Chapter 2, these writing and analytical activities are best paired with texts, assignments, and assessments that are a regular part of your curriculum; they are intended to help your students write stronger nonfiction texts and be able to think critically about the theme, tone, and perspective of the nonfiction texts they read. And as in the previous chapter, I've included a few student-written nonfiction pieces you might want to use to facilitate this transfer. In both Chapters 2 and 3, the use of film has been like the use of a tool that helps us to isolate and practice the skills and knowledge students need to be successful: the documentary clips described here are not end points, but rather a part of the process that includes all of the other strategies and approaches we regularly use in our classrooms.

Practice Nonfiction Print Texts

A Uniform Improvement

By Emma Dobbins

My daughter came home to me in tears. She slammed her backpack on the floor with considerable force and stomped away. I delicately opened the door and peeked into her room. She was lying there, face down on her bed, her body shaking from sobs. I walked in and asked her what was wrong and she said to me through deep gasps, "They never stop, mom." I left the room angry, not towards my daughter, but towards the many students at her school who have teased her for years about her clothing. My daughter is not alone. At least half of the students in that school have been criticized and ridiculed for their clothing at one point or another. Yet this teasing is the least of our school's problems. In Detroit, a fifteen year old boy was killed over a pair of 86 dollar shoes. Another boy lost his life when

---

he was struck by a stray bullet during a robbery of a student's designer jacket. He was just an innocent bystander.

Statistics show that uniforms decrease the rates of in-school violence, fights and theft. An article from *Psychology Today* in September of 1999 reported that schools in Long Beach California found uniforms extremely effective. They saw a dramatic 91% drop in overall school district crime and a 90% decrease in suspensions. The article also noted that sexual offenses were down 96% and vandalism down 69%. Other communities have also seen similar decreases in violence, theft, and discrimination.

High school fashion has become increasingly provocative and distracting. The latest styles are portraying girls as sexual objects, having them flaunt more skin than ever. Not only is this distracting for the classrooms but it creates an unprofessional and inappropriate atmosphere for our schools. Schools are supposed to be institutions designed to promote an education for the future, not a place to advertise the latest fads. Uniforms could instill a professional semblance into our classrooms that could enhance and sharpen the academic climate of our schools.

Furthermore, uniforms help to instill a sense of community. Arnold Goldstein, Ph.D., head of the Center for Research on Aggressions at Syracuse University, feels that uniforms help, in particular, our troubled students in that they promote a unified sense of community in which all students can feel a part of. He says, "there is a sense of belonging" which, in many cases, can make all the difference. Teens can relate to each other on an academic level as well as a social one. Our students and teachers will be able to easily establish professional relationships. This student to teacher interaction has the ability to heighten the overall academic performance of many of our students.

Uniforms have obvious potential to enhance our schools in more ways than one. Not only do they help to keep children safe, but they also create a purely academic community that facilitates learning and personal progress in all students. Teenagers could even begin to define their identity by character and moral originality rather than by existential and superficial means. The positive effects of uniforms are immeasurable and needed now more than ever. I know of one little girl who would come home a whole lot happier.

An Eye for an Eye

By Ann Kaleshnik

Since when have two wrongs made a right? The majority of us were raised with our parent's constant reminder that two wrongs don't make a right. Taking someone's life is a wrong, however, taking the murderer's life is also wrong. As the French philosopher Albert Camus stated, "[Capital Punishment] is the most premeditated of murders to which no criminal's deed, however calculated, can be compared. For there to be an equivalence, the death penalty would have to punish a criminal who had warned his victim of the date at which he would inflict a horrible death on him and who, from that moment onward, had confined him at his mercy for months. Such a monster is not encountered in private life." The death penalty in no better than murder itself and it should be banned.

Execution is irrevocable and can be used on the innocent. Recently, many prisoners have been released from prison after being proven innocent and after spending years of their life in jail. How is that just? 95 people have been released from death row in the USA since 1973 after being proven wrongly convicted. How many people have we already killed that weren't guilty?

Capital Punishment is a cruel, inhumane way to die. Many of the forms of death such as lethal injection or execution can take several minutes before the person is actually dead. In one case, a prisoner was to be executed and after getting jolted three times with 1.900 volts during a 14 minute period was finally declared dead. During the first electrical charge, the wire hooked up to his leg burned through and severely burned the prisoner's leg. The second jolt caused smoke and flames to erupt from his left temple and his leg. It needs to be remembered that criminals are people too, who have life and with it the ability to feel pain, fear, and the rest of emotions we are capable of feeling. Every form of execution causes the prisoner physical suffering along with psychological trauma. How would you feel knowing you would die next Thursday at 9:00 am?

The death penalty is a vicious, unfair, inhumane way of punishment. As Albert Peierrepoint, Britain's chief hangman for 25 years, said, "All the men and women I have faced at the final moment convince me that in what I have done I have not prevented a single murder." The death penalty goes against everyone's basic and most important right—the right to life. With the death penalty in effect there is always the risk of putting an innocent person to death and that is not worth putting a guilty person to death. Besides, wouldn't it be more effective having the prisoner sit in jail for the rest of their life without a chance of parole? Then they will have a good amount of time to carry the guilt on their conscience and that would be punishment enough.

Reading in the Reel World: Teaching Documentaries and Other Nonfiction Texts by John Golden © 2006 NCTE.

Justice Served?

By Jon Coon

Coral Eugene Watts may be one of America's most prolific serial killers ever. After already admitting to killing over 12 women and believed to have killed a dozen more, Watts is about to be set free. What is wrong with this picture?

In America, mass murderers are not supposed to be let go unaccosted though sadly a deal with the devil was made in the case of Coral Watts.

Inevitably the question should be raised, why isn't this man on death row? The answer is that the prosecutor of the case felt it necessary to find the remains of a number of known slayings with the help of Watts. In return he was granted a sentence of 60 years in prison which turned into a mere 24 due to future court rulings.

Considering myself an educated American, I understand that families need solace. But is one really to think that if the families of the slain women were asked if they would rather see Mr. Watts dead or alive that they would respond with the latter. When one of the detectives questioned Watts before he was sentenced the conversation leaves any human to wonder about the true evil inside this man.

(The officer) "I said, 'Coral, I haven't got enough fingers and toes to count the number of people you've killed, have I? And he looked around the room and said, 'There's not enough fingers and toes in this room.'"

Oh and by the way the room contained five police detectives.

What is the true rational reasoning behind not killing a convicted murderer? Should we instead have the law-abiding citizens of America pay for a ruthless criminal to breathe the air of life? As documented in the ACA's (American Correctional Association) report of 2003, a majority of states pay over $18,000 dollars a year to feed, clothe and look after the felons of our country. Now let's for a minute stop and think about how much money we could save if we killed those who could be proven without doubt to be deserving of the death penalty.

The average stay in prison before execution is 12 years. An especially conservative estimate puts the cost of keeping 3300 death row inmates alive at roughly $67 million dollars a year. If you were wondering, you could pay for 1500 new teachers to educate our youth. We could spend the money to buy 1250 new police officers to protect our communities. Instead we use these funds to extend the lives of the most evil of our society.

In addition to the funds lost to convicts there are also serious moral reasons to use the death penalty. Do you believe that it is fair for a convicted felon to receive a life saving transplant paid for by the taxpayers? While outside the walls of the penitentiary innocent individuals with chronic illness await their chance at survival. This is a pitiful flaw in the system which deserves to be addressed. When someone commits a horrendous crime they should not be given the advantage of free healthcare. All decisions come with a consequence; one would think that felons should have this ideal engraved in their minds.

After reading the story of Coral Eugene Watts do you think that justice has been served? After analyzing the cost of holding inmates for years before killing them do you think justice is being served? After realizing that criminals on death row have been given life saving transplants, do you believe justice has been served? I for one do not think that any of the listed situations are adequate for our modern world. There is no need to abolish the death penalty. The need is to help society vanquish those who commit atrocities with the hope of no more harm being done.

Reading in the Reel World: Teaching Documentaries and Other Nonfiction Texts by John Golden © 2006 NCTE.

Class Sizes and School Funding

Ben Zarov

Here I have a joke for you; what do you call a school where roll call takes 15 minutes, classes are so full heaters are the new seats, and there are traffic jams . . . in the halls? Give up? A public school! Portland Public Schools has reached a ridiculous status. Changes need to be made. No, not talked about, but actually made.

The solution to PPS's problems is abundantly clear. Plain and simple we need more funding. The National Education Association reported that the national average funding per pupil is $5,712 a year. Oregon's funding is $147 less. For some reason unbeknownst to me, no one seems to be willing to take action. With more funding more teachers could be hired. The average salary for teachers in Oregon is $1,624 less a year. More teachers equals more classes which, in turn, leads to smaller class sizes! I don't think the majority of people understand the importance of class size. Studies suggest that a 1 to 15 student to teacher ratio is the most effective for students' success. Current class sizes have double to triple this ratio.

A few years ago I was also a victim of overcrowded classrooms. I distinctly remember walking into my physics class on the first day of school and being directed towards the back corner of the room. The chair beneath me had probably been rotting away since the time of our forefathers. Not only was I squished between my neighbor and the wall, but the board was about a mile away. Every day was a battle over getting the one desk in class with all four legs, and being able to sit in a seat where you could actually learn something. Oh those were the good ol' days.

Schools need funding for many other reasons too. Without proper funding, many programs like the arts and sports suffer. Although it may seem that these programs aren't as important to schools as the fundamental classes, they are a vital part of any student's education.

Many people underestimate the value of sports and arts to students, not only do they provide more depth to school, they also allow students to get involved in healthy activities that they may have otherwise missed. Sports provide athletes with a structured environment where they are able to learn good values like the importance of hard work, responsibility, commitment, and teamwork. All of which are things necessary to success that are not always taught in school.

   With more funding a much needed change to our school system could be brought about. We could increase the effectiveness of the classes that exist, and increase the interest of students in Portland Public Schools. Trust me, the joke of Portland Public Schools needs a better punch line.

4 Teaching a Complete Film

Up to now, this book has focused mainly on using clips from documentaries to accomplish a specific goal, but there are a number of reasons why you might want to show a *complete* nonfiction film. Maybe the topic of the film coincides with your curriculum, or maybe you want to examine a filmmaker's ability to construct reality and manipulate an audience, or maybe you need some grading time right before the quarter ends.

Every one of these is an honest reason for wanting to show a complete film (except the third one, if you're reading this, Boss), but the most important consideration to keep in mind is that, just as you would never allow students to read *Romeo and Juliet* straight through without stopping for discussion, you should not do this with a complete film. This book is about helping you teach students new ways to think about nonfiction film, and students need an opportunity to talk about a film, review key parts, and hear from you and their peers. Also, students have been watching documentaries for years, but they have been asked only to copy down facts that the film presents. They need to be actively engaged—through directed note taking and discussion—by looking at how the filmmaker has constructed the reality that he or she is presenting. Before jumping right into teaching a complete documentary, be sure to:

1. Decide on a film that meets your curriculum goals and your students' interests and age.
2. Secure the necessary approval from your building supervisor. (I am continually amazed at the resistance to film in the classroom that still exists these days, so be sure to use your best professional judgment. My experience has been that if you can articulate your purposes and curricular connection for your administrator, approval comes fairly easily.) A quick rant, though, about ratings of films is necessary. Some districts have a blanket policy about the use of films with particular ratings, and you certainly need to be aware of your district's standards, but ratings for documentaries are often difficult for me to fathom. *Born into Brothels*, for example, received an R rating for two scenes of vulgar language that is simply a natural part

of the situation of the film: growing up in a world of prostitution. It certainly is not gratuitous, and to cut it out (or to not translate it) would have certainly made these scenes less real. Think too of *Bowling for Columbine*, which also carries an R rating, mainly for including the real footage from the school shootings; ironically, its rating would keep it out of the reach of many high school students, for whom its lessons are most important. In *This Film Is Not Yet Rated*, a fantastic exposé of the Motion Picture Association of America, one of the directors of *Gunner Palace*, which is a documentary about soldiers in Iraq who say the *f*-word a few too many times for the ratings board and which originally received an R rating, said, "Reality cannot be rated." He and his producers, unlike many other documentarians, successfully petitioned the board and got its rating changed to PG-13 without changing any of the content. My point is: know your students, know your community standards, and know that the ratings of films are often arbitrary.

3. Plan out your "mini-unit," leaving a day or two before and after the viewing of the film for introductory and closing activities.

4. Reflect with your students about what they learned from the film. We want students to be able to articulate more than just the facts presented.

I have separated each of the following films into viewing days. A typical viewing day in my classroom includes a brief discussion about what we saw or did the previous day, viewing of a thirty- to thirty-five-minute section of the film (during which I do not speak: very, very difficult for me!) as the students take notes (sometimes using a specific note-taking form included in this section and sometimes using a generic one found in the appendix), a review of a key sequence, and class discussion for the remainder of the period. Just as you would for any print text, I also include activities that can be completed before watching any of the films and extension projects students might do afterward.

One of the most difficult parts of writing this book was determining which films should be included. This section is not intended to be exhaustive or even representative of the best documentaries ever made, but I did try to keep a few factors in mind as I constructed this section. My main criterion was whether I think the film gives students an opportunity to view the world in a way they have not had before. Another factor I kept in mind was availability. There are many amazing documentaries out there, but if you are not able to locate them easily, it would be a waste to include them here. So, with only one notable exception that I describe below, I was able to find all of these films on Amazon.com, usually at very low prices. All but the *High School* films can also be rented for a reasonable fee from Netflix. Next, I thought about how a film might match up to curricula at various grade levels; I tried to articulate these connections in the Rationale section. From there, I tried to give some balance to subject matter, gender, race, culture, and different types of documentary forms and styles. Some of the films—*Super Size Me, Bowling for Columbine, Spellbound, Hoop Dreams, Mad Hot Ballroom*—are contemporary and probably familiar to you and your students, while others are older—*High School* and *Night and Fog*—or had limited releases—*The Gleaners and I, The True Meaning of Pictures, Six o'Clock News, Girlhood*. I have taught all but two of the very recent films, and my suggestions by grade levels are:

> **Middle school**: *Spellbound* and *Mad Hot Ballroom*
>
> **Grade 9**: *Hoop Dreams* and *Girlhood*
>
> **Grade 10**: *Night and Fog, Amandla!*, and *Born into Brothels*
>
> **Grade 11**: *Bowling for Columbine, Super Size Me, The True Meaning of Pictures*, and *4 Little Girls*
>
> **Grade 12**: *High School, High School II, The Thin Blue Line, Six o'Clock News*, and *The Gleaners and I*

In Appendix C, I have also included a list of other documentaries, by topic, that I have not taught or did not include here.

While I do think that your students will be successful with any of the films presented here without a lot of background in documentary film, their appreciation of and ability to analyze the films would increase if they were exposed to at least some of the information included in Chapter 1. At the end of that chapter is a Putting It All Together section that offers a plan for introducing your students to nonfiction film.

Be prepared for resistance from students at first to working with documentaries this way, because, as I noted in the introduction, they are used to looking at nonfiction films much less critically. But I receive the strongest and most positive feedback from students when we examine a nonfiction film. They know that when they watch a documentary they are seeing something that is supposed to be the "real world," and they genuinely seem to appreciate learning to look at this world with new eyes.

Spellbound

2002, Rated G, Directed by Jeffrey Blitz

Summary

Among the highest-grossing documentaries of all time, *Spellbound* follows eight middle school students as they prepare for and compete in the National Spelling Bee. In this mostly affectionate look at an American tradition, we learn about the spellers' families and their varied motivations for competing. (Approximately 95 minutes)

Rationale

This film, while appropriate at any grade level, might be a great first encounter with analyzing documentary form and style. It will also appeal to middle school students because most of the kids in the film are in the eighth grade and many middle school students will be participating in this year's and future spelling bees. The spellers in this film face conflicts and challenges that resonate with students who participate in sports or other types of competitions. Because the subjects of the film come from such diverse backgrounds, it is also a good text for helping students with compare and contrast writing.

Previewing

1. Just about every student has had to or will soon suffer through a spelling bee (I say suffer because I was eliminated from my eighth-grade bee on the word *mellow. Mellow*?!), so ask students to write about their experiences or expectations. I would bet that most are like me and can still remember the word that bumped them from the competition. Their narratives should focus on the feelings and the pressures at the time or what they expect they will feel. Also, ask them to include a reflection on the purpose and value of the National Spelling Bee.

2. Read the following words aloud:

   a. *banns*: An announcement, especially in a church, of an intended marriage

   b. *distractible*: Capable of being turned away from the original focus of attention or interest; likely to be diverted

   c. *hellebore*: Any of various plants of the genus *Veratrum*, especially *V. viride* of North America, having large leaves and greenish flowers and yielding a toxic alkaloid used medicinally

d. *clavecin*: Harpsichord, a keyboard instrument

e. *terrene*: Of or relating to the earth; earthly

f. *ecclesiastic*: Of or relating to the clergy

g. *logorrhea*: Excessive use of words

These are some of the words asked during the national competition. Ask students to try to spell them correctly. Identify how many people got them all correct (not only did I not get a single one correct when I first saw the film, but even my computer thinks some of the words are misspelled).

3. Discuss with students the value of proper spelling in the age of spellcheckers. Do we still need to spell things correctly these days? Is spelling getting worse due to e-mail and instant messaging?

4. Give out the chart (Figure 4.1) of the spellers and ask students to keep track of the details they learn about each of them as the movie goes on. You will probably want to practice with Angela, the first speller profiled, and pause briefly after her segment to check how students are doing with the note-taking form.

Viewing Day 1: 0:00:00–0:31:42; Chapters 1–5 on DVD (about 32 minutes)

- Begins with opening titles
- Ends with the sequence on Ashley

Things to Notice

The opening sequence is hilarious and an effective attention grabber. It shows a young boy (Harry, as we learn later) trying to spell a word. He's framed in a close-up and then there is a series of quick cuts, emphasizing his discomfort. He starts and stops, and just as he is about to commit himself to spell the word, the movie cuts off and moves to the title card. We'll have to wait to see what happens to him later on. This title page shows pictures of eight kids and is used throughout the film to reveal when one of the spellers has left the competition.

It quickly becomes clear that there will be no voice-over narration, but we still have a form of direct address through the text track, which provides background information on the National Spelling Bee; the text track will act as a narrator throughout.

The rest of the day's viewing consists of short (approximately five minutes each) sections on five spellers (Angela, Nupur, Ted, Emily, and

Spellbound: Character Chart			
Eight spellers are documented in this film. As you watch, keep track of the information presented about each speller, how it is presented, and what the outcome of the competition is for each.			
Name	Information Presented	How Information Is Presented	Outcome
Angela			
Nupur			
Ted			
Emily			
Ashley			
Neil			
Harry			
April			

Figure 4.1. *Spellbound* character chart.

Ashley). Each one of them is distinct from the other based on race, geography, class, and personality, and each seemingly has his or her own story to tell. You can point out to your students how each vignette establishes the speller in his or her surroundings: Ashley's story is wrapped up in the larger plight of Washington, D.C.'s, Angela's is also the story of south Texan immigrants, and so on. All speakers and locations are identified, and the songs on the sound track remain consistent throughout the background on all the spellers. The filmmaker, though, focuses on key elements that purport to explain that speller's life. A close-up on a sign warning of firearms on school property is featured in Ashley's scene, while Emily talks about her au pair and is seen horseback riding. These are visual shorthands that establish and distinguish each of the spellers. The funniest moment for me is when the manager of Hooters wants to acknowledge Nupur's win by putting "Congradulations" on a huge billboard outside the restaurant.

Key Sequence: 0:08:30–0:11:00; Chapter 1 on DVD

In this sequence, Angela competes in the finals of her regional spelling bee against another girl. As they go on and on for many rounds, the shots are edited more and more quickly, the sound becomes a blur of words, until finally the bell rings, signaling a missed word. It is an extremely effective and well-constructed scene that communicates the tension of the spellers and the audience to the viewers. When Angela finally wins, ask students about their emotions and whether they would feel the same way if the scene were edited differently.

Discussion Questions

1. Update the chart on the spellers. How has the filmmaker been able to communicate so much information about the spellers so quickly? Why were these spellers chosen? What contrasts are being drawn between them?

2. Has a tone been revealed so far in this film? What do you think the filmmaker thinks about spelling bees? In Emily's segment, she facetiously states that spelling bees are a form of child abuse. Do you agree? Why could they be called that?

3. Emily also states, and many other spellers would agree, that she feels a lot of pressure to not disappoint people. What are the expectations this film has set up for each speller? Is this fair to them? Why or why not?

Viewing Day 2: 0:31:42–1:04:20; Chapters 5–10 on DVD (about 33 minutes)

- Begins with sequence on Neil
- Ends with Ashley losing

Things to Notice

The first part of this day's viewing introduces the three remaining spellers: Neil, April, and Harry. Neil's house overlooking the beach in San Clemente, and his high-powered father who waxes eloquent about hard work and the American dream, are directly contrasted with April's modest home and her father who admits that his life is "not a real success story." Interestingly, the shortest sequence is on Harry, about whom we learn very little except some of his eccentricities and his bizarre robot voice.

By 0:45:05, we have met all the spellers featured, and it might be worthwhile to pause to ask students to examine their charts for what we know about each of them and, most important, how we know it. It also might be fun to ask your students who they think will win, who will go out first, and which speller they are rooting for.

The rest of today's viewing involves the first three rounds on day one of the competition. Watch how the filmmaker uses various montages to show how the original 249 spellers are reduced to 104 spellers. During this day, Ted, Angela, and Ashley go out; the title card we have seen throughout the film is reduced by three.

Key Sequence: 0:52:00–0:54:30; Chapter 10 on DVD

Like the sequence from viewing day 1, this section shows the power that editing can have to move time and create feelings of anxiety in the audience. During Ashley's first word, we see close-ups of her breathing hard, and then the filmmaker cuts to an earlier interview with Ashley about the pressures she and her family feel, and then cuts back to Ashley beginning to spell the word. This is a technique employed several times in the film and again with April in this section, so that the cutaways seem almost like a visual of what's going on inside the spellers' heads. Notice too the montage of close-ups of the spellers' faces, contorted in frustration and fear, and the cutaways to the cameras taking pictures of Ashley as she struggles with the word that gets her out.

Discussion Questions

1. A lot of care has been taken to establish cultural, racial, and socioeconomic differences among the spellers. Is this done to

be inclusive and multicultural by making sure that different groups are represented, or is there another point the filmmaker is trying to make? What do the three spellers who went out first have in common, from what we know? One possible answer: socioeconomic status.

2. Look back at the interview with Nupur's brother. He talks about Nupur's appearance in the spelling bee in the past tense, while all of the other interviewees we saw before the competition started talked about the Bee in the future tense. What does this fact mean for the construction of the film? Why do you think that Nupur's interviews were done after the competition? (**SPOILER ALERT:** Nupur ends up winning.)

3. Think back on the music so far in this film. Describe the main music and explain its effect on the tone.

Viewing Day 3: 1:05:20–end; Chapters 10–14 on DVD (about 30 minutes)

- Begins with the title card with Angela, Ted, and Ashley missing
- Ends with closing credits

Things to Notice

The filmmaker includes a brief sequence of interviews with past winners of the National Spelling Bee who express pride in their accomplishment and in the overall experience. We also return to that opening scene in which Harry is struggling to spell a word; he eventually misspells it, though he later blames the pronouncer. When the live ESPN coverage begins, the announcers refer to the action as if it were a football game, handicapping the odds for each speller to win. Interestingly, the filmmaker decides to introduce a rival to our spellers—Georgie—who is a favorite to win this year. Your students might speculate as to why the filmmaker did not include Georgie from the beginning since we learn a lot of the same kind of information about him as we do about the others.

The scenes move very quickly now, and our spellers drop out in this order: Neil, Emily, and April. After each of their final words, we see each participant and his or her family praising their kids' efforts, and Emily sums up her experiences with a phrase that is probably true for them all: "This part of my life is over." Finally, Nupur is alone on stage and wins the National Bee.

Key Sequence: 1:31:27–credits; Chapter 12 on DVD

Just as Nupur receives her final word for the championship and before she begins to spell it, the filmmaker cuts to an American flag and then to the announcer in an interview declaring that spelling in America has always been a community process and that education is the great leveler of class and social status in this country. We see a montage of images of the spellers that reconnect us to the spellers' families and their stories, contextualizing and, in some cases, rationalizing their participation in the Bee. We then return to Nupur as she confidently, quickly, and correctly spells the final word.

Discussion Questions

1. Why do you think the filmmaker chose to use the text track instead of a voice-over or on-screen narration? How might the film have been different with the narration? Why?

2. What is the purpose of the spelling bee, according to those who participated in it? Emily says that now she can "throw the books away," and Neil's father says that the work Neil put into the competition will serve him well in the future. What is the purpose of the Bee, according to your students? Is there value in participating even if you don't win? In this way, is spelling just like athletics?

3. What is this film saying about race, class, and social status in this country? Are those children of foreign-born parents better students? Do they value education more than other Americans? Why?

4. A question students often ask after seeing this film is how the filmmaker was able to know which spellers would go so far in the competition. But if you look closely at the clothing worn in and the surroundings of some of the interviews, you can tell that a number of the interviews were conducted after the spelling bee, even though they were presented as taking place before the competition. So at times the families were talking while already knowing the outcome of the Bee (Nupur in particular). Is it unethical of the filmmaker to rearrange the time and conceal this from the viewers? Why or why not?

Closing Questions/Activities

1. Overall, this film expresses a generally positive tone toward the idea of spelling bees. What are the key visual, sound, and text track elements that create and support this tone? Imagine that the filmmaker wanted to suggest that spelling bees are a danger to education, families, and children. To demonstrate this new tone, what scenes would you need to eliminate, add, or extend? How would they demonstrate this new tone? Describe the music you would add and other textual information you would put on the screen. Students could create a treatment as de-

scribed in Figure 3.4 (see also the "Nonfiction Film Treatment" form in Appendix B) from a scene from the new, negative *Spellbound*. The advertising tagline for the original film is "Everyone Wants the Last Word." What could be a tagline for this new film?

2. Return to the seven words that you read to your students before you started this film. Give them a copy of the words and ask them to try to memorize the spellings. What are the skills and the kinds of effort needed to do this? How often are our students asked to study this way? Is there value in it?

3. Read the novel or view the film *Bee Season* or see/read the musical *The 25th Annual Putnam County Spelling Bee* (the cast album is widely available) and contrast its tone and theme to this film.

Mad Hot Ballroom

2005, Rated PG, Directed by Marilyn Agrelo

Summary

The feel-good documentary of the summer of 2005, this film follows groups of fourth and fifth graders from New York City public schools who take classes in ballroom dancing and participate in citywide competitions. We see interviews of the children about their home lives, their goals for the future, and their views on dancing with members of the opposite sex. I love the openness of the kids as they talk about one another, and the filmmaker makes every part of New York City look glorious. The film is a lot of fun, and unfortunately for my wife's toes, it has also inspired me to take up dancing. A film of this activity might be called something like *Bad Sad Ballroom*. (Approximately 105 minutes)

Rationale

Mad Hot Ballroom and *Spellbound* are perfect films to introduce documentary form and structure to middle school students. The subjects in this film are just a few years younger than middle schoolers, so students can relate to the feelings and the pressures the subjects face. The film provides lots of opportunities for students to write narratives of similar experiences and to see how music and image choices create meaning.

Previewing

1. Start with a discussion about what kinds of dancing your students are familiar with. Ask them to compare the dancing they do at their

school dances with the dancing they see at a wedding. You may want to define *ballroom dancing* for your students and identify some of the most famous ones: tango, foxtrot, rumba, and so on. You could show clips from two recent and successful TV shows, *Dancing with the Stars* and *So You Think You Can Dance*.

2. The children in this film are mainly fifth and sixth graders. Ask students to try to describe themselves at that time. You could have them pretend they are back in elementary school and direct them to write a journal entry in the voice they would have used at that age. Ideally, their entry should focus on their feelings about the opposite sex and about their dreams for the future. Remind them that they are acting as if they were in elementary school.

3. In a lot of ways, this is a uniquely New York film. The kids come from different parts of the city, some of which are more affluent than others and some of which are more ethnically diverse, and people—including the kids themselves—have expectations for them based solely on the neighborhood they live in. If your students are unfamiliar with the city, you might want to spend a little bit of time illustrating the areas of New York, specifically the Washington Heights, Tribeca, Queens, and Bensonhurst neighborhoods. You could do this by assigning students to do a quick Web search of a specific area or, if you have the ability to project from a computer in your classroom, you could take them on a "virtual tour" of the city offered by various Web sites online.

Viewing Day 1: 0:00:00–0:29:00; Chapters 1–5 on DVD (about 29 minutes)

- Begins with opening titles
- Ends with Washington Heights School practice

Things to Notice

The film opens with a black screen text track that describes the city's ballroom dancing program in which over 6,000 students are required to participate. (Notice the word *required*. It might be interesting to consider whether the children we see are the ones being "required" to attend.) This type of text track information will serve as the only narrative voice; there is no voice-over or on-screen narrator.

After images of New York City streets and gentle, light piano music, we see the outside of the first school that we will follow throughout this film: Washington Heights PS 115, in Manhattan (**SPOILER ALERT**: this is the team that wins). Inside we meet one of the instructors of the program, who directs the boys to tuck in their shirts so that they look presentable. From the very first scene with kids, the film is suggesting that the program is about more than just dancing: it's about helping young people to grow and mature. The camera then travels for a while down the city streets to the next school, PS 150, in Tribeca, downtown Manhattan. The principal of this school talks about the positive reasons she chose to have her school participate in the program. The camera then takes us outside again to introduce us to the third and final school, PS 112, in Brooklyn, where we see tree-lined streets and well-kept homes. In this school, students get to practice in a large, clean auditorium, unlike one of the previous schools, where they danced in some kind of makeshift space.

After these brief introductions, we begin to meet the children, though unlike other documentaries, such as *Spellbound*, this film doesn't give us a lot of background information about any of the dancers (there are a lot of them). We are meant, I think, to see the children more collectively than individually. This is a choice, made perhaps by the sheer number of kids or perhaps in order to universalize their experiences.

The text track begins its countdown to the competition—eight weeks at this point.

We learn from the principal of PS 115 that the student population is mainly from the Dominican Republic and over 75 percent live in poverty, and we also see how much the students of this area love the merengue, probably influenced by their culture, which the filmmaker reinforces through nondiegetic merengue music on the sound track.

You should note how the filmmaker uses sound as a bridge between the schools; we often start in one school but move to another while the music stays the same; the schools, regardless of race and class, are united in purpose. The film takes care to show that everyone is included, even Taja and Mohammed, who are prohibited from dancing due to their religion but who act as the class DJs and unofficial coaches.

At 0:15:35, we get another sequence of kids from all the schools talking about one another; again, little or no distinction is made between the three schools. I love the girls who talk about the kind of man they want to marry; they talk so wisely about making good choices in relationships.

About halfway through this day's viewing, we learn that not all the kids get to compete, and we start seeing signs of pressure and how much some of the people, including teachers, want to win. Even so, the tone of this film is always positive, and the scene in which the kids get to line dance just for fun, not for competition, softens the effect of the

Figure 4.2. Even if the scene is probably staged for the film *Mad Hot Ballroom*, it's still a beautiful image: kids ballroom dancing in Central Park.

pressures; the kids are smiling, laughing, and having a great time—some even have their shirts untucked. The shots at 0:25:11 of the kids practicing their moves in Central Park with the New York skyline behind them are probably staged for the film, but accompanied by soft, light music, they are beautiful (see Figure 4.2).

As noted previously, we don't get a lot of background information on the kids, but at the very end of the day's viewing we learn about Wilson, one of the best dancers, who does not yet speak English but is doing well, his teacher says, because of the dancing (we also get this information because he will play a large role at the end of the film).

Key Sequence: 0:08:12–0:11:45; Chapter 2 on DVD

To establish the idea that this film is about more than just dancing, you might want to reexamine this clip in which the boys and girls talk about each other. The film makes quick cuts back and forth between sets of boys and of girls talking about why they like or don't like dancing with each other. The scene then continues with a lesson at the Tribeca school where the teacher is encouraging the kids to make eye contact with each other; notice how difficult it is for them (and the other teacher), as well as for the next group the film cuts to, which is at a different location and time. The nature of this editing is important to point out to students. While three separate schools are competing, there are so many similarities in their experiences that the film will cut back and forth among them to show this.

Discussion Questions

1. Are there differences between the three schools? What are they and why is the filmmaker either illustrating these differences or downplaying them?
2. According to the film so far, what does this dancing program do for the children? How is this illustrated in the film?
3. Why do we not learn much about individual children?
4. What do the boys think of the girls and what do the girls think of the boys? Is this what you remember from elementary school?

Viewing Day 2: 0:29:00–1:05:20; Chapters 6–11 on DVD (about 36 minutes)

- Begins with a boy leaving school in Brooklyn
- Ends with the kids from Brooklyn looking back on the competition

Things to Notice

At the beginning of this section, the kids start talking more specifically about who they like to dance with and who will get to compete or not. Some kids are very excited, and one girl notes a change in the boys' attitude and behavior when they dance. The teacher at the school in Tribeca breaks down on camera talking about how difficult it is to decide who gets to compete, but just as the film often does when it gets too serious, the filmmaker immediately cuts to an upbeat montage of the kids playing (see the following key sequence).

At the teachers' meeting about judging the upcoming competition, great emphasis is placed on being sure the kids' feelings aren't hurt too much when they don't win the competition. The instructors also have fun with this competition, and we get to see them dancing too, with quick cuts back to the kids dancing the same dances.

At about 0:40:00, the schools have to start cutting kids from the competition, which you would expect to be the most painful part of the film so far, but again, note for your students how the filmmaker does not include images of kids crying or include interviews with anyone who was cut. This is not that kind of movie.

Figure 4.3. What a perfect shot from one of the competitions in *Mad Hot Ballroom* to illustrate the awkwardness of growing up.

At the quarterfinals, the Brooklyn and Tribeca schools compete (Washington Heights, because of its high finish the previous year, goes right on to the semifinals), and one of my favorite shots comes from the warm-ups when one of the Brooklyn boys has to dance with a girl who is easily a foot taller than he, after which he quickly runs away (Figure 4.3). During the competition, the film focuses on kids we have seen a lot of during the film so far; we better understand how the construction of the film led us to know these kids better than we thought we did. As they dance, we hear the kids on the sound track talk about their experiences with the dancing and how enjoyable it has been. Interestingly, the film cuts away from the quarterfinals to show the girls of the Washington Heights team trying on costumes for their later competition.

At the end of the quarterfinals, each of the kids wins a ribbon for meeting designated levels, but neither team gets to move on to the next level of the competition. For the first time in the film, we see some negative reactions from the Tribeca team: tears, frustration, disbelief, and even anger from the kids. Later in this day's viewing, the teacher holds a debriefing session during which the kids are still wrestling with the loss. Conversely, from what the filmmaker shows of the Brooklyn team, they seem happy with their placement and think it was all worthwhile.

Key Sequence: 0:59:05–0:37:09; Chapter 6 on DVD

If one clip could illustrate the tone, structure, and style of *Mad Hot Ballroom*, it would be this one. Right after the Tribeca teacher breaks down crying, we see the kids playing on the playground at each school. The music is the same gentle and light tune we've heard before. All kids, the film suggests, play and have fun, regardless of race and class. Then the film cuts between several of the kids talking about what it means to be ten or eleven years old. Some are confused by changes in their bodies and the difficulties of the schoolwork, and some are excited about getting older. Again, the editing is done thematically, not chronologically; be sure to point out that these interviews could have taken place any time throughout the year. The sequence ends with images of the children at home or play with one of their parents: rollerblading, studying, riding on the back of a motorcycle. If these are single-parent homes, they're great ones. This sequence provides only positive images.

Discussion Questions

1. Is competition good for kids? Should they be protected from the kind of disappointment these teams felt until they are older?
2. Has there been a shift in tone in this part of the film? How does the filmmaker signal this shift?
3. What does this film seem to be saying about childhood? How do you know?

Viewing Day 3: 1:05:20–1:40:03; Chapters 12–18 on DVD (about 35 minutes)

- Begins with the Washington Heights team going to their competition
- Ends with closing credits

Things to Notice

During the competition, the film cuts away to a group of girls expressing their concerns about their partners and their chances. But their concern is undercut by the visuals that show them dancing well, especially compared to the dancers we saw in the previous competition. Look at how the merengue is filmed and edited. After every move that Wilson and his partner make, the director cuts back to the team cheering, laughing, and clapping. We also see the girls again, this time talking about how great Wilson is. The Washington Heights team moves on to the citywide finals.

At 1:13:17, for the first time the film seems to make it a point to illustrate differences between schools when we get to see Forest Hills in Queens, the defending city champions. The neighborhood looks orderly, quiet, and privileged. One of the dance teachers comes across as harsh ("Straighten up!" she barks), and there are at least six adults helping out as the students practice in a large, clean gymnasium (remember that Washington Heights was often shown practicing in the library). The team also seems to gloat over the trophy they won the previous year. The contrast continues in the dressing rooms before the competition: the team from Queens is going over last-minute instructions, while the Washington Heights kids are laughing and joking with one another.

The final twenty minutes of the film focus on the finals competition. We see all five of the dances (plus the alternates' dance) in their entirety, with cutaways to close-ups of the kids cheering them on, to the Washington Heights teacher, and to the parents of the kids. During the second dance, we hear a voice-over from the Washington Heights principal talking about Michelle, who used to be a discipline problem until she joined the dance team. During the fourth dance, we hear the mother of one of the girls talking about supporting her daughter's dreams. After the first five dances, there is a "dance off" between three of the schools. During the first of these, we hear about Kelvin, who is described as having been on his way to being a criminal until the dance team taught him leadership and responsibility. The final dance, the merengue, is appropriate since it's the national dance of the Dominican Republic, the nationality of most of the children on the Washington Heights team, which is then crowned the city champion.

Key Sequence: closing credits; Chapter 18 on DVD

Instead of looking back at a key sequence, let your students watch the closing credits, in which we see additional interviews with the kids that did not make it into the finished film. A lot of them are very funny. Afterward, you could discuss where these interviews might fit if they were to be included.

Discussion Questions

1. Why did the filmmaker introduce the school from Queens so late in the film? What did their inclusion add to the film?
2. How would this film have been different if it had focused only on the Washington Heights team? What is lost and gained by the filmmaker's decision to follow three teams?

3. For the finals, why did the director choose to show all five of the dances in their entirety?

4. The filmmaker got lucky since one of the teams she followed ended up winning. Would your feelings about this film have been different if one of the teams highlighted had not won?

Closing Questions/Activities

1. Overall, this film demonstrates its positive tone toward the dancing program in many ways, including music and image selection. Imagine yourself as a filmmaker who wants to paint a less sunny picture of the program. First, brainstorm reasons why someone would not think the program is valuable (waste of money, too competitive, etc.). Then describe the interviews, B-roll, music, and any text track elements you would include that would express this more pessimistic tone.

2. Pretend you have been asked to make promotional trailers for this film for two different audiences. One trailer will be shown before a cartoon and is intended for teenage and younger audiences. The other trailer will precede an adult romantic comedy and is intended for adults. What scenes would you include in each? Why? Write out the narration that would be delivered in both. What are some of the differences between the two?

3. What is another activity in which students in elementary or middle school can participate that might have an effect similar to the ballroom dancing program? Write a letter to your school's superintendent proposing your program. Be persuasive and detailed in your description of the program's benefits.

4. Write a narrative about a time that you competed in an activity similar to the dancing in this film. Be sure to include details of the preparation you had to undertake as well as the outcome and your feelings afterward.

Girlhood

2003, Not Rated, Directed by Liz Garbus

Summary

Girlhood follows two teenage girls, Shanae and Megan, for three years as they move through the juvenile justice system in Baltimore, Maryland. Both have been convicted of violent crimes, and they must prove to the court officials that they—and their families—are prepared for their return. Garbus shoots mainly in the observational mode, capturing the various interactions the girls have with counselors, family members, and court officials, though she does include some individual interviews with the two. The documentary is beautifully filmed and edited and uses music as effectively as any documentary I've seen. (Approximately 80 minutes)

Rationale

I was watching PBS one night when I saw a viewer's emotional response to a documentary she had seen previously about welfare reform; she said, "I forget because I don't see." Her words reminded me why documentaries like this one are so important for us to watch. As I wrote in the introduction, nonfiction films often take us to places we cannot go to or might not even want to go. *Girlhood* takes us into the juvenile justice system that very few people experience but about which everyone seems to have an opinion. Remember the nine-year-old Florida boy who killed his neighbor by imitating a wrestling move he had seen on TV? The public screamed for blood and wanted him locked away for life. But what does that mean? Do we throw away the lives of children out of desire for revenge? Is rehabilitation possible? How much should a child be held responsible for his or her actions? These are the questions that *Girlhood* attempts to address, and its portrayal of the two girls is brutally honest and extremely emotional. I have shown this film to ninth graders as part of a Coming-of-Age unit, but be sure to preview the film because some scenes include profanity and discussions of sexuality and drug abuse.

Previewing

1. Ask students to describe their own or a friend's or a family member's experience with the justice system. In what kinds of ways and places would you expect to come into contact with the legal system of this country? I, for example, have had to deal only with traffic court (one win, three losses, by the way), but others I know have had to deal with family court and small-claims court. If students have had no experiences, ask them: what are your expectations about the justice system in this country?

2. Write the phrase "an eye for an eye" and ask students to consider its meaning. Do we practice this in our country? Are our prisons set up for rehabilitation or for punishment? How do you know? Do you think that a young person who killed someone in a fight can be rehabilitated?

3. Describe for your students the competing theories about human development: nature versus nurture. Are we a product of our genes (nature) or of how we are raised (nurture)?

4. Because it becomes important later in the film, ask students what they would ask for if they could have any three wishes granted. What do these wishes reveal about them? About humanity in general?

Viewing Day 1: 0:00:00–0:39:53; Chapters 1–13 on DVD (about 40 minutes)

- Begins with opening titles
- Ends with Megan moving into her foster home

Things to Notice

The film opens with a stark white-on-black text track that states that the number of young girls committing violent crimes has more than doubled. In a quick montage that includes home movies, observational images, and interviews, we meet Shanae, a little girl with pigtails who talks of stabbing her friend, and Megan, a little older, who has been convicted on various assault charges. The pace is fast and the images of the girls in and out of jail come and go very quickly. The film settles in once we see the girls inside the juvenile facility, and we learn more about their backgrounds. We see Megan working with hair, her own and others', and we see that she tries to manipulate everyone around her. The observational mode Garbus uses puts us right in the middle of this facility, with short interviews to fill in some gaps.

Garbus loves to crosscut between the girls, as when Shanae gets a home visit while Megan stays behind at the facility. During the visit, Shanae's family makes it clear that they don't think she's ready to be released yet. Megan tries so hard to manipulate the staff ("You don't love me"), but she's not very good at it, and she seems to know it. One of the most interesting sequences (0:18:33) is when a man tries to present to Shanae images of "effective" dress for men and women by showing her pictures of professionally dressed people, but Shanae refuses to judge them by their outward appearance.

The filmmaker shows us the evaluation process that both Shanae and Megan have to go through in order to be released. Shanae is moving in the right direction more quickly than Megan, but because her charge is more serious, she is released to a "step-down program" while Megan can be released to a foster care arrangement. The day's viewing ends with one of my favorite shots in the film: a close-up of Megan, in the home of a total stranger, staring out the screen door.

Key Sequence: 0:20:50–0:22:08; Chapter 7 on DVD

This short section in which Shanae confesses her drinking and sexual experiences is worth reviewing to examine how carefully and effectively Garbus uses music, framing, and editing to create a powerfully emotional connection. When Shanae talks about drinking for the first time and losing her virginity at age ten, we see pictures of her as a young girl (probably younger than ten), sitting on Santa's lap in one and staring plaintively at the camera in another. The music is just a slow, simple repeating organ sound. As she begins to describe her slide into alcohol abuse and we learn she was pregnant, we see another picture of her, looking older, sexualized, but still "only eleven years old."

Discussion Questions

1. Compare and contrast the two girls. What support does each girl have? What motivates each of them?

2. What impressions do you have of Waxter, the facility where we meet the girls? What did Garbus include to give you these feelings?

3. How has Garbus connected us to these girls? Think of the editing, sound, and framing.

Viewing Day 2: 0:39:43–1:21:10; Chapters 14–end on DVD (about 40 minutes)

- Begins with Megan meeting with a counselor
- Ends with Megan's rap and the closing titles

Things to Notice

In her first postrelease conference, Megan is instructed to stay away from "undesirables," which she turns around on the counselor by saying that her own mother would fit that description. Garbus then cuts to images of Megan walking down the street looking for her mother, Vernessa, and then to a scene in which Megan meets with Vernessa, who is currently serving time and sees being released as being "evicted."

On her way to the interview for a group home, Shanae talks with other girls about her assault charge, and she appears remorseful or at least certainly takes no pleasure in talking about it. During the course of the interview, we learn that Shanae was gang raped when she was eleven and never told anyone about it. Shanae's departure from Waxter is emotional, with lots of hugs from the counselors, but she says she's ready to move on, and by everything Garbus has shown us, we would probably agree.

Vernessa, Megan's mother, is out of jail, working, and trying to convince Megan to go to family counseling. After the scene described in the following key sequence ("vicious cycle"), we see Megan back on the street, getting high, and hear her saying that she won't ever change and doesn't want to. In one of her few intrusions into the on-screen action, Garbus asks Megan what she would do if she had three wishes. After a long pause and shots of the desolate street where she's hanging out, Megan finally says there's no real point in wishing. A little later, we see that she has a place of her own, which upsets Vernessa for a lot of reasons, mostly because she feels abandoned by her own daughter.

After completing her time at the group home, Shanae is going home with her mother, who dies later that summer. As we see pictures of the two of them together, Shanae says that she won't let herself get too far down. Garbus then crosscuts to Megan waiting for her mother, who is also sick. There is a huge explosion between Vernessa and Megan, who tells her mother that she doesn't want anything to do with her anymore. The scene that follows is a quieter one in which Megan and a friend sit on a pier, while Megan now says that she is nothing like her mother.

We catch up again with Shanae, a senior at the top of her class, getting ready for her senior prom. One of the Waxter counselors is there to see her off; the scene probably has been staged somewhat, but it is a metaphor for Shanae's growth, and it creates an ending to Garbus's film. Surrounded by her family and friends, we hear Shanae saying that she's going to keep pushing on, no matter what. The final image of Shanae has her waving in the back of a limo. After we learn that Vernessa is back in prison and that Shanae will be attending community college, we see shots of Megan, who is back in Waxter, singing a song she wrote.

Key Sequence: 0:59:05–1:01:40; Chapter 18 on DVD

This devastating scene between Vernessa and her own mother, Lorraine, raises the issue of who is responsible for how a child turns out. Lorraine's sad eyes and the close-up of Vernessa's finger pointing at her mother when she says "I wanted your love" tells volumes about their relationship. Lorraine does not take responsibility for how Vernessa turned out yet blames her for how Megan behaves. This scene could not have been more effective if it had been scripted, nor would it have had the realism and power if it had not been captured in observational style.

Discussion Questions

1. Why does Garbus use the text track for narration instead of voice-over?

2. What is the role of music in this film? How does it affect your feelings at key places?

3. On the audio track of the DVD, the filmmaker says that one of the differences between the girls is that Shanae tries to help herself but that Megan needs help from others. How do you see this playing out in the film?

4. Garbus does not clearly state her feelings about the juvenile justice system, but after experiencing it for eighty minutes, what do you think her point is? Do you agree with it?

Closing Questions/Activities

1. Research mandatory sentencing guidelines (feel free to use my own state of Oregon's draconian Measure 11) that sentence juveniles to minimum sentences regardless of the circumstances or their age. Write a persuasive essay calling for either the continuation or the repeal of these guidelines.

2. The juvenile facility, Waxter, comes across as a good place. What would a filmmaker probably show if he or she wanted to portray it in a negative light?

3. Do prisons rehabilitate? Research this issue and present your findings in visual form: charts, diagrams, photos, a film, etc.

4. Make a list of institutions in your city or neighborhood that you have never been to. You might include prisons, drug rehabilitation centers, the courthouse, and so on. What do you know about these institutions, what functions do they serve, and why have you never had to go there?

Hoop Dreams

1994, Rated PG-13, Directed by Steve James

Summary

One of the highest-grossing documentaries of all time, *Hoop Dreams* follows William Gates and Arthur Agee for five years as they pursue their dreams of playing in the NBA. Mixing interviews, thrilling game footage, and an observational approach, director Steve James uses the boys' efforts as a way to explore the challenges and pressures of the American dream. (Approximately 2 hours and 46 minutes)

Rationale

I love this film. I used to teach it every year as part of a Coming-of-Age unit for ninth graders, but for some reason I hadn't used it for a while until I started this book project. While I think that *Hoop Dreams* might be best suited for ninth graders, I taught it this year to eleventh graders in a unit on the American dream, and it worked wonderfully. We come to know the boys and their families so fully that their struggles with poverty, pressure, and families become, in the truest sense of the word, "real" to us in a way few documentaries are. The only downside is that the film is long (it takes four full class days just for the viewing), but for the right class in the right situation, it is an extremely valuable experience. Because of the length, I do not have time to review a key sequence from each viewing day, but each day (except for day 3) should allow enough time for an abbreviated class discussion.

Previewing

1. At several points in this film, Arthur and William say that basketball is their ticket out of the ghetto. Ask your students for examples of NBA players or other celebrities who have come from poverty. What do you imagine are the challenges and difficulties of making it to the NBA?

2. Ask students to identify and describe the American dream. Does it always include money? Is the American dream the same for everyone? What prevents people from reaching their dreams?

3. Discuss the issue of recruiting students to a particular school with scholarships and other incentives in order to play a sport, which happens at high schools as well as at colleges. Are the schools exploiting these athletes? Are the schools wasting money that should be spent on academics? In 2005 the NBA changed its rules, saying it will not draft anyone who is not at least one year out of high school. Is this a necessary and/or worthwhile change?

Viewing Day 1: 0:00:00–0:29:03; Chapters 1–7 on DVD (about 29 minutes)

- Begins with opening scene
- Ends with basketball coach explaining why Arthur is coming back to his neighborhood school

Things to Notice

The opening shows the Cabrini Green housing project in Chicago, and the very first interview shows a fourteen-year-old, already-dunking-the-ball William Gates saying that he dreams of playing in the NBA "all the time," which is important to note because William, who also has the last words of the film, strikes a different tone four years later. Before the titles, we also meet fourteen-year-old Arthur Agee, whose mother and father both mention their son's obsession with basketball and making it to the NBA.

When Arthur goes to a basketball camp run by a private school in the suburbs, he comments on the different scenery and ethnicities outside of his neighborhood, and when he gets a chance to play one-on-one with his idol, NBA star Isaiah Thomas, he is all smiles, shot in slow motion. But Isaiah's shadow looms large at this school, St. Joseph's; his pictures and trophies are everywhere, and throughout the film Arthur and William will be measured against Isaiah's success. William's brother, a former high school basketball standout, plainly admits that since his own dreams of making it are gone, all of his dreams are now invested in William. Note the playful game of one-on-one that Arthur and his father play in this day's viewing, because it will be starkly contrasted with other games as Arthur grows up.

Once their first year of high school has begun, we see Arthur and William making the three-hour round-trip commute to and from St. Joseph's, and Arthur talks about the difficulty of fitting in with a school of mainly white people. The filmmaker crosscuts often between Arthur's and William's contrasting experiences in school and on the basketball court. We get the first taste near the end of the day's viewing of the real-life drama of the film when director Steve James is able to capture William's team's last-second loss.

An interesting situation arises when William's partial scholarship from his neighborhood runs out and a donor from St. Joseph's comes forward to pay the remaining amount for the next three years. Arthur's family has some financial setbacks, and when they are unable to pay tuition, St. Joseph's suspends Arthur until the family can come up with the money. No donor comes forward for Arthur, who blames the coach for not helping him. The day's sequence ends with the startling contrast between the quiet, ordered halls of St. Joseph's and the chaotic, crowded hallways of Arthur's neighborhood school, Marshall, whose coach plainly states that Arthur was bumped from St. Joseph's because he was underperforming on the basketball court. Though he talks fondly of it sometimes throughout the film, Arthur never does return to play ball at St. Joseph's.

Discussion Questions

1. What has the director done to establish contrasts? Consider contrasts between the boys, schools, families, etc. What is the effect of these contrasts on you as a viewer?
2. What are some of the pressures the boys face? How does each handle this pressure?
3. Watching the day's viewing, you get a sense that the filmmaker spent a lot of time following the boys, but think back on the specific scenes you saw. Where and when do you think the filmmaker shot footage? How much time do you really think he had to spend to get what he did?
4. Was Arthur treated unfairly by St. Joseph's and its basketball coach? Why or why not?

Viewing Day 2: 0:28:03–1:12:09; Chapters 8–18 on DVD (about 44 minutes)

- Arthur joining the sophomore basketball team
- Ends with William's second surgery, after the season

Things to Notice

In the beginning of this section, in two of among the most emotional sequences I've seen in any documentary, the film shifts just slightly away from the boys to concentrate on other people in their lives. The first is about Curtis, William's older brother, who was a high school and junior college basketball star but who "couldn't handle it." Sandwiching pictures and archival footage of Curtis in his glory days between images of him working as a security guard, the filmmaker nearly brings me to tears every time I hear Curtis say that he's "just a regular guy on the street now." It's even more emotional for me since I've learned that Curtis was murdered in a street dispute a few years ago. The other powerful scene is when Bo, Arthur's father, who had moved out of the family home, shows up to shoot baskets with Arthur at the local playground. Afterward, the camera catches Bo buying drugs, with Arthur watching not more than a hundred yards away. I've read that there was considerable debate about whether to include this footage, but Bo himself, after kicking his drug habit, gave permission and, in fact, requested that the scene stay in.

Isaiah Thomas comparisons abound for William, and the director cleverly edits the footage to show that William feels the weight of the entire team and school on his shoulders, though he has a serious knee injury that keeps him off the court for most of the year. Money problems continue for Arthur's family, and the filmmaker shows the family's home without any lights; the family grows to include Arthur's older sister and his best friend. We also learn that William has a baby daughter, and we see footage of him doting on her. William continues to benefit from his basketball skills when he gets his ACT prep course paid for, in contrast to Arthur, whom we see cutting up in a large, unruly classroom.

A key scene in this viewing comes when William's coach, knowing that William is injured, allows William to decide whether he wants to play. Of course William says yes, but it is this injury that continues to plague him throughout his career. We then see another last-second, heartbreaking, season-ending loss for William and his team.

Discussion Questions

1. Documentary filmmaking often raises certain ethical considerations. The director of *Hoop Dreams* surely had enough money to help Arthur's family get the lights turned back on. Should he have given them money? Why? Also, what factors did the director have to consider when deciding whether to include the footage of Bo buying drugs? Would you have included it if Bo had objected? Why? The film says that Bo had abused his wife. If that had happened during filming, should the filmmakers include it? Should they stop the beating? Why or why not?

2. Describe your feelings about Coach Pingatore. What has the filmmaker done to give you this feeling? Should the coach have allowed William to play? What are the pressures that William and other top-tier athletes face, especially with injuries?

3. Describe the use and role of music in this film so far. When is it used and what is the effect?

Viewing Day 3: 1:12:09–2:03:00; Chapters 19–30 on DVD (about 51 minutes)

- Arthur and family going to church
- Ends with Arthur's meeting with St. Joseph's coach

Things to Notice

The opening of today's viewing could be called "A study of fatherhood." We first see that Bo is back with the family, and the shot selection of Arthur implies that he is suspicious of his father, whom he calls irresponsible and hypocritical. Next we see William with his own father, whom he has not seen in about three years and who, William suspects, got in touch with William only because of a potential future payoff with William in the NBA. Finally, we see William with his own daughter, and they are clearly close; William says that he would never leave his daughter alone like he was left by his father.

We then witness one of those "only in a documentary" moments when Sheila and Bo have to go to St. Joseph's to arrange for payment so that Arthur's academic credits can be released; the school's financial director is clearly uncomfortable with the chitchat after the transaction and especially with Bo's hugging him. Arthur's and William's summers are contrasted: William at Nike's prestigious summer camp and Arthur working at Pizza Hut and playing on the playground. Spike Lee shows up at William's summer camp and articulates a theme that has been hinted at in the movie: young black men are being used for their basketball skills because they make the schools a lot of money; I'm guessing this was the last time Spike Lee was asked to speak at the camp, though many of the coaches and scouts say roughly the same thing.

As William enters his senior year, recruiting season hits full stride. While offers pour in for William, the director shows us that Curtis, growing more overweight, can't dunk any more. The most unintentionally funny moment in the film is when a white assistant coach at St. Joseph's, talking with William about his recruiting visit to Marquette, asks whether he had talked with the "leading . . . black people on campus." After William asks what he means by "*leading* black people," the coach clarifies by saying, "You know, whoever is in charge of the black students on campus." St. Joseph's generally doesn't come across well in the film, and this scene certainly doesn't help. The filmmaker also captured a wonderful scene (probably initiated by the director) of William shooting baskets in his old grade school gym while we hear him on the sound track reflecting on how he has recently lost some of his drive as a player.

One of the best crosscuts in the film is between the silent St. Joseph's players on the bus on the way to their game and the rowdy Marshall bus. Without ruining the ending for you, this could be seen as foreshadowing of Marshall's on-court success, because basketball is supposed to be fun, especially as articulated by William.

I read an interview with Arthur Agee that took place in about 2003 in which he says that when people see him in person they usually ask him two things: did he ever make it to the NBA and how's his mom? Sheila's determination and pride is shown here when she completes a nursing assistant program with the highest grade in the class and doesn't even seem to notice that her graduation takes place in an empty room.

The filmmaker returns to the beginning of the film, in a sense, by interviewing the scout who recruited Arthur for St. Joseph's four years earlier. The scout has begun to have reservations about the treatment of boys like Arthur at the school and has stopped working for them. Arthur visits St. Joseph's and watches William's team lose again, denying him the opportunity to go to the state tournament. After the game, we see Arthur and William hugging, and it takes a moment to realize that this is the first time in the film we have seen them together.

Discussion Questions

1. Is the recruiting process fair, according to this film? Does Marquette take advantage of William?

2. Why does the film spend time with the peripheral subjects (Bo, Sheila, Curtis)? What do they add to the film or relate to the theme and tone?

3. In this day's viewing, much has been made of the importance of getting into college. Do William and Arthur seem to want to get an education, or is attending college a way to get into the NBA? How has this experience changed recently since so many players like Kobe Bryant and LeBron James are going into the NBA directly from high school?

Viewing Day 4: 2:03:09–2:46:00; Chapters 31–40 on DVD (about 43 minutes)

- Arthur's play-off game
- Ends with closing credits

Things to Notice

The first section of this final viewing day deals with Arthur's Marshall team's improbable run through the play-offs, winning the city tournament and coming in third in the state. The games are extremely close, and they are shot and edited to create even more drama. As I was reviewing the film for this project, I kept finding myself watching the games that I've seen many times, forgetting to write.

After the season ends, Arthur goes on a recruiting visit to a junior college in southern Missouri where all the basketball players (six of the seven black students on campus) live together in a tiny house. One of the final times we see Arthur and his father Bo together is in their third one-on-one game. It starts off a bit humorously as Bo lies, cheats, and fouls, but it becomes more serious as Arthur stands up to him and wins the game. Taken together, the three one-on-one games throughout the film show the changing nature of their relationship.

After William's season, he reflects on how he is no longer obsessed with basketball the way he once was or the way Coach Pingatore still is. It had become like a job for him, and he stopped respecting Pingatore when he told William to "write off" his family and their problems. "What kind of advice is that?" he asks. The final meeting between William and Pingatore is awkward and forced; the director shows through editing, framing, and pauses that there is a gap of understanding between the two.

Both boys graduate and the film crosscuts between their graduation parties, even though they did not happen simultaneously. The same effective parallel editing occurs again when Arthur and William leave their families for college. There's a nice moment when William's mom, who has been pretty quiet through most of the film, asks one of the filmmakers if William is going to make it. It's one of the very few times when the subjects have acknowledged the camera, and it seems genuine because she knows that those working on the film have spent a lot of time with William.

The last images of Arthur include a return to the scene where the fourteen-year-old Arthur meets Isaiah Thomas, and then we see him at his junior college still talking about making it in the NBA, but adding that if he doesn't, he'll still do something productive, legal, and worthwhile. Then we see William at Marquette, sounding much less enthusiastic about basketball than his fourteen-year-old self we heard in the opening. He says there's more to life than basketball, and to illustrate this, we see him in his dorm room, pictures of his daughter plastered on the walls, listening to a message from his daughter and girlfriend. The final lines of the film, spoken by William, are perfectly chosen to illustrate many of the ideas this documentary has raised: "People say to me, 'When you get to the NBA, don't forget about me.' I should say to them: 'If I don't make it, don't forget about me.'" The titles give an update of the boys' lives since the film was shot, though I always stop the film before they run so that students can predict what happened to them.

Discussion Questions

1. What are the differences between Coach Pingatore and Coach Bedford of Marshall? What role do you think editing plays in the different feelings we have about the coaches?

2. How are the Marshall games in the state finals edited to create more drama? How are they similar to or different from fiction films about sports?

3. While the film's title and the boys' obsessions make us think that this documentary is mainly about NBA dreams, what other dreams are explored? What does the director seem to be suggesting about dreams in general?

Closing Questions/Activities

1. Before students learn where William and Arthur are today, have them make some predictions about their futures. In 2005, they would be in their midthirties. Do you think they make it to the NBA? Why or why not? What about their families?

2. Research the probability of making it to the NBA. How many spots are available, how many are recruited from college, how many try out each year, etc.?

3. Look at excerpts from the fiction film *He Got Game* (directed by Spike Lee and rated R), which covers a lot of the same territory as *Hoop Dreams*, especially the pressures of "making it" and the corruption of the recruiting process. Compare the representations of the players, the coaches, and the families with those in *Hoop Dreams*. Other fiction films on this topic include *Above the Rim* and *Blue Chips*.

4. There was considerable debate among the filmmakers about including the scene in which Bo Agee was buying drugs. What are the ethical considerations of including this scene and what other scenes do you imagine caused some kind of ethical discussion?

5. Did any people in the film come off badly? Do you think anyone was upset about his or her representation in the film? Why or why not?

6. Read excerpts from *Our America: Life and Death on the South Side of Chicago* (LeAlan Jones and Lloyd Newman, 1998), a series of audio documentaries created for National Public Radio by two boys who live in Cabrini Green, the same neighborhood as William and Arthur's, or watch scenes from the fiction film version titled *Our America*. How is their picture of the neighborhood and America similar to or different from that in *Hoop Dreams*?

Amandla! A Revolution in Four Part Harmony

2002, Rated PG-13, Directed by Lee Hirsch

Summary

For more than forty years, black South Africans suffered under the racist policies of apartheid, and throughout that time, their music both sustained people's hopes and provided a message of resistance. Through interviews with major musicians and politicians, but especially through the music itself, *Amandla!* explores the role that music played in bringing down the apartheid system. The title means "power," and this film has a lot of it. (Approximately 103 minutes)

Rationale

Does the story of apartheid still matter? Yes, it's been over fifteen years since Nelson Mandela was released, and South Africa has moved on to a new chapter of its history. But what is so powerful about this documentary is that, while the struggle is unique to South Africa's time and place, the desire to protest one's condition is universal. Students of all ages (though I think the film tends to fit best within a tenth-grade world literature or history class) love music and to protest things, and they find real connections to their own lives through the struggles of the past depicted in this film.

Previewing

1. Students have limited knowledge about Africa, though some are familiar with South Africa and apartheid, mainly through movies. I tend to start with a simple KWL chart, asking students to write down under the *K* portion what they already know or think they know about South Africa, apartheid, Nelson Mandela, and Desmond Tutu. Next, students work in pairs or small groups to write under the *W* portion questions they have about any of these topics. Students then could do some brief research that addresses some of these questions. After viewing the film, I ask students to return to their charts and write down in the *L* portion what they've learned about the topics.

2. Since music plays such a large role in this film, I suggest playing some South African music for students to familiarize them with the rhythms, instrumentation, and language. You might want to share a song or two of some of the musicians featured in this film: Hugh Masekela, Miriam Makeba, and Vusi Mahlasela; the sound track to this film is widely available. On the DVD of the film, in the Extras section, is some concert footage of Mahlasela and sing-alongs with some of the major songs in the film. The film version of the musical *Sarafina*, about life in the South African townships, is also widely available and includes many songs representative of the style and substance of the music found in this documentary.

3. I also like to ask students to think and write about the role of music in their own lives. What purpose does it serve? Does music in this country unite or separate people? Do young and old people listen to the same music? What are some protest songs throughout American history? Is music today used for protest?

Viewing Day 1: 0:00:00–0:33:03; Chapters 1–9 on DVD (about 33 minutes)

- Begins with opening titles
- Ends with black-and-white footage of the Sharpeville Massacre

Things to Notice

The first image of the film is an opening text track that starkly and boldly identifies apartheid as "one of the most brutal systems of segregation the world has ever known." In a film about music, this is one of the few silent sections. From there, we quickly move into the music and the connection between it and the act of protesting, with a montage of various protest marches, burials, and a solitary dancer on a rooftop, all to the rhythm of the music.

The film itself really begins with a scene from 1998 at a pauper's cemetery, where protest singer Vuyisile Mini was unceremoniously interred after being executed by the government forty years earlier. From there, the film takes us back in time to 1948 to see the very beginnings of apartheid and hear about the policy from one of its chief architects, Hendrik Verwoerd, about whom one of the first protest songs was written; Verwoerd calls apartheid "good neighborliness." Here we see the first of a type of construction this film employs in which it's clear that director Lee Hirsch has asked various groups and individuals to perform particular songs for him, in this case "Watch Out Verwoerd," which the filmmaker edits with Mini's family singing as well. Each time the film does this, it effectively creates a sense of community and unity of purpose across generations and time periods.

In another type of reenactment, a black mother and her little girl do not get on a whites-only bus. The film continually works to keep its story in the present tense, and after a discussion of "Nkosi Sikelel iAfrika," the subversive national anthem for blacks, the film jumps to present-day hip hop and a group of young people talking about the history and effect of the protest songs of the earlier years.

Another issue explored in this section is how black women took care of white babies, which Sophie Mgcina articulates in the song

"Madam Please," and which the director visualizes through B-roll images of black domestic servants contrasted with images of black poverty. This segment ends with the first of several violent clashes with the government over the mandatory use of passbooks, and we see archival footage of a very young Nelson Mandela wondering how to maintain peaceful protests in the face of government violence.

Key Sequence: 0:24:50–0:28:26; Chapter 7 on DVD

This sequence exemplifies an editing structure the film uses often as it moves back and forth between primary footage, in this case of Hugh Masekela in concert singing "Stimela," and archival footage of black South Africans riding on the train and men working in the mines below. The director crosscuts between these images to create the sense that the past is never too far removed; he even merges and overlaps the sounds between the past and the present so that the bells on the train become Masekela's bell and his singing becomes the train whistle.

Discussion Questions

1. Why did the filmmaker choose to start the film with the exhumation of Vuyisile Mini in 1998 rather than in 1948, the beginning of apartheid?
2. What are some of the different ways the filmmaker uses archival footage?
3. Why do we not always get translations on the text track of the songs?
4. How is the music represented in the film similar to or different from the music we listen to today?

Viewing Day 2: 0:33:03–1:05:12; Chapters 9–19 on DVD (about 32 minutes)

- Begins with the sequence called "Thina Sizwe" (lamentation)
- Ends with Thandi Modise talking about her daughter being born

Things to Notice

Today's viewing begins with one of the film's most beautiful and affective scenes, which I recommend below for reviewing. This scene also signifies a change in the tone of the film that reflects the change in the mood of the country in 1964 when Mandela and other leaders were sent away to prison. The songs selected in this section are more somber, and the text track gives us new information about subjects we had met earlier in the film: now we learn that these subjects were exiled and jailed. Even the archival footage selected here is grainier and fuzzy as the anti-apartheid movement loses strength for over a decade.

The turn came in the 1970s, we learn, through the children, who began protesting the mandated teaching of Afrikaans in black schools, which led to uprisings in the townships. These are mainly shown in archival footage as peaceful protests, with more upbeat songs on the sound track. Another change in tone comes when the armed wing of the African National Congress (ANC) is formed (notice that the text track identifies some of these subjects as "freedom fighters"; other phrases, depending on your perspective, could of course be used). The songs now are more militant and strident. We also learn about Radio Freedom, an illegal radio station, and the pains that had to be taken to disguise the protest messages in code.

This day's viewing ends with two beautifully sad songs, as Thandi Modise, a "freedom fighter" tortured in prison while pregnant, shares how she nearly tried to commit suicide but was saved by the kicking of her daughter. Afterward, she sang songs of defiance until her daughter was born in prison. Notice the B-roll of the prison and the dull light of the scene.

Key Sequence: 0:33:16–0:35:40; Chapter 9 on DVD

This scene (see Figure 4.4) is called "Thina Sizwe" (lamentation), and notice how, like other scenes, this one is probably staged for the film, but it is filmed even more theatrically. Alone and isolated on a bare patch of land, shot from a long high angle, the singers are in constant movement but in slow motion. They sing of their land taken away as we see archival footage of their leaders being taken to jail. This is a great scene to reexamine for how the film connects the music to the political and the past to the present.

Discussion Questions

1. An interesting anecdote to discuss with your students is how the Zulus, who fought in wars against the British a hundred years earlier, would always sing before battle, which of course gave away their position to the enemy. Do these songs work the same way in this struggle against apartheid?

2. What does the film do to personalize the struggle? What stories and images are most affecting? Why?

3. How does the filmmaker establish the tone? Trace the shifts in tone throughout this day's viewing. Why are there shifts?

Figure 4.4. This stirring dance in *Amandla!*, probably enacted for the film, illustrates the merging of music and politics in South Africa.

Viewing Day 3: 1:05:12–1:37:12; Chapters 19–29 on DVD (about 32 minutes)

- Begins with image of outside Pretoria Central Prison
- Ends with closing credits

Things to Notice

The final viewing day begins with a continuation of the chapter titled "Birth and Death in Prison," where we meet prisoners on death row and see an extreme close-up of a guard who worked there; while he says he became "addicted" to the power of killing, it's clear he also feels regret. We learn in this section that when Vuyisile Mini was hanged, he went to the gallows singing. As a poet reads an ode to Mini, we see reenacted B-roll of the condemned men walking toward the noose and hear defiant singing on the sound track.

In the 1980s, the violence intensified, which the film documents through the powerful archival footage of a teenager's funeral and illustrates again through a shift in the songs presented, which are identified as those with a new sense of militant urgency, especially the *toyi-toyi*, described as a "tool used in war." This dance, accompanied by song, was successful, it seems, in scaring the white police officers, according to former members of the riot squads, whom the filmmaker interviews to reveal just how far apart the two sides were at the time. This sequence ends at 1:20:00, with an upbeat pop tune and the images of large crowds doing the *toyi-toyi*. The dance doesn't seem scary anymore, but it communicates a sense of historical inevitability.

The next sequences start the movement toward the release of Nelson Mandela with songs praising him, images of more protests, worldwide support, and a contemporary hip-hop song. When Mandela is finally released in 1990, we hear upbeat, joyful music on the sound track and see huge crowds (with smiling faces probably for the first time in the entire film) on the visual track. In the same montage, we see black South Africans going to the polls for the first time in history, and we learn that Mandela has been elected president. The film ends with a sequence of ordinary South Africans dancing, singing, and laughing, which the film intercuts with archival and primary footage of Mandela dancing: he may be a "messiah," but he is still one of them.

Key Sequence: 0:59:05–1:01:40; Chapter 18 on DVD

Just before the closing montage, the director takes us back to the beginning of the film with the same shots of Vuyisile Mini being taken out of his pauper's grave, but now we see the aftermath of that exhumation as he and other heroes of the struggle are given a large and official state funeral; on the sound track, we hear a song about remembering our ancestors. This clip elicits in viewers various moods ranging from joy to anguish, all created by the music and the images.

Discussion Questions

1. What do you think the film's subtitle means: "A Revolution in Four Part Harmony?"
2. Why does the film start and end with the images of Vuyisile Mini?
3. Describe the film's tone toward Nelson Mandela. How is this tone established?
4. Editing means that certain information is included and some is left out. What do you think was not included in this film? Why was it not and how might the film have been different if it had been included?

Closing Questions/Activities

1. Choose a time period and place of social conflict in this country, such as the Revolutionary War, slavery, the civil rights movement, the 1960s,

etc. Or select another country at a time of social unrest, such as the Troubles in Northern Ireland, the Holocaust, World War I, the Israeli-Palestinian conflict, and so on. Research the leading protest musicians of the era and their influence on the conflict. Locate samples of the lyrics and compare them to the songs found in *Amandla!* Is there a universal theme in protest music?

2. Watch one or more of the fiction films that cover the same subject and time period of *Amandla!*, such as *Cry Freedom*, *A Dry White Season*, or *Sarafina!* How does the documentary present the issue of apartheid differently? What did you learn from the fiction film that you did not from the documentary?

3. Make a list of the issues facing people today in this country. These could be political, economic, social, or personal conflicts. Try your hand at writing the lyrics (and the music?) of a protest song about an issue you have identified. Before writing, be sure to consider the following: Who is your audience? What is your purpose? What do you hope to convince your listeners to do? You may also want to take it a step further and create a music video of your song, or at least a storyboard of what it would look like if you were to film it. What images and text would accompany your song? Why?

4. Read the original English translation of "Nkosi Sikelel iAfrika," the South African National Anthem translated in Figure 4.5. Look back at how it is performed and discussed during 0:18:04–0:22:34. Analyze the song for tone and theme. Explain why it became the rallying cry for the anti-apartheid movement. Research its origins and adaptations, especially how it has changed since the end of the apartheid era.

5. Conduct research on postapartheid South Africa. You may want to examine the Truth and Reconciliation Commission that was set up to address abuses of the apartheid era, or you might look at the effect that AIDS is having on the South African population. Describe what a documentary on this subject would be like. What might its tone be? What images and music might be used?

Born into Brothels: Calcutta's Red Light Kids

2004, Rated R, Directed by Zana Briski and Ross Kauffman

Summary

An Academy Award–winning documentary, *Born into Brothels* is a portrait of children who live in the red-light district of Calcutta, India. One

"Nkosi Sikelel iAfrika": South African National Anthem

Original Lovedale English Translation

Lord, bless Africa;
May her horn rise high up;
Hear Thou our prayers And bless us.

Chorus
Descend, O Spirit,
Descend, O Holy Spirit.

Bless our chiefs
May they remember their Creator.
Fear Him and revere Him,
That He may bless them.

Bless the public men,
Bless also the youth
That they may carry the land with patience
and that Thou mayst bless them.

Bless the wives
And also all young women;
Lift up all the young girls
And bless them.

Bless the ministers
of all the churches of this land;
Endue them with Thy Spirit
And bless them.

Bless agriculture and stock raising
Banish all famine and diseases;
Fill the land with good health
And bless it.

Bless our efforts
of union and self-uplift,
Of education and mutual understanding
And bless them.

Lord, bless Africa
Blot out all its wickedness
And its transgressions and sins,
And bless it.

Figure 4.5. South Africa's national anthem, "Nkosi Sikelel iAfrika."

of the directors, Zana Briski, lived in the district and taught a group of kids to take photographs; she felt compelled to help these children out of the fate that is in store for them, especially the girls, by getting them into good schools outside of their troubled neighborhoods. Not only do we get a glimpse of a world we would never see otherwise, but we also learn about the universal, transformative power of art. It also doesn't hurt that the documentary is beautifully filmed and scored. The DVD version includes a follow-up with the kids three years after the events chronicled in the documentary. (Approximately 87 minutes)

Rationale

My wife traveled to India a few years ago and visited a village of extreme poverty, even by India's standards. There, a woman asked my wife to take her child home with her to the United States; my wife was so stunned at the desperation of such an offer that she could barely shake her head to say "no." Director Zana Briski feels the same hopelessness we all feel in the face of such seemingly insurmountable circumstances, but she acts nevertheless. This is a perfect film for a tenth-grade world culture or literature class, though some graphic language is spoken in a few places throughout the film, which is rated R for those scenes. In the following sections, I have marked where this language occurs (the scenes could be skipped, or you could turn off the subtitles and your students won't be able to read the swearing unless they can understand Bengali), but you will want to preview these scenes closely based on your school and community standards.

Previewing

1. Provide students with background on India and Calcutta. Since our students are so geographically challenged these days, I always start with a world map and then proceed to a map specifically of India to show the major cities, especially Calcutta. I also like to ask students to guess India's population. According to the *CIA World Fact Book*, the population in India as of July 2005 is estimated to be 1,080,264,388, compared to the U.S. estimated population of 295,734,134. It is also interesting to take students on a "virtual tour" of India and Calcutta; a number of Web sites (search for "virtual tour + Calcutta") provide slide shows of pictures that you can project for your class. In the ones I have seen, the business and tourist districts of Calcutta look beautiful, clean, and cosmopolitan, which will offer striking contrasts to what students will see of the red-light districts in this film.

2. If you have the DVD version with the Special Features section, show students the segment with Charlie Rose, who interviews both directors. This feature is only about six minutes long, provides some background about Zana's early involvement with the brothels, and includes pictures of each of the children. Ask students whether they would do what Zana does and why or why not.

3. An activity intended to introduce students to the power of photography is to have them take pictures of their lives—school, family, friends—for about a week before you begin showing the film. If this is not feasible because of cost, time, or equipment, ask students to look through some family photographs. Ideally, these should be snapshots of daily life and special occasions, not formal portraits. In either case, have them describe what someone might conclude about their lives from these photos if that person knew nothing else about them. Afterward, hold a discussion about what photographs can and cannot reveal about people's lives. I suggest that you show a few of the photo sequences from the Calcutta children's work. The DVD chapter menu clearly identifies "Photos By . . ." You might also want to have students consider the idea that it can be dangerous and perhaps unethical to assume too much about a person's life from a series of snapshots.

Viewing Day 1: 0:00:00–0:27:12; Chapters 1–7 on DVD (about 27 minutes)

- Begins with opening titles
- Ends with Gour talking about Puja

Things to Notice

The opening image of the film is of a lightbulb with moths—drawn to the light—buzzing all around it (though the director says on the commentary track that they are really flying ants); not too often in film can you capture such a clear metaphor that sums up much of the film in a single shot. The rest of the opening is described in the following key sequence section.

After the titles is a close-up of a rat scavenging for food and an interview of a young girl (who we learn later is named Kochi) who talks about the men who come into the brothels and who says that she often asks when she "will join the line," which we assume means becoming a prostitute. We then hear director Zana Briski for the first time as she gives us some background on how and why she came to live in the brothels. Throughout the film, her narration is an interesting one: it is

Born into Brothels **Character Chart**			
Use this form to keep track of details about each of the children throughout the film (see also Figure 4.7).			
Name	**Personality**	**Family Life**	**Significant Actions**
Kochi			
Shanti			
Avijit			
Suchitra			
Manik			
Gour			
Puja			
Tapasi			
Make predictions about what you think each of the children will be doing three years after the events in this film. Watch the follow-up documentary on the DVD to see if your predictions were correct.			

Figure 4.6. *Born into Brothels* character chart.

Figure 4.7. To help you identify each of the children in *Born into Brothels* (left to right): Puja, Suchitra, Kochi, Avijit, Tapasi, Gour, Manik, and Shanti.

not constant or authoritative, but decidedly personal. She narrates her own story and struggle within the larger events, but she doesn't try to sum up Indian history and culture for us, nor does she try to speak for the children or their experiences; their photography does this for them.

The next sequence is an essential introduction to each of the children. I suggest putting the kids' names up on the board or using the chart in Figure 4.6 to help your students keep them straight. In the order of how they are introduced, here are their names and brief descriptions: Kochi, the quiet, shy one we met earlier; Shanti, the one who needs to get her way all the time and sister of Manik; Avijit, the one around whom much of the movie will revolve because he is clearly a gifted photographer; Suchitra, who doesn't like to fight or disagree; Manik, Shanti's brother, a good-natured, funny boy; Gour, intelligent and articulate, whom the filmmakers call an activist in training; and Puja, funny and feisty (evidenced by her smacking Gour on the side of the head and her running commentary throughout this sequence about each of the children). This sequence culminates in the group photo that appears in the film's promotional material and other times later in the film. There is an eighth student in the picture and in the photography class, Tapasi, who is not introduced in this section.

Notice the shift in music and tone immediately after we see Kochi working in the kitchen. The film will often signal these tone shifts between the children's joy in taking pictures and their awful home lives with changes in music. Be warned that Tapasi's segment (0:09:04) contains a short section of profanity; it's clearly included by the filmmakers to illustrate just how rough and unchildlike the brothels are, and it would be best if you could show it; nevertheless, keep your community standards in mind. You could easily cover up the subtitles.

After more street scenes and a lesson with "Zana Auntie" about developing a critical eye, we see the first of the sequences of the children's photography that run throughout the film. While the photos are the children's, the filmmakers in each sequence have selected the images, set them to music, edited them together, and decided when to zoom in, zoom out, and so on. It is important to point out to your students that even though we are, in a sense, seeing the brothels through the kids' eyes, we have to remember that we are seeing the entire film through the eyes of the filmmakers. In this case, we see Kochi's photos accompanied by slow, soft music that accentuates the otherworldliness of the subjects of her pictures. Later in this day's viewing, we see a markedly different tone in Manik's and Shanti's photos.

In one of the most devastating interviews, Manik talks about picking up his mother from the police station, and Shanti talks about how she and her brother have to go the roof when their mother is "working" behind the curtain in the one room where they all live. The kids spend *a lot* of time up on that roof. In another interview, we learn that Kochi's father tried to sell her.

Zana begins to take a larger role in the narrative about halfway through this day's viewing as she begins what will be her central quest in the film: to get these kids into good schools out of the neighborhood. If your students are familiar with the different documentary modes, you can discuss how Zana's interaction with the events in the film is changing those very events. She admits that she cannot be a passive observer (as someone working in the observational mode would be) in the face of the horror she witnesses. This film clearly is not merely documenting events as they occur; the filmmakers are trying to change the events.

When the children take the first of several trips out of the neighborhood, the pop tune on the sound track is upbeat, reflecting the kids' mood and excitement (Figure 4.8), even though the trip is to a rather depressing zoo. We get a sense of Gour's compassion (which is his defining trait) as he expresses his concern for the animals' health. The zoo, with many shots of bars and cages, could be read as a metaphor of the

Figure 4.8. A rare moment of escape for the children of *Born into Brothels* on an outing to the zoo.

children's own lives. The day's sequence ends with Gour discussing Puja's home life and how he wants to take her away from it all.

Key Sequence: 0:00:07–0:02:17; Chapter 1 on DVD

The opening of the film is such a powerful way to begin that it is worth looking at again more closely. The ominous music accompanying the shot of the lightbulb dissolves into nondiegetic voices, low and indistinct murmurings, which then lead into an up-tempo, driving, Indian-sounding song with high-pitched flute, drums, and plaintive vocal. The visual track, meanwhile, cuts quickly between images of the brothels and close-ups of children's eyes. The images we see of the brothels, often blurred and dark, are of women standing in lines, often in bright-colored saris; men counting money; alcohol being poured and consumed; and children playing amid it all. Obviously, the children are not watching these street scenes at this time (and were probably not filmed at the same time at all), but the shots are edited together to give us the impression that this is what the children have to see each day. The images of the streets around the brothels are shot from a very low camera angle, suggesting a child's view (though on the commentary, one of the directors says he had to film the brothels surreptitiously, with the camera down by his side, to avoid being caught). In just over two minutes, with powerful juxtaposition and effective sound layering, this clip establishes the central premise of the film: these children need to get away from this life.

Discussion Questions

1. What is the filmmakers' tone toward the brothels? What do they do to establish this tone?

2. What is the filmmakers' tone toward the children? What do they do to establish this tone?

3. The filmmakers say on the commentary track that Kochi's pictures reflect her desire to photograph her dreams. How did the music and the editing of her photo sequence capture this desire?

4. What do you think of Zana? Why? What role does her narration play in the film?

Viewing Day 2: 0:27:12–0:51:51; Chapters 7–14 on DVD (about 25 minutes)

- Begins with the kids in a circle discussing their photos
- Ends with HIV testing that proves negative

Things to Notice

Today's viewing begins with interviews that remind us of the danger the girls are in because the families are so desperately poor that it will not be long before the girls go "on the line." When Suchitra is asked if she sees any solution to this problem, she just shakes her head and says an untranslated "no." Maybe as an answer, the filmmakers insert Suchitra's beautiful photos here, perhaps to say, "Art can be a way out." But to reinforce the depth of the kids' plight, we hear from a nun who runs a boarding school where Zana is trying to place the children, who says that "no one will take them."

We've been meeting the children slowly throughout the film, and now we get to learn more about Avijit, who is the most talented of all the children (later he will be invited to Europe to show his work) and who lives in the bar of the brothel.

The children's trip to the beach is described in the following key sequence. The next section highlights a fight that erupts in the brothel (warning: a lot of profanity at 0:44:28), and the film shows the women yelling and cursing, a child (Manik) being beaten, and a lot of close-ups of the children's faces, watching.

Again, this film does have a chronological story going and it is driven by Zana's voice-over about getting these kids some help. In this case, she struggles to find the paperwork they need to enroll in school. There are some lighter scenes at the end of the day's viewing in which the kids get passport pictures and have blood tests taken. The editing is quick and often played for laughs, even though the test is for HIV. All the tests turned out negative.

Key Sequence: 0:39:40–0:43:53; Chapter 10 on DVD

In this short sequence, we see the children arrive at the beach for what looks like the first time ever. We see them in bright light, running, jumping, and laughing and smiling a lot. The devotional music is upbeat and filled with life and energy, just like the children. Notice the shift in feeling and mood as the children return to the brothels. Now the camera is jerky and the images are blurred; the girls begin dancing on the bus in a sexualized way (because they are on their way back to the red-light district?). The music has become harsh and discordant. Next we hear the diegetic sounds of the neighborhood: car horns, shouts, cries, and whisperings. The music that starts up sounds sinister, and the camera follows the children as they move quickly through the brothels with their heads down; through the framing and camera movement, we appear to be stalking them through the prying eyes of the people on the streets. The contrast between the kids on the beach and the kids back home is devastating.

Discussion Questions

1. How does this film illustrate the influence of the brothel environment on the children? Consider images, music, and dialogue.
2. How do the filmmakers construct their story? What is the rising action? What are the main conflicts?
3. How do the kids' photographs—and how they are shown in the film—reflect their personalities?

Viewing Day 3: 0:51:51–1:23:03; Chapters 14–20 on DVD (about 32 minutes)

- Begins with kids playing on the roof
- Ends with closing credits

Things to Notice

After an interview with Tapasi about her mother, with B-roll of Tapasi washing pots and she and her family packed into a small room, we get to see her photographs. They are much different from the other kids' pictures; most of hers are indoors, claustrophobic, and harsh. The accompanying music is equally mournful.

The film jumps in scope a bit here when we learn that Zana has been exhibiting the children's work around the world, and the kids get to see video of their show at Sotheby's in London. This leads to a teacher from New York coming to work with the kids. Notice how the focus is more and more on Avijit: dialogue of him talking about photography like a grad student and images of him at work with his photos. The scene of the kids preparing for and later attending their exhibition is beautiful; the kids are so proud of their work, and the film includes great cuts of the kids laughing and smiling.

Avijit's mother was murdered, and the film traces his withdrawal from the group through close-ups of him, the music, and Avijit talking about how he had wanted to be a doctor, then an artist, but now, there is no hope. We also hear a phone call from Zana expressing frustration with Avijit.

Zana manages to find placement for some of the girls at a boarding school, and we see the children at the school for the first time, as well as the mothers listening closely to the rules of the school as they try to decide whether to enroll their daughters. The scene at school—one of hope and progress—is immediately juxtaposed with more images of the prostitutes of the red-light district. Kochi, who is leaving it behind by enrolling in the school, looks out the window of a moving taxi but doesn't get out: another effective metaphor. When Zana goes to another school, Future Hope, for the boys, you might have your students speculate about how much of Zana's decision to enroll them is influenced by the filmmaking itself. It's also a great place to remind your students about the construction of the film: we can see how the organization and the editing have created a narrative out of events that did not necessarily occur chronologically. I love the contrast of the girls leaving the neighborhood: Kochi is crying and Puja is all smiles, as always.

An effective use of the visual and text tracks occurs as Avijit and Zana are trying to get his passport so that he can go to Amsterdam for the showing of his photographs. We see a huge crowd of people in front of the office and a tiny Avijit nearly swallowed by the crowd; then there's a fade-out and a text track that says "8 hours later," fading into a picture of Avijit's passport. The next sequence is of Avijit in Amsterdam and includes, in addition to a lot of "fish out of water" images (he is on ice skates!), many quick cuts of Avijit taking picture after picture of nearly everything he sees. He appears supremely confident and self-possessed, whether talking about photographs or walking down the street; this is a kid, the film suggests, who is ready for the world.

While it's clear that the film found its upbeat ending with Avijit's successful trip and decision to attend school, the reality of the challenges facing these kids is illustrated in the closing, in which we get updates on each of the children. We learn who is attending school and who is not: of the eight children, only four, at the time the film was finalized, were still attending school. As does the rest of the film, the end leaves the viewer with both hope and sadness.

Key Sequence: Deleted Scenes under Special Features on DVD

Instead of a key sequence from this last section, I like to show one or more of the deleted scenes from the DVD. There are about seven to choose from, and it does not necessarily matter which one you select. After students look at the scene, I ask them to think about why the scene might not have been included, and if it were in included, where it would fit in best.

Discussion Questions

1. Are Zana's actions ethical? Though it is clearly desirable for the kids to get out of the red-light district, when she tries to get them into boarding schools, she is breaking up families and changing their ways of life. Is she imposing an outsider's view of the world onto these children?

2. Think back on the construction of this film. What did the filmmakers do to make the "climax" of the film—Avijit in Amsterdam—as powerful as it is?

3. What does the film seem to be saying about the women in the red-light district? How are they portrayed? What about the men and the fathers of the brothels?

Closing Questions/Activities

1. Look back at the photo sequences by the children in this film to see how the filmmakers constructed each of them differently. Take five to ten pictures of your own life and insert them into a PowerPoint presentation. Decide how long each image will stay on screen, how each will transition to the next (cut, fade, dissolve), and add music to create a particular effect. Show your sequences to a peer or to your class to see if your audience was affected in the way you intended.

2. The directors of this film created a foundation called Kids with Cameras designed to empower children through the arts. They are also selling a book of the children's photography, the profits from which are directly subsidizing the children's educations. Identify a social problem, either in your local community, in the country, or out in the world. Research its causes and its victims and describe a foundation that you might set up to address this concern. How would you raise money and awareness? Who would you contact for support?

3. Look over the character charts you have been keeping throughout the film. Make predictions about what you think the kids will be like three years later. Have some kind of reason for your prediction based on the kids' personalities, home lives, or previous actions. Look at the Reconnecting special feature on the DVD to see how the kids are doing three years after filming had stopped. Were your predictions accurate? Make more predictions for three more years later.

Night and Fog

1955, Not Rated, Directed by Alain Resnais

Summary and Rationale

This powerful exploration of the Holocaust is like a long poem, an ode to the horrors of man's ability to hurt others. While it provides facts, statistics, and dates like any other documentary, *Night and Fog* transcends many other Holocaust texts mainly because of its narration, written by poet Jean Cayrol, a political prisoner during the war, delivered in an all-knowing but world-weary and detached manner, and because of its stark and shocking visual track. Made only ten years after the end of World War II, the film, which focuses on the concentration camps and the "Final Solution," is extremely explicit, and you should take care to preview the film ahead of time. But the explicitness of the images is exactly the point: we cannot forget the Holocaust because the ability to commit these atrocities lies within mankind and is not limited to the events of this one war.

The film is only thirty-two minutes, though it feels much longer (in a good way), so I tend to show the film twice. After we do some of the following previewing activities, students watch the film once without any note taking, interruption, or discussion. Whenever my colleague Dave Lickey teaches this film, after the viewing he suggests silence: no talking, writing, or discussion; he likes to time it so that class ends just as the film does, forcing students to see the real world through the lens of the horrors they have just witnessed. I like to ask students to write in their journals their initial thoughts and feelings, though I too like this to be done in silence. I have never had a class that has not been profoundly and deeply affected by what they have seen: be prepared for anger, tears, and confusion. When students watch the film the second time, I ask them to pay attention to the construction of the film and the details noted below, particularly the narration and the director's contrasting use of primary and archival footage.

A Holocaust study is a mandatory part of many districts' curricula, and I have generally taught this film as part of my regular tenth-grade class, which has a world culture focus. An English teacher and a history teacher could easily team up with this film, each class viewing it for different but related purposes.

Previewing

1. While it might seem amazing that students come to high school with little knowledge of World War II and the Holocaust, I have stopped being surprised after years of blank looks when I ask about the Final Solution, so I start with a KWL chart about various topics: concentration camps, causes of the war, Allied and Axis powers, etc. After the *K* part of the chart, you can ask students to conduct a brief Internet research on further topics they need to know to understand the film, which they put under the *W* column. After they share their research, have students fill out the *L* portion of their chart.

2. What is "evil"? This is an essential question for the class to discuss since too often we say that the Holocaust happened because Hitler was evil. But as the film suggests, evil is within humanity and we need to be ever vigilant of evil within ourselves.

3. Read the following section of the narration from the film written by poet and survivor Jean Cayrol, and ask students to identify and describe the speaker of the passage. What is the tone? Theme? What images come to mind?

> At the moment I speak to you, the icy water of the ponds and ruins is filling up the hollows of the charnel house. A water as cold and murky as our own bad memories. War is napping, but with one eye always open.

Viewing Day: 0:00:00–0:32:03; all chapters on DVD (about 32 minutes)

- Begins with opening scene (see Figure 4.9)
- Ends with closing credits

Things to Notice

As noted earlier, it is essential that students have at least one uninterrupted viewing, but once students have seen the film, I pause it at various times to discuss certain points. The following are some of the key parts of the film you might want to note on second viewing:

Time Code	Description/Comment
0:01:43	The first shots appear to be of a beautiful, open landscape, until the camera moves downward to reveal that we are behind a barbed wire fence. Each of the initial camera movements starts in the open and moves toward and into the camps, with the wire dominating the frame. The narration repeats the word *ordinary* and notes that the camp is silent now with "no footstep heard but our own." Clearly, the director wants us to be here in the present day, long after the atrocities, for a reason, though we may not know why just yet.
0:02:56	The first switch to black and white is signaled with a drumbeat and images of the Nazi party (many taken from *Triumph of the Will*) gaining power, but the film quickly returns to the concentration camps, focusing on the construction and mechanisms of the camps and including archival footage of people boarding the trains.
0:07:15	A piece of narration here always strikes me as odd. As the trains pull away, a piece of paper falls out of one of the cars, and the narrator says, "A message flutters to the ground. Will it be found?" The narrator is clearly not an objective one, and he also appears to be commenting on the actual footage included in the finished film, not just on the historical events the film is recounting. It's a good place to discuss the role of this narrator and contrast him to a typical narrator in a historical, expository documentary.
0:07:35– 0:10:54	We return to the present, signified by the color pictures of the "same tracks . . . looking for what?" The color images are now beginning to be established as our conscience: our

Even a peaceful landscape...

Figure 4.9. I wish this could have been printed in color, because this shot from the opening of *Night and Fog* shows the camp as it is today in contrast to images in black and white of the camp during the war.

need to know and understand what happened in the black-and-white images. As the narrator asks later (0:09:14): "Who does know anything?" We begin to notice that there are no living, moving things in any of these color pictures. The camera, though, never stops moving in the color shots. It is, perhaps, continuing to search for something.

0:12:20– Listen to the music—slow, mournful—in the past images
0:12:50 of prisoners starving, contrasted with the more strident, angry tones of the present images of latrines. The music in this film is constantly changing, keeping us unsettled.

0:16:00 Here are more images and descriptions of contrast: men staying sharp intellectually with letters, politics, and religion versus their bodies, which are withering away from hunger and exhaustion.

0:20:20	1942: Plans are made to convert the prisoner camps into death camps as the Final Solution is put into place: the gas chambers and crematoriums. The images become steadily more graphic and explicit. The shots in color explore the intricate details of the mechanisms of the camps, sometimes slowing down just enough to let certain details sink in.
0:26:00–0:28:20	These are some of the toughest images in the film as the Nazis explore various ways to dispose of the bodies of the dead and to use whatever they can from them in the war effort. Then, once the camps are liberated, the Allies—and we—see mountains of corpses. We know all of this, of course; we've read about it, but *seeing* the sheer numbers of dead has a paralyzing effect. I rewatched this sequence three times before I remembered to write about it. When the narrator says, "All the doors," we see lines of German female soldiers leaving the camps, healthy, well fed, and clean, contrasted with the skeletal corpses being thrown into common graves.
0:29:17	The ending of the film begins here (see Figure 4.10) when a camp's *kapo*, officer, and commandant each says, according to the narrator, "I am not responsible." Over another shot of the mountain of corpses, the narrator asks, "Then who is responsible?"
0:29:56–end	We stay in the present for the rest of the film. The narration here includes the section that students looked at before beginning the film, about "war is napping," and also says that the "faithful grass has come up again," which implies that we are in danger of forgetting what happened here as soon as the grass comes in to cover things up. As the narrator delivers the final section (see Figure 4.11), we see the wreckage of the camps, and as the camera finally comes to a halt, we hear the words that implore us to be vigilant.

Discussion Questions

1. Complete a SOAPStone for the final portion of the narration (see Figure 4.11) and write an analysis of the theme and tone.

2. How is this film similar to or different from other Holocaust films you have seen?

Figure 4.10. This shot from near the end of *Night and Fog* captures the central question of the film: who is responsible for the Holocaust?

3. Describe the delivery of the narration. How does the narrator's tone of voice, pace, and diction affect the audience?

4. Select a particularly powerful image on the visual track. Why was it included and how does it relate to something you heard on the audio track?

Closing Questions/Activities

1. In groups, research contemporary genocides before or since the Holocaust. Unfortunately, there is no shortage of possibilities, including such peoples and places as Armenians, Iraqi Kurds, Cambodia, Bosnia, Rwanda, Darfur, etc. Has the world forgotten the lessons of the Holocaust, which this film suggests it must not forget? Read excerpts from Samantha Power's *A Problem from Hell: America and the Age of Genocide*, which addresses this topic.

2. Philosopher Theodor Adorno wrote that "to write poetry after Auschwitz is barbaric." What do you think he meant by this, and is it

Night and Fog **Analysis**

Reread the final portion of the narration of the film, complete a SOAPStone for this passage only, and then write an analysis of how the tone of the piece reflects the theme.

> The crematorium is no longer in use. The devices of the Nazis are out of date. Nine million dead haunt this landscape. Who is on the lookout from this strange tower to warn us of the coming of new executioners? Are their faces really different from our own? Somewhere among us, there are lucky Kapos, reinstated officers, and unknown informers. There are those who refused to believe this, or believed it only from time to time. And there are those of us who sincerely look upon the ruins today, as if the old concentration camp monster were dead and buried beneath them. Those who pretend to take hope again as the image fades, as though there were a cure for the plague of these camps. Those of us who pretend to believe that all this happened only once, at a certain time and in a certain place, and those who refuse to see, who do not hear the cry to the end of time.

Speaker	
Occasion	
Audience	
Purpose	
Subject	
Tone	
Analysis	

Figure 4.11. SOAPStone analysis of *Night and Fog*.

true? Read examples of Holocaust poetry by such writers as Miklós Radnóti, Primo Levi, and Paul Celan. How does this poetry fit with Adorno's statement?

3. Select a Holocaust poem and imagine that it is the narration for a documentary. Create a storyboard for it. What images, sounds, and graphics would you use and why?

4. Watch scenes from *Schindler's List*, *The Pianist*, *Life Is Beautiful*, or another Holocaust fiction film. How does a fictional representation of the Holocaust differ from a documentary? Are your feelings similar to

or different from those as you watch a nonfiction film on the subject? Why or why not?

Super Size Me

2004, Rated PG-13, Directed by Morgan Spurlock

Summary

Morgan Spurlock, the director of *Super Size Me*, decides to eat nothing but McDonald's food for one month and to document the effects on his health. Along the way, he interviews lawyers, nutrition experts, and industry figures to determine the role that fast food plays in our culture. (Approximately 100 minutes)

Rationale

This film is just like a persuasive essay, so I have shown it to students before starting a unit on persuasive writing to show the way in which Spurlock uses facts, personal experiences, and humor to make his points. While one scene, noted below, refers to sexuality, the film is appropriate for just about any grade level, though I like to use it with eleventh graders, especially if I am going to have them work with Upton Sinclair's *The Jungle* or the writings of other muckrakers.

Previewing

1. Ask students to take a survey about their eating habits (see Figure 4.12) before they view the film, and hold a class discussion/debate on their responses.

2. Have students keep a log of advertisements they see during one full day. Identify how many ads were for food and drink, specifically for fast-food restaurants. Discuss the health benefits of the products found in these advertisements compared to other products they probably did not see advertisements for, such as milk, vegetables, and whole grains. What ads did they see in school?

3. Morgan Spurlock, the director of this film, puts himself at serious health risk to complete the experiment that constitutes his film. Ask students a hypothetical question about how far they might be willing to go in order to prove a point: would they risk jail, expulsion, health damage, etc., to stand up for what they believe is right? In what types of scenarios can students see themselves doing this?

Previewing Survey: *Super Size Me*

1. How often do you eat at a fast-food restaurant?
every day   once a week   once a month   never/very rarely

2. Why do you eat fast food? (circle all that apply)
tastes good   it's quick   nothing else to eat   don't eat it

other reasons:

3. How often do you eat your school-provided lunch?
every day   once a week   once a month   never/very rarely

4. What words best describes your school lunch? (circle all that apply)
excellent   terrible   healthy   too few choices

other words:

5. How much exercise do you normally get in a week?
a lot   some   little   none

6. Do you think that people should be able to sue tobacco companies for their addictions?
yes   no   maybe   don't know

Comments:

7. Do you think that people should be able to sue fast-food companies for their health?
yes   no   maybe   don't know

Comments:

8. In what ways do you think fast food can affect your health?

Figure 4.12. Previewing survey for *Super Size Me*.

Viewing Day 1: 0:00:00–0:29:03; Chapters 1–10 on DVD (about 30 minutes)

- Begins with opening scene
- Ends with Spurlock playing in a McDonald's playground

Things to Notice

The film opens with a group of young kids singing a song about Kentucky Fried Chicken, Pizza Hut, and McDonald's. No context is provided for the scene (we do not know if it was shot for the film or for some other purpose), and there is no narration at this point, but if you were to look back at this opening after you view the next section, you would notice that many of the kids the clip focuses on are both overweight and extremely enthusiastic about fast food.

Next we hear a narrator (director Morgan Spurlock, we learn shortly thereafter) list a series of facts about the obesity problem in the United States, which the visual track supports with many shots of overweight people, charts, graphics, and newspaper articles. He sets out his main questions here: are fast-food companies responsible for the obesity in the United States, and where does personal responsibility stop and corporate responsibility begin? These questions, of course, lead Spurlock to his "super size me" experiment of eating nothing but McDonald's food for every meal for a month. As the opening titles run, we hear the song "Fat Bottomed Girls" and see more pictures of overweight people eating fast food. This establishes a tone that is both serious and mocking; Spurlock is not above using sophomoric humor to make a more serious point throughout the film.

When Spurlock goes to his three doctors (see Figure 4.13), a nutrition expert, and a fitness guru for a checkup, notice how effectively he is able to communicate his overall healthiness in a very short sequence, and how each of these individuals makes a prediction about his experiment that ultimately will not be dire enough. You will want to point out how Spurlock uses the artwork to divide many of the chapters on the DVD and to add comments to his own work; for example, one from this section depicts a cartoon version of the Last Supper that introduces Spurlock's own final meal before embarking on his McDiet.

The film then settles into its rhythm of moving chronologically through Spurlock's thirty-day experiment, with short intercuts (like the one described in the following key sequence) that support his exploration of the role of fast food in this country. Day two is extremely funny, revealing, and gross as he cannot keep his food down; these scenes are well edited and shot with close-ups and fade-outs to emphasize

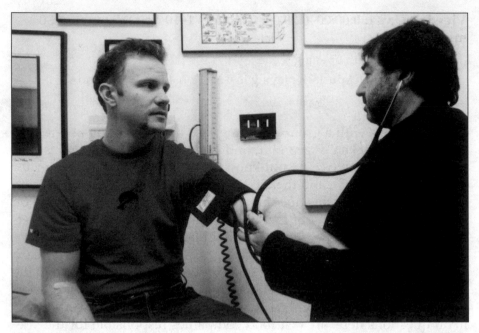

Figure 4.13. Spurlock faces real health risks in his experiment in *Super Size Me*.

Spurlock's sickness. It also makes you wonder—as you should through-out this film—whether Spurlock is a good actor aware of what would make a good film, or a detached, objective researcher interested in find-ing the truth of fast food. Think again about Spurlock's structure here: right after getting sick on day two, he includes an exploration of the effects of fast food called "Toxic Environment." He also meets with a law professor who links fast food with tobacco by discussing the "life-long branding" that both industries do to kids, as the images of kids playing and having fun at McDonald's are shown on the visual track.

Key Sequence: 0:16:29–0:21:14; Chapter 7 on DVD

In this sequence, Spurlock offers up a side to the argument that he seemed to ridicule earlier in the film: people sue the fast-food industry for their health problems. Notice how he constructs his argument here. He starts with interviews of people on the street talking about how silly it is to sue over this, which is probably the position that most of his audience holds; certainly it was mine as well. While these people pro-pose seemingly logical opinions, they are not experts, unlike *everyone* that Spurlock interviews next on the other side of the argument: a law-yer, professors, and a former surgeon general. This side offers facts, sta-tistics, and well-reasoned arguments. (Though he does take a little dig at the lawyer by not letting him finish a sentence about why he is suing McDonald's for reasons other than monetary compensation.) Look to see how Spurlock supports with visuals what these experts say: Ronald McDonald drawing the kids in, cartoons, advertisements, and close-ups of drinking cups to the scale of a New York street. In just about five minutes, Spurlock, through his choice of interviews, his editing, and B-roll, makes the idea of suing the fast-food industry seem not quite so ridiculous.

Discussion Questions

1. How do you think Spurlock feels about suing the fast-food industry at this point? What does he include on his visual, text, or sound track that reveals this?

2. Is his experiment a fair one? Is he an unbiased investigator? How else could he have tried to answer his central questions?

3. What are some of the parallels Spurlock tries to draw between the fast-food and the tobacco industries, and why?

Viewing Day 2: 0:29:03–1:04:04; Chapters 11–22 on DVD (about 34 minutes)

- Begins with the title "The Impact" and a picture of Ronald McDonald
- Ends with Spurlock in Texas on day sixteen of his experiment

Things to Notice

This section begins with a focus on disease and then moves to the effect of obesity on body image. As the teenage girl talks about her self-image, Spurlock visually agrees by showing pictures of beautiful, skinny fashion models that begin covering the frame, eventually obscuring the teenager entirely; it is an extremely effective way of blending the audio and visual tracks.

Since the effect of Spurlock's diet on his health is an important part of the film, we see two weigh-ins during today's viewing. Spurlock started at 186 pounds; after five days he was at 195; and after twelve days he was 203: a 17-pound gain.

Spurlock returns to his central question of whether McDonald's is responsible for its customers' bad health by showing—and highlighting—a phrase from a court document stating that it is a "matter of common knowledge that any processing that [McDonald's] foods undergo serve to make them more harmful that unprocessed foods." Spurlock cuts to an extremely graphic and highly critical animated sequence about the processing of chicken McNuggets, and then he moves to a huge list of ingredients in the product; halfway through he has a picture of Frankenstein's monster pop up. Without saying a word, Spurlock makes his point quite clearly: chicken McNuggets sure are scary.

The diet experiment continues, and Spurlock is just about halfway through by the end of this viewing day. Meanwhile, he explores the role of advertising (see the following key sequence) and the nature of school lunches, contrasting three schools: one where students buy lots of junk food under the "watchful" eye of the nutritionist, one where the "cooks" only heat up government-supplied food, and one where students' behavior reportedly improved when they were put on a diet of fresh fruits, vegetables, and grains. Notice how the selected close-ups of the food tell the story and reveal Spurlock's opinion about which school is better. The section ends with an attack on the cutbacks of physical education classes and recess due to the testing requirements of the No Child Left Behind Act.

Key Sequence: 0:44:10–0:47:14; Chapter 18 on DVD

This is a short but devastating section in which Spurlock uses his visual, sound, and text tracks to effectively persuade his audience about the destructive power of advertising to children. Rather than list on his text track a series of statistics about the number of commercials children see and the amount of money that is spent on this advertising, he uses animation sequences to make comparisons between the money Pepsi spends on advertising versus the money the government spends on healthy-food programs. He also uses shots of four children who can readily identify pictures of Ronald McDonald but not Jesus. Whether this is reflective of national surveys is not addressed; it's funny and telling—but accurate?

Discussion Questions

1. How reliable and objective a narrator is Spurlock? Obviously he is interested in critiquing the fast-food industry and he wants to make an entertaining film. Does he do any "acting" in this film? Is he "playing up" to the camera? Is this unethical? Is he *supposed* to be objective?

2. Are you changing your position on the fast-food industry? What evidence seems to be most compelling to you? What is Spurlock's position? How does he reveal this?

3. You are two-thirds of the way through this movie. Whose point of view has not been represented so far? Why do you think Spurlock constructed the film this way?

Viewing Day 3: 1:04:04–1:36:23; Chapters 23–36 on DVD (about 32 minutes)

- Begins with news footage of a snow storm
- Closing credits

Things to Notice

This section starts with a fight between Spurlock and his girlfriend, a vegan chef, over his diet, after which you need to be aware that she speaks rather frankly about their sex life during this experiment; it's a short sequence that could be easily skipped if you are concerned about its content. Several times in this section, Spurlock is presented with scary information about his health as a result of his McDiet, but he does not stop and even seems to resist taking a daily aspirin. We have to wonder as an audience about the ethics involved here and the filmmaker's own motivations: is he more interested in making a compelling film than in his own health?

Listen for Curtis Mayfield's "Pusherman" on the sound track during visuals of McDonald's products as Spurlock and his interview subjects consider whether fast food could be an addiction; his sound track answers the question for them.

An excellent example of how documentary filmmakers can make visual points that may be effective but not accurate is when Spurlock learns that Haelth, the site where he was getting his nutrition counseling, is closing. Spurlock shows boxed-up offices and fitness equipment as he says, "Apparently we don't put much emphasis on health in America." The visuals of the closed club are supposed to support this assertion, but we don't know anything about why Haelth closed. It could have been for any number of reasons specific to Haelth (bad business plan, poor location, and so on) and not have anything to do with the larger issue in the United States, as Spurlock claims. This is a very short scene, but it's a perfect place to point out how documentaries are constructed and how carefully we need to watch them.

Spurlock then visits with a man who is having surgery to staple his stomach. On the sound track during shots of the surgery (pretty graphic ones), Spurlock plays Strauss's "Blue Danube Waltz," which gives the scene a lighthearted feel that seems to be in contrast to the seriousness of the procedure. I have, for some classes, turned down the sound during this sequence and then compared my students' reactions with and without the song.

As noted in Chapter 1, documentaries often use cinematic techniques normally associated with fiction films, and Spurlock effectively uses dissolves in this sequence, in which he wakes up sick in the middle of the night and then slowly disappears (dissolves) from the shot, creating a feeling of impending disaster.

The voice that has been absent throughout this film is that of the McDonald's corporation itself, and Spurlock shows us a series of quick cuts demonstrating his futile attempts to reach someone from the organization to comment. Did these calls take place on a single day, over the course of a week, or throughout the entire month? We have no way to know the time sequence, but we clearly get the sense that McDonald's is an unresponsive company not interested in addressing the issues raised in the film.

Near the end, we see Spurlock's final blood tests and weigh-in to learn that he is now 210 pounds, for a total weight gain of 25 pounds in one month. After this we learn that the lawsuit that raised the question which prompted Spurlock's film was thrown out because the (plaintiff) girls had not been able to prove that McDonald's had actually been harmful to them. As with many sections in this film, we do not know the genuine sequence of events. The film makes it seem as though the lawsuit was dismissed only after Spurlock finished his experiment, but it's entirely possible the lawsuit had resolved even before he started filming. Spurlock's placement of this material is narratively effective, but that does not mean this is the true order of events.

Spurlock ends the narrated portion of his film on a positive note about how some school districts are fighting back against the fast-food industry, and he shows an animated tombstone of Ronald McDonald with the dates 1954–2012, implying that the fast-food giant's days are numbered. The last sequence before the credits is an epilogue with updates on various people in the film.

Key Sequences: (see below for time codes)

Rather than a single key sequence, I suggest that you give students a chance to look back at several key scenes that demonstrate how documentaries construct reality. A scene to point out that illustrates the power of editing is when Spurlock interviews the lobbyist from the Grocery Manufacturers Association (1:22:55), who at one point in the interview says, "We're [the food industry] part of the problem." When he says this, Spurlock treats this comment like a "gotcha" and freezes the lobbyist on screen and covers the rest of the frame with logos and names of companies the lobbyist represents. We can only guess how long the original interview lasted, but Spurlock edited it to include a twenty-second clip that lends the greatest support to his argument. The lobbyist made a true statement, and it's not at all wrong or unethical to include it here, but its inclusion reinforces the point that students need to learn that documentaries are constructs of reality. That one comment is probably not at all reflective of the overall tone and subject of the lobbyist's comments. Another scene through which to examine a documentary's construction is a sped-up shot at day twenty-five (1:25:35) of Spurlock eating his McDonald's meal as a very large woman comes up behind him, the song "Fat" by the Violent Femmes on the sound track. Spurlock is clearly reacting to the woman behind him and "acting" somewhat for the camera. This scene is also representative of the simultaneously serious and mocking tone he uses throughout. Spurlock's last McSupper (1:28:07) includes several people we have seen in the film and takes place in the manner of a kid's birthday party, with "Yummy, Yummy, Yummy" on the sound track. The last shot is extremely cinematic and probably staged: Morgan alone in his party hat, slumped in his chair, looking sick as the camera slowly pulls back and fades to black (Figure 4.14). All of these scenes happened and are therefore "real," but the power and effect of the scenes lie in how they were constructed during either production or postproduction.

Discussion Questions

1. Should Spurlock have stopped the experiment when his health began to deteriorate? Did the doctors and crew involved in the production of the film have a responsibility to no longer participate if they thought he was damaging himself?

2. At the beginning of the film, Spurlock asked the question, "Where does personal responsibility end and corporate responsibility begin?" While he does not directly answer this question, how would he answer it at the end of his film? Why?

3. Look back at your notes. Is Spurlock "fair and balanced" on this issue? Why or why not? On which side of the issue are most of the people interviewed? Is a documentarian supposed to be "fair and balanced"?

4. This film often balances humor with seriousness. Which scenes do you think demonstrate this conflicting tone, and why do you think Spurlock chose to take this tone?

Closing Questions/Activities

1. Read excerpts from the popular text *Fast Food Nation* by Eric Schlosser. On what points would Spurlock and Schlosser agree and on which

Figure 4.14. Spurlock on the last day of his experiment in *Super Size Me*.

would they disagree? The DVD of *Super Size Me* includes a short interview between Schlosser and Spurlock.

2. In 2005, Morgan Spurlock began producing a show for the FX Network called *30 Days*, in which people try a thirty-day experiment of some kind while Spurlock films and narrates the results. The pilot episode features Spurlock and his fiancée trying to live on a minimum wage

(a nice connection would be to have students read an excerpt from Barbara Ehrenreich's *Nickel and Dimed* before or after viewing this episode), while other episodes include such scenarios as a Christian fundamentalist living with a Muslim family.

3. Write a press release or a script from an interview with a McDonald's corporate executive that addresses the major points raised in the film.

4. Research the eating habits of students in your school. Who eats the school lunches, how healthy are the food choices, what options are available, are sodas and snacks sold, etc.? Write a letter to your principal that presents your findings and makes recommendations.

5. Keep a log of the food you eat for one week. Compare its nutritional value with those recommended by the federal government.

6. Imagine that someone wanted to make a film suggesting that personal responsibility is more to blame than McDonald's products themselves. Who would this filmmaker interview and what other information would be included? Songs? Visuals?

Bowling for Columbine

2002, Rated R, Directed by Michael Moore

Summary

Michael Moore explores the role of gun violence in the United States in the wake of the shootings at Columbine High School in Colorado. He examines the possible factors—social, racial, cultural, and political—that make the United States unique in its number of murders. *Bowling for Columbine* is often funny, yet poignant, and always powerful. The film is rated R for what I assume is some mild profanity and images of violence. (Approximately 120 minutes)

Rationale

Michael Moore takes a lot of heat: some of it is deserved, but much of it reveals people's unfamiliarity with documentary forms. Critics—often Republicans, since his film *Fahrenheit 9/11*—like to suggest that his films are not really documentaries at all because he manipulates images, sound, and time. Their criticism is absolutely true, as we will see when we examine this film, but their conclusions are not. Yes, Moore constructs "reality" to suit his purposes, but as we have seen throughout this text, every nonfiction film does this: as soon as a filmmaker turns that camera on and off, he or she has presented a constructed version of reality. Because Moore's films are so popular and often funny, they become the perfect place for students to see the construction that goes on in documentaries. We will look at individual sections in which Moore is clearly being manipulative, and we can judge his actions and, more important, examine our reactions. It is not my intention to somehow show that Moore is "lying" in his films (several books and Web sites already try to do that), but I like to point out places where, if you're not paying close attention, you might not notice how he is manipulating us. This doesn't make Moore a liar, merely a "constructor of reality," as is any documentarian. Moore, whether you agree or disagree with him, is an accomplished filmmaker, and his films should be a call to teachers to teach students to be more aware of the methods filmmakers use to influence an audience. The film is rated R, so it might be most appropriate for older high school students and would be most effective in an American literature class or in a unit on persuasive or expository writing.

Previewing

1. Michael Moore is considered to be a "liberal" by people who consider themselves "conservatives," but oftentimes we use these terms without discussing with our students what the labels signify. I like to introduce these terms by starting a chart like the following (which the careful reader will notice I stole from myself in the section on perspective in Chapter 2) and having students add to it:

	Liberal/"The Left"	Conservative/"The Right"
People	John Kerry	George W. Bush
Political Party	Democrat	Republican
Abortion	right to choose	right to life
Gun Control	more limitation	believe in strict interpretation of the Second Amendment
Gay Marriage		
Education		
Death Penalty		
Assisted Suicide		

2. Ask students to closely analyze the text of the Second Amendment: "A well-regulated Militia being necessary to the security of a free State, the right of the people to keep and bear arms shall not be infringed." What rights does this amendment give and what are its limitations?

3. Michael Moore is popular with a lot of students because he is often funny and sometimes sophomoric. His TV show, the *Awful Truth*, is widely available on DVD and contains two- to three-minute skits that demonstrate his humor and filmmaking style. Try to find one in which he ambushes a corporate executive or politician, making him or her look ridiculous (trust me: such a scene is not hard to find).

Viewing Day 1: 0:00:00–0:29:33; Chapters 1–10 on DVD (about 30 minutes)

- Begins with opening
- Ends with trucks carrying rockets through Littleton

Things to Notice

The movie quickly establishes its ironic tone with the opening scene, which purports to document April 20, 1999, a typical day in the United States: idealized shots of the Washington Monument, a farmer, a milkman, a foreign city bombed by the orders of our president with the "Battle Hymn of the Republic" playing on the sound track. The filmmaker edits an image of a bikini-wearing babe holding a gun right into a picture of the Statue of Liberty. Moore is many things: subtle is not one of them.

Even before the titles, we see Moore's first "stunt," in which he opens a bank account to receive a free gun from the bank (Figure 4.15). The scene is a stunt because as with many others in this film, the events as they transpired on screen would not have happened if Moore himself were not filming: it is a textbook example of the interactive mode of documentary filmmaking. It also typifies Moore's style of deadpan delivery and allows the audience to see the irony of the situation.

After the opening titles (the song's chorus is "Take the skinheads bowling"), Moore takes the time to establish himself as a gun owner, from a gun town, who is a lifelong member of the NRA, though he immediately contrasts this with images of gun-owner stupidity ("Dog wearing gun shoots owner") and the Michigan militiamen who once trained with Timothy McVeigh and Terry Nichols. Then we get an interesting scene that forces us to question the ethics and the role of the filmmaker who uses the interactive mode: Moore interviews Terry's

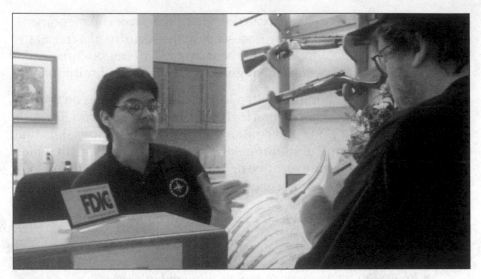

Figure 4.15. One of the earliest scenes in *Bowling for Columbine*, this is quintessential Moore: through humor he illustrates the idiocy of giving away a free gun in a bank.

mentally unstable brother, James, who—at Moore's insistence—shows Moore the gun he sleeps with under his bed; he even puts it to his own head, all while Moore's crew continues to film. Again, Moore's (and his camera's) presence initiates and extends a potentially dangerous situation. This is a wonderful place to discuss the ethics issues of documentary filmmaking.

Almost half an hour into a film ostensibly about Columbine, Moore finally gets to Littleton, Colorado, where the shooting took place, though he goes not to the school but to defense contractor Lockheed Martin, the largest employer in the area. The day's viewing ends with shots of Lockheed Martin trucks driving the company's missiles through a sleeping town. Moore's point is clear: military violence—represented by Lockheed Martin—is associated with the individual, personal violence of the Columbine shootings.

Key Sequences: 0:19:45–0:20:48 and 0:26:00–0:28:26; Chapter 8 on DVD

These are two very short scenes, but they effectively demonstrate how Moore uses montage and music to create irony. In the first sequence, to the tune of The Beatles' "Happiness Is a Warm Gun," we see various images of happy people with their guns, including a blind man who has received his handgun license, though at the end of the sequence the images start turning violent and we see the results of the guns: people shot and killed in an increasingly graphic manner. Happiness is killing?

Moore uses this method again with Louis Armstrong's "What a Wonderful World" playing on the sound track while the text track identifies various U.S. interventions around the world since 1953 and the visual track displays extraordinarily brutal pictures of dropping bombs and dead bodies: this is clearly not a Wonderful World.

Discussion Questions

1. In a movie that includes "Columbine" in its title, is it odd that Moore has barely mentioned the school shooting? What has he established instead? Why did he choose to construct his film this way?

2. What are the funniest scenes? What makes them funny? What are the most emotionally powerful scenes? What makes them effective?

3. What is Moore's argument at this point? What is he saying about violence? What is his strongest piece of evidence at this point? What is his weakest?

4. Describe Moore's relationship to the people he interviews. How do you think they feel about how they appear on screen?

Viewing Day 2: 0:29:34–0:58:54; Chapters 9–18 on DVD (about 29 minutes)

- Begins with title card that reads "April 20, 1999"
- Ends with President Bush talking about the "evildoers"

Things to Notice

Moore continues to make the connection between military and personal violence by starting his section on Columbine High with shots of the U.S. bombing of Kosovo that took place on the same day. After his depiction of the fateful day at Columbine, described in the following key sequence, the film fades out and then we hear, before we see, Charlton Heston saying, "From my cold, dead hands." Watch carefully here because the editing makes it seem as though Heston says these words at the rally that took place in Denver immediately after the shooting, but he's clearly wearing a different suit and the background is different when he discusses the mayor of Denver. Again, this is not unethical or immoral; Heston did say these words—just not at the time and the place the audience might believe. More important to Moore, the words are effective here as a counterpoint to the suffering of the victims of Columbine. As teachers of critical reading, it is important for us to help students see the construction of the film.

From here, Moore examines how tough high school is for those who don't quite fit in and how Americans are becoming more afraid of kids; notice the deep, foreboding music and the word choices of those interviewed describing children ("guerilla warfare," "enemies," "little time bombs"). There is also a too-good-to-be-true promotional video of a metal detector company that shows how a young boy with baggy pants can hide over twenty guns on his body, from which Moore cuts to idealized images of children at play, in Boy Scouts outfits, and other wholesome scenes with light music on the sound track.

After a surprisingly insightful interview with shock rocker Marilyn Manson, who comes off as one of the more reasoned voices in the film, Moore finally gets to the central question he wants to explore: what makes Americans so different from people of other countries? He compares the statistics of gun violence in other countries to ours and quickly dismisses a series of commonly held reasons for the difference: poverty, violent entertainment, violent history, etc. Notice how sometimes he refutes these assumptions not with a fact or a statistic, but with an observation of his own or an interview with someone less than an expert. Moore ends this day's viewing with an answer of his own that he will continue to explore throughout the rest of the film: fear. He includes an animation sequence that appears to have been created specifically for the film and a montage of scary news stories set to the earlier ominous music, which turns into a heartbeat slowly speeding up to the breaking point.

Key Sequence: 0:29:36–0:35:00; Chapter 10 on DVD

Moore could have represented the day of the Columbine shootings in many different ways, but look back at this section to discuss the reasons for Moore's choices. We hear the 911 calls made during the attack, which at first are surprisingly calm, though that will change, and we see images of the empty hallways that Moore filmed himself long after the incident. The effect of the contrast is startling: panicked voices and now-quiet hallways and classrooms. Soon we also begin hearing the calls from the media requesting interviews, which, without context, appear to be going to the 911 operator as well, though the impression is made that the covering of the event is as important as the event itself; one of the media bookers even seems to be crying about not getting information. Then Moore shows the security camera footage of the schoolchildren running and the shooters stalking the library with their guns

Figure 4.16. Moore chooses to depict the shooting at Columbine through archival footage: the security cameras at the school.

(Figure 4.16). The phone calls keep coming in, slow, somber guitar music playing on the sound track. The song continues, louder, on top of images of bullet holes, kids crying, and media interviews.

Discussion Questions

1. Are young people influenced by violent movies, music, and video games? Does Marilyn Manson bear any responsibility? Why do some people want to blame him and other forms of media?

2. What is the effect of the black-and-white security camera footage of the attack? In what other ways could Moore have portrayed the event? Is Moore exploiting the victims of the tragedy to make his movie and his point?

3. What makes Americans different from people of other countries in terms of violence against one another, according to Moore? What other factors might lead to more gun violence?

Viewing Day 3: 0:58:54–1:28:05; Chapters 19–25 on DVD (about 30 minutes)

- Begins with discussion of south central Los Angeles
- Ends with Moore talking with the principal of a Flint, Michigan, school

Things to Notice

In this section, Moore continues to explore the role that fear plays in the minds of Americans, especially in whites' fears of African Americans, by reminding the audience of the Susan Smith and Charles Stuart cases; both individuals blamed black males for the crimes they themselves committed. Moore singles out the reality show *Cops* as particularly notorious for the racist and fear-inciting imagery it presents (some of which Moore selectively edits to include as evidence); during an interview with the show's producer, Moore pitches him a fictitious show called *Corporate Cops*, and he includes a clip from this fictitious show.

When Moore asks Americans why there is less violence in Canada, he gets a variety of answers. Just as he did in the previous section, he refutes all of these answers with a wide range of support. When one person says that Americans watch more violent movies, for example, Moore refutes this with "That's wrong. Hordes of young boys all throughout Canada eagerly await the next Hollywood bloodbath"; he then supports this visually with a scene from a violent movie and interviews with two groups of Canadian teenagers. This is classic Moore. There is no lie, no deception, but no real answer either. How many, exactly, is a "horde"? He does this again when referring to the Canadian news, which he says features less violence than American news, but instead of citing a particular survey or study, he includes a ten-second portion of one Canadian broadcast. Now, my local news is—probably like yours—obsessed with blood and guts, but I can guarantee that I could find a ten-second clip from them that *isn't* about violence.

The day's viewing ends with the sequence described below about another school shooting, this one in Moore's hometown of Flint, Michigan.

Key Sequence: 1:22:25–1:28:59; Chapter 25 on DVD

Just after one of the Canadians Moore interviews says, "If more guns made people safer, America would be one of the safest places in the world," Moore fades to black and, once again, we hear a 911 call; the connection between Columbine and this new shooting is made very clear to us through this device. Moore further connects the Flint and Littleton shootings through quiet music and shots of empty school hallways, and he ends with a shot of a tattered American flag, symbolizing a school and a town that has been left out of the American dream. Moore then turns his gaze to the news media: we see one TV reporter give an emotional delivery about a little girl who was shot and then immediately begin haranguing his producer and worrying about his hair before resuming his "act." The scene ends with Moore comforting the principal of the Flint school as we hear Heston's words again "intruding" on someone's grief: "from my cold dead hands."

Discussion Questions

1. This day's viewing does not directly address Columbine; how does it relate to the central issues that the school shooting raises?

2. How does Moore depict the differences between the United States and Canada? Who is interviewed and what evidence does he include?

3. Who is the villain(s) of this film? Clearly, Moore is trying to demonize Charlton Heston and the NRA. Why? How does Moore establish this tone? The true villains of the tragedy, the shooters at Columbine, are shown briefly and almost never discussed. Why do you think this is?

4. What do you make of the structure of this film? It does not seem to move chronologically, as do so many documentaries. Why did Moore choose this way of telling his story and what do you think will be presented next? Why?

Viewing Day 4: 1:29:54–1:57:39; Chapters 25–end on DVD (about 28 minutes)

- Begins with Charlton Heston
- Ends with closing credits

Things to Notice

Today's viewing starts off with another sequence to pay close attention to. Obviously, Heston did not say "from my cold, dead hands" again, this time in Flint, though the film is edited to perhaps give that impression. More important, though, you need to keep track of what Moore says or doesn't say, because it is clear that he is trying to make Heston and the NRA seem insensitive to the victims of gun violence. In the sequence from the previous day's viewing, Moore said that Heston and the NRA held a rally *ten days* after the shooting, but here Moore says only that Heston "showed up in Flint." According to news reports, the shooting in Flint took place in February and yet people in the audience of Heston's speech have "Bush/Cheney" signs for the 2000 election (Bush was not nominated until August), so that rally must have taken place much closer to the election, at least *six months* after the shooting; there is also no evidence from the footage that this was an NRA-sponsored event: it looks like a political rally for Republicans. This is not to defend Heston or the NRA, but only to point out how carefully we need to examine nonfiction texts. Moore does not lie here, but he tries to give an impression that may not be wholly accurate.

Moore then moves into an exploration of the role that poverty played in this particular school shooting, by looking at how the welfare-to-work laws might have contributed to the tragedy and by showing us the same eighty-mile bus trip the shooter's mother had to take, which, Moore claims, did not allow her to properly supervise her son. Because the mother once worked for one of Dick Clark's restaurants, Moore decides to confront Clark outside his office. This "gotcha"-type interview is also classic Moore, but it presents the audience with a problem. Clearly, Clark comes off badly (as do most people interviewed by Moore), but is this the "real" Clark? Maybe he had more to say on the issue than he had time for or knowledge about at the time Moore stuck a microphone in his face. But, then again, maybe these surprise encounters reflect the true person more than if he or she had time to put on makeup, consult with lawyers, prepare a statement, and so on. As you've probably noticed throughout this book, I don't seem to have many answers to questions like these; I just like asking questions.

After more images of U.S. fears in the wake of 9/11, Moore visits with two survivors of the Columbine massacre and convinces them to visit the headquarters of Kmart, the seller of the bullets that wounded them. Here is a clear example of the interactive documentary mode: the boys would not have done this without Moore (we assume that Moore paid for their travel expenses), and Moore is doing it because he is making a film. Some critics wonder if Moore sometimes exploits his subjects' tragedies for his own gain. Me? I'm torn a bit. This scene does feel a bit manipulative, but because of the film and the boys' involvement in it, Kmart announced it was discontinuing the sale of handgun bullets, which is a positive outcome for the boys and for the country.

Continuing to interweave the two school shootings, Moore interviews Charlton Heston (see the following key sequence) about the little girl who died in Flint, and then ends his film with more images of fear and guns and a story about three employees murdered at a bowling alley in Littleton, home of Columbine High School. The titles run as the Ramones sing a punk version of "What a Wonderful World."

Key Sequence: 1:47:18–1:56:30; Chapter 31 on DVD

The scene with Charlton Heston is an accumulation of all the best—and most manipulative—elements of a Michael Moore film. As Moore enters the Heston compound, he chooses to walk in, even though his equipment van is behind him and we hear the theme song to "Mr. Rogers' Neighborhood" on the sound track. While Heston is aware of the interview, unlike Clark, it becomes clear that Moore is still in "gotcha" mode, because he puts Heston, who looks and acts quite old, at ease by showing him Moore's NRA membership card. Moore badgers Heston for a while about going to cities after they've had a school shooting (if you think about the six-month lapse between the Flint shooting and Heston's visit to Flint that probably happened as described earlier, he doesn't look quite so insensitive at his inability to recall the trip or when he wonders why he should apologize for going there) until Heston gets up and leaves. Moore follows him and plaintively asks him to look at the picture of the little girl who was shot in Flint. I have some questions about the feasibility of this sequence. If you look at it closely, Moore would need to have two cameras (one to get Moore's close-up and one over Moore's shoulder to get Heston's leaving) moving very quickly to get into position, and I'm not entirely convinced that Moore did not re-create the close-up shots afterward. I do not really have an opinion about the ethics of this construction—if it did in fact happen—but I do like to hear student reactions when they are presented with the possibility of what Moore might have done here. When Heston leaves, Moore places the girl's picture and walks solemnly out of Heston's compound. Moore is "acting" in a very true sense: he brought the picture and left it for a purpose; the scene is real, if not entirely authentic.

Discussion Questions

1. How do you feel about Moore's "gotcha" interview style? Is it fair? Is it revealing?

2. Earlier, Moore had dismissed the idea of poverty as a cause of gun violence, but in this section, he seems to think it might have some relevance. Why do you think he includes the section on welfare-to-work in a film about guns? Is it effective?

3. Would it matter to you if Moore did re-create some of the reaction shots with Charlton Heston? Why or why not?

4. How would you respond to a critic who says that Moore makes fiction films, not documentaries? How would Moore respond?

Closing Questions/Activities

1. Test Moore's theory on the perpetuation of fear by tracking the lead stories in the news for a week. Assign one student to each of the major channels, local and national, to keep track of the types of stories featured in the first five minutes of the broadcast. Tabulate the results as a

class and create pie charts that represent the main topics of the news. Also, keep track of another assertion Moore makes: TV news overrepresents minorities in stories about crime. Do your conclusions support or contradict Moore's? Explain.

2. Watch the fiction film *Elephant*, directed by Gus Van Sant, which also depicts a school shooting. What similar or different conclusions do these films draw about violence?

3. Choose one of the factors Moore explores in this film that may lead to gun violence—poverty, fear, easy access to weapons and ammunition, etc.—and research it further. Alternatively, find research that does a side-by-side comparison of U.S. violence rates and those of other countries. Do you come up with the same conclusions that Moore does?

The True Meaning of Pictures: Shelby Lee Adams' Appalachia

2002, Not Rated, Directed by Jennifer Baichwal

Summary

The True Meaning of Pictures examines the work of photographer Shelby Lee Adams, whose photographs document the life of rural Appalachia. The filmmaker interviews Adams, residents of Appalachia, art critics, and a sociologist; some feel his work is exploitative, whereas others see it as a celebration of a culture. By presenting the photos themselves, along with the stories behind them, the filmmaker tries to figure out what a photograph really means. (Approximately 70 minutes)

Rationale

I discovered this wonderful film in the course of writing this book, but it has quickly become a favorite of mine to teach because, even though it is about the nature of still photography, it raises many of the issues of documentary filmmaking that I love to explore with my students: how does the presence of the filmmaker affect the subject, how much "construction of reality" is allowable for a film to still be considered nonfiction, can pictures and/or films exploit their subjects, how do outsiders tell someone else's story, etc.? This would be a wonderful documentary to look at with any age group, though it might fit in best with units on world culture and literature (often tenth grade) because the images that Shelby Lee presents are thought by some to be culturally insensitive and playing to stereotypes. At the same time, it could be at home in an eleventh-grade American history/literature course.

Previewing

1. Students should have an opportunity to see some of Adams's work before they watch the film, since a lot of what the director is after here is to get us to confront our own feelings and prejudices. You can accomplish this in several ways: locate Web sites that highlight Adams's work and then project them using an LCD projector; have students peruse his books, which are widely available (though expensive); or you could pause the DVD on a few key photographs (there is a series of them at the very end of the film). Ask students to give their impressions of these pictures and of the people in them. What stereotypes of rural Americans do these photos include? Can a picture include elements of a stereotype but not be stereotypical?

2. Demonstrate the popularized and simplified version of the Heisenberg principle that I discussed in Chapter 1 (the very act of watching, photographing, or filming a subject affects that subject) by bringing in a camera (or video camera) to take pictures of students. Ask other students to notice how the subjects react to having their pictures taken. Are these pictures "real," or have the subjects of the photo altered themselves or their behavior in some way: fixed hair, smiled, stopped misbehaving, etc.?

3. Brainstorm what the title of this film might mean and what the film might be about. Are films more truthful or accurate than still photos? Why or why not?

4. Identify the Appalachia area for students and tell them about or allow them to research some information on the area, especially the history and culture of the residents, as well as the roles that poverty, coal mining, and agriculture have played in the region.

5. Hand out the graphic organizer for this film (Figure 4.17), which provides space for students to keep track of what various people (including themselves and the filmmaker) think about Adams's work. This film explores four central questions that you might want to write on the board ahead of time for students to keep track of on the chart:

   a. Do Shelby Lee Adams's photos present stereotypes of Appalachia?

   b. Are his photographs documentaries of true life in Appalachia or staged theater? How does his presence affect the pictures?

c. Do his photos exploit or make fun of his subjects?

d. Who "owns" the pictures after they are published: the photographer, the subjects, the audience, the culture, etc.?

Viewing Day 1: 0:00:00–0:35:08; Chapters 1–6 on DVD (about 35 minutes)

- Begins with opening titles
- Ends with photo of a girl on a screened porch

Things to Notice

The film opens with the enthusiastic voice of a preacher as the visual track begins to show pictures of lush, green forests and then fades out and fades in on a black-and-white picture of two men huddled over a Bible. Then we see a series of black-and-white photographs of people who are white and appear to be of low socioeconomic status, and everyone is looking at the camera in clearly staged poses; the sound track plays quiet, gentle outdoor sounds such as birds, crickets, and wind. In the first of a series of beautifully effective juxtapositions, the camera slowly zooms in on one picture, passing the subjects' faces to a black spot in the corner of the photo, and when the camera fades back in, we see patrons at an upscale urban art gallery sipping wine and looking at some of the same photos we just saw. Within the first two minutes, the director has established her central questions: How do people look at pictures? What do we as an audience bring to a picture? Are photographs truths? Does everyone who looks at a picture see the same thing?

As we continue to see more pictures, we hear a critic talking about Shelby Lee Adams's work ("I just can't stand to look at them for long periods of time"), and when we see a photograph of a family on a porch with a dog, we cut to primary footage of Shelby at work creating this very picture. Throughout the film, we will experience this pattern of seeing a photo and then learning about its creation. Adams also states what will become his key defense against later charges of exploitation of his subjects: the people he photographs in Appalachia accept themselves for who they are, and they accept him.

After the title card, we see a variety of still Adams photos; the last one dissolves into a film shot of that picture and then moves on to more moving images of rural Appalachia, continuing the pattern the filmmaker has established of examining the area outside and around the frame—the context—of one of Adams's pictures.

While the film presents many images of many different subjects, the film is organized mainly around three different families whom

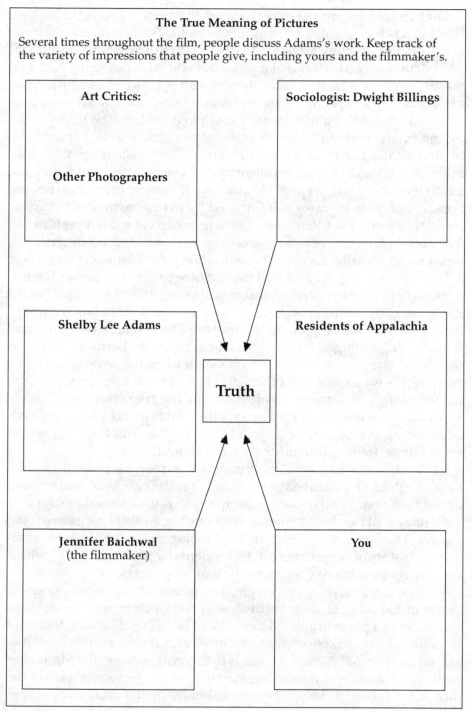

Figure 4.17. Graphic organizer for *The True Meaning of Pictures*.

Adams has photographed over the years (his own home video of these families has been included in this film as well). The first family we meet is the Napiers, whom Adams describes as a historical and traditional mountain family. The filmmaker does not add subtitles to the Napiers' words, even though their accents sometimes make them difficult to understand (it also seems to me that Adams's accent is much more pronounced when talking with his subjects than it is when he is interviewed by the filmmaker). After we've met the Napiers, we see some of the photos Adams has taken of them and hear from a sociologist, Dwight Billings, who says that the problem with these pictures is that they are left to the viewer to interpret. He also says that more often than not the "reader" of these pictures is influenced by over one hundred years of stereotypes, and the filmmaker cuts here to clips of the fiction film *Deliverance* with its representations of Appalachians as inbred, ignorant, violent, and sexually deviant. Through editing, the filmmaker constructs a "debate" between Adams and the sociologist about whether the images in his photos are stereotypical or authentic; Adams says that "nothing is made up, nothing is staged" in a photo of Berthia Napier smoking a pipe and wearing boots. A montage of the real, alive, authentic family going through its daily life is included, with Berthia singing on the sound track. Two art critics then weigh in on the issue of Adams's "staging" of his photos, one of which becomes the subject of debate (see the following key sequence). Before leaving the Napiers, the filmmaker shows us a series of family funerals that Adams has photographed, culminating in a picture of Berthia in her casket, with her song on the sound track, leading into other Adams photographs.

In the next sequence, the filmmaker explores a little of the history of Appalachia, focusing specifically on the effects of coal mining on the inhabitants and on the landscape, effects the filmmaker supports with images of the devastation of strip mining and still pictures of coal miners. The film also includes archival footage from the 1960s to establish the history of exploitation of the residents by the news media, which came to Appalachia to document the war on poverty.

The day's viewing ends with a key debate about Adams's exploitation of his subjects, as a resident who has since moved away takes exception to a photograph Adams took of her sister. She wonders why he couldn't have taken a "pretty picture" and claims that he has "disgraced our family." Adams responds to this criticism and the filmmaker ends the discussion by zooming slowly into the picture, showing the face of the little girl. This is an interesting moment because four separate people (Adams, the resident, the filmmaker, and the viewer) are all looking at this one picture and responding differently. Personally, I agree with Adams: the picture is beautiful, but I always open up the issue to debate because not all of my students agree.

Key Sequence: 0:17:50–0:22:30; Chapter 4 on DVD

When the New York art critic talks about the photo of a hog killing, she raises a central issue I have tried to explore throughout this book about the ways in which documentary films construct reality. She muses that "if this is an honest re-creation of something that did happen" at one time, then the photo could be "useful as well as beautiful," though, she says, it should be labeled as such (which it is not). Without this label, the viewer is being sold an inauthentic situation as "real." The filmmaker then moves to the archival home video footage of Adams preparing to take the picture of the hog killing: there is a great deal of "intrusion" on reality, including the positioning of the subjects and the fact that Adams himself arranged for the purchase of the hog, which he says the family could not afford. Adams defends his actions by saying that hog killing is a traditional practice that a family like the Napiers would do, though he admits that before he took the picture it was already in his mind: he only had to re-create it (this is not typically the role of a documentarian). Clearly, the picture cannot be considered "real," which the other art critic explains by invoking the Heisenberg principle, but Adams fully admits to not being "objective."

Discussion Questions

1. At the end of the day's viewing, Adams discusses whether the photo of the girl on the screened porch is "disgraceful." How do you think director Baichwal feels about the issue? How do you know this? How would she have shown that she felt differently?

2. Is Adams documenting or constructing reality? Is there a difference?

3. How do you feel as you look at Adams's pictures? How does the additional information revealed about the subjects in the film itself change your feelings?

4. Some documentaries include subtitles for people who are speaking English but are difficult to understand because of low volume, accents, or enunciation, to help the audience understand what the subjects are saying. This filmmaker did not. Why do you think she chose not to?

Viewing Day 2: 0:35:10–1:08:27; Chapters 7–12 on DVD (about 33 minutes)

- Begins with shots of the river and the rattlesnakes
- Ends with closing credits

Things to Notice

This next section deals with Wayne Riddle, a Pentecostal snake handler from Appalachia. When I first saw this film, the idea of demonstrating one's faith by handling poisonous rattlesnakes and copperheads was as unusual and extreme as I could imagine. Adams says often that he knows these people and they trust him; this is what the film tries to do for us. We learn about Wayne's life and family, and even if we cannot agree with the practice, we can understand what motivates them to do what they do, because they clearly live what they believe. We see Adams's home video of the serpent handlers drinking strychnine without suffering ill effects. In this case, unlike previous and later sequences, the filmmaker saves the most devastating picture—Wayne after a severe snakebite—until after we learn about the subject's life situation. Adams also comments on the difficulty he has remaining a true documentarian because he cannot be simply an observer; he admits that he has become a participant and even a subject in one of his photos.

The next section of the film deals with the issue of exploitation and representation. We hear once again the male art critic, who finds many of the images in Adams's work to be "spooky" and admits that he would not want to meet the subjects of these photos in a dark alley; remember, however, that we have "met" many of these people through the film, and it is clear that this critic is viewing the photos through his own urban experiences. The filmmaker shows Adams meeting with the subjects of his photographs and receiving permission to use the photos before publishing them, clarifying that he would never use a photo against the wishes of his subjects. Meanwhile, the critic basically says that the people in the photos are not sophisticated enough to know that they are being exploited, while a fellow photographer counters that everyone knows what a picture can do, no matter their literacy. Again, the filmmaker seems to support the latter sentiment by moving into another sequence about home funerals, in which we see Adams's sensitive treatment of a very difficult issue.

The last section of the film is recounted in the following key sequence, which deals with the Childers, the third family with whom the film documents Adams working closely. At the end of the section, it becomes apparent that the sociologist the filmmaker has been interviewing is either screening the filmmaker's footage or hearing her accounts of Adams's involvement with the family, because he reacts to what we—the audience of the film—have just learned. This makes it especially clear that the film is both reflexive (because it deals with issues of documentary filmmaking) and interactive (because the film itself is changing the action on screen). To reinforce the reflexivity, we hear Adams talking about how his images force us to confront that which we would normally not want to see, and then the filmmaker slowly zooms in on one of his photographs (in which Adams is hiding in the back of the frame, just an eye looking at us) and dissolves it into a close-up of a camera lens that in a sense is now taking our picture. The film ends with a soundless (except for a camera's shutter) series of still photos that we have been seeing throughout the film, but now we know the stories behind the pictures and probably—hopefully—think of them differently now. The film's final image is a still photo of a bridge that dissolves into a moving picture of that same bridge with Adams walking across it, which dissolves again, erasing Adams from the frame, cementing the notion that reality is a construct of the photographer and/or filmmaker, who in this case just eliminated her subject from her frame. It's a beautifully executed idea.

Key Sequence: 0:52:07–1:05:08; Chapters 10–11 on DVD

For me, the most powerful scenes in this film come from Adams's work with the Childers family because they ask the viewers to confront their own discomfort with difficult issues, in this case, mental and physical abnormalities. The sequence starts, as this film often does, with a still Adams photo without much context provided. We see two men, shirtless, and hear the sociologist discussing the stereotypes of inbreeding and incest, and then we hear from one of the photographers, who believes that the subjects are presented in a favorable light. When the art critic hears about the story of the knife used in the photograph, he wonders whether the picture captures the subjects' lives, or "Shelby's inner life"? Or, as the filmmaker seems to suggest, these photos reflect our own perceptions and thoughts. We see shots of Adams at work with the family and how he treats Homer and Selina with respect and tenderness, and we hear Adams tell a story about working in an institution where handicapped people like them are hidden away from society's view. In two interviews, it is clear that the family does not have any problems with the pictures, and once the sociologist hears of Adams's views on institutionalizing those who are different, he says that's interesting, but this is not a story that is told in the book of Adams's photos. The photos, he says, do not tell enough of the story; without context, the pictures can only be seen as stereotypical, and the film then cuts back to the Chicago gallery featuring Adams's work, with shots of people looking at the pictures, uninformed about the stories that the viewers of this film and the critics and sociologist now know.

Discussion Questions

1. The closing credits note that "Adams's living subjects who were featured in the film saw and approved their parts before it was released." What does this statement tell you about the film-maker? Why do you think that not all documentary filmmak-ers do this before releasing a film? Do you think that a film-maker like Michael Moore does this? Why or why not?

2. Look back at the chart you completed during the viewing of the film and consider the following:

    a. Do Shelby Lee Adams's photos present stereotypes of Ap-palachia?

    b. Are his photographs documentaries of true life in Appa-lachia or staged theater? How does his presence affect the pictures?

    c. Do his photos exploit or make fun of his subjects?

    d. Who "owns" the pictures after they are published: the pho-tographer, the subjects, the audience, the culture, etc.?

3. Think back on how many times this film moves into close-ups of one of Adams's photographs, revealing more detail to the viewer and emphasizing certain parts more than others. Also, think back on the number of times we learned—through the film, not the pictures—about the context that allowed us to properly understand the photos. Is the filmmaker saying that film is a documentary form superior to that of photography? Why or why not? Do you think it is? Does the filmmaker be-lieve her own title? Is there a "true meaning of pictures"? If so, what is it? How do artists, viewers, critics, and sociologists arrive at "truth"?

4. Adams describes himself as both a documentarian and an art-ist. Is there an inherent conflict between these two roles? Is there a conflict within Adams's work?

Closing Activities/Questions

1. Ask students to bring in a photo of a significant event in their lives and hand it to another student without saying anything about the event. The second student should write down what he or she knows and feels about the picture and the event. Then the first student writes a narra-

tive about the event the picture captured and give it to his or her partner, who should read the narrative and comment on whether knowing the background of the story changes his or her feelings about the picture. Debrief the activity by asking what this reveals about the "truth" of pictures. Also, ask students to identify elements of the Heisenberg principle in the photos. What information was present in the scene but not captured in the photo because of how it was framed? How does this affect the "truth" of the picture?

2. Compose a letter to Adams, one of the art critics, or the sociologist about the issues raised in this film: stereotypes, representation, constructing reality, etc.

3. This film explores the stereotype of "the hillbilly." What other stereotypes are presented in the media and popular culture? Select one of these stereotypes that exist or once did exist in this country. Imagine yourself as a documentary filmmaker. How might you go about exploring this stereotype? What footage would you collect? Who would you interview?

4. Compare the issues raised here with those in other films about Appalachia:

   a. *Stranger with a Camera* is an outstanding documentary available at *www.appalshop.org* about an Appalachian filmmaker who investigates the murder of a Canadian filmmaker who was killed by a local man who objected to the media's representation of Appalachians.

   b. *Songcatcher*, a fiction film about the exploitation of Appalachian culture, with Janet McTeer as a music teacher who begins to collect the folk music of the area.

   c. *Deliverance*, the film discussed in this movie as the one responsible for cementing the public's prejudice against the "hillbilly." Note that the film is quite graphic and clearly presents the residents in unflattering ways.

4 Little Girls

1997, Not Rated, Directed by Spike Lee

Summary

Spike Lee's first documentary examines the 1963 bombing of a church in Birmingham, Alabama, that killed four girls who were attending Sunday school. He interviews family members, prominent members of the civil rights movement, journalists, and even George Wallace, the governor of Alabama at the time. The film puts the bombing into the larger context of the struggle for civil rights in the South, but at the same time, it never loses focus on the subjects in the title. (Approximately 100 minutes)

Rationale

This film, unlike most of Lee's fiction films, can be shown at any grade level, though there are some graphic pictures of the girls after the bombing. It would fit in perfectly with an eleventh-grade American literature/history course, and it would be an effective introduction to a study of African American literature or for Black History Month.

Previewing

1. Begin by having students create a KWL chart about what they know, what they want to know, and (eventually) what they have learned about the civil rights movement. Give them time to share the *K* portion of their charts with a partner.

2. Read the poem "Ballad of Birmingham" by Dudley Randall and/or the song "Birmingham Sunday" by Joan Baez (both are widely available online). Ask students about the tone of the pieces (a SOAPStone activity—see Chapter 2—might work well here) and how the writers communicate this tone. Ask students what they have learned about the Birmingham church bombing from these texts. They should add this information to their KWL charts.

3. Share a list of Jim Crow laws with students (also widely available online) to give them a sense of exactly how much of life in the South was segregated.

Viewing Day 1: 0:00:00–0:33:55; no chapters on DVD (about 34 minutes)

- Begins with opening titles
- Ends with discussion of "Bull" Connor

Things to Notice

For viewers coming to this film without any background or context, Lee effectively uses the opening song "Birmingham Sunday" by Joan Baez to introduce us to the girls, with shots of their graves and pictures superimposed on the screen; he also introduces us to Birmingham and the civil rights movement through archival footage as the song sets a mournful tone. Lee then quickly establishes his pattern for the first third of the film by providing interviews of family members, neighbors, and childhood friends of each of the four girls. Even though the events recounted in this film are more than thirty years old, the pain these people feel and communicate is still vivid and real. At one point, one girl's sister is so emotional that she is unable to finish the interview, though Lee does not cut away from her on-screen breakdown. In between each of the short biographies of the girls, Lee includes information on Birmingham, the civil rights movement, and Eugene "Bull" Connor, the police commissioner in Birmingham. Through file footage and current interviews, Lee casts Connor as the face of racism in the South and the "bad guy" in his film.

Key Sequence: 0:07:32–0:12:18

After interviewing the family of Denise, one of the girls, Lee gives us a brief history of Birmingham, through which we can see much of how Lee constructs his film for maximum effect. Interview subjects tell us that Birmingham was a steel town that grew up quickly and had to bring in a large unskilled labor force to maintain its growth, which caused it to be a violent town. Even though no one mentions lynching, Lee cuts to a series of graphic pictures of black men being lynched by smiling mobs, to an upbeat drumroll on the sound track. The pictures seem to be of rural areas that are not identified as being in or around Birmingham. The filmmaker gets an ironic laugh in when he cuts from a white circuit judge saying that Birmingham in the 1950s was a quiet, wonderful place to raise a family to archive footage of a KKK group (complete with kids in white robes) marching through the streets. The real power of this sequence lies in Lee's ability to make the concept of segregation felt in such a personal way. Denise's family recounts a time when she wanted to eat at a whites-only lunch counter and they had to teach a six-year-old girl about racism. A quiet, simple song starts up on the sound track, and when the father talks about his daughter's reaction, Lee probes with a question and slowly moves into a tight close-up on the father and holds for a moment or two after he finishes.

Discussion Questions

1. What do we know about each of the four girls? How does Lee present this information? Who is interviewed? Why *these* interview subjects?

2. What do we know about Birmingham at the time before the bombing? How does Lee present this information? What are your feelings about Birmingham at the time?

3. Describe Lee's organization so far in this film. He has presented very little information about the bombing at this point. Why?

4. At the very end of this day's viewing, we see a sequence on Eugene "Bull" Connor. Why do you think Lee introduces Connor at this point in his film?

Viewing Day 2: 0:33:55–1:07:12 (about 33 minutes)

- Begins with George Wallace's inaugural speech
- Ends with a woman identifying her sister's body

Things to Notice

The last words spoken in the previous day's viewing claimed that Bull Connor could have existed only with the blessing of others, from which Lee immediately cuts to Governor George Wallace's famous line: "Segregation today, segregation tomorrow, and segregation forever," which dissolves into a current interview with an elderly (senile?) Wallace. Throughout this interview, Wallace appears disoriented and repeatedly mentions his "black friend," who never speaks on camera and is not identified by Lee, but who might be a caretaker for Wallace. In today's viewing, Lee interviews most of the major players in the civil rights movement, which is probably a testament to Lee's own celebrity. It would be interesting to consider how this film might have been different if it were made by a filmmaker without Lee's reach. Just before he examines the day of the bombing, Lee includes a sort of foreshadowing by showing a close-up of the monument dedicated to the girls and by including interviews with people about premonitions they had before the bombing. When he does get to the bombing itself (almost an hour into the film), the effect is tremendous because of the emotion and the detail the interview subjects share about that day. Lee also adds nondiegetic sound effects of bombs going off before each of his subjects describes that day; he even includes graphic pictures of the girls' bodies in the morgue.

Key Sequence: 0:47:43–0:51:00

This sequence on the protest at Kelly Ingram Park is interesting to re-examine for how Lee uses editing to create new contexts that allow his audience to connect with images of the civil rights movement; we have seen these images so many times that we are in danger of becoming immune from shock. We all know about the use of dogs and water hoses during this era, but Lee cuts this scene with energy, including music (specifically drums); close-ups of snarling dogs and wounds; the sounds of water, barking dogs, and screaming; interviews with people who were there—all to remind us of the horrific effects of the violence and racism of the period. He also gets another opportunity to mock the white circuit judge, who says that much worse could have happened. What Lee shows us and makes us hear is awful enough; it's difficult to imagine much worse.

Discussion Questions

1. When he wanted to make the film *Malcolm X*, Lee famously said that a black director could tell Malcolm's story better than a white director. Do you think this statement is true for *4 Little Girls*? Why or why not? How might the film have been different if someone else had directed it?

2. Are the pictures of the dead girls necessary for Lee's intended effect? What would be the arguments for their inclusion and their exclusion?

3. Lee's framing of his interview subjects is often as an extreme close-up. What is the effect of this on you as a viewer and what does it reveal about the filmmaker?

4. About half an hour of the film remains. We've learned about the girls, Birmingham at the time, and the bombing. What's left for the film to explore? What else do you as a viewer want to know about?

Viewing Day 3: 1:07:12–1:41:50 (about 34 minutes)

- Begins with newspaper headline of church bombing
- Ends with closing credits

Things to Notice

The family of one of the girls, Carol, does not take part in the mass funeral, despite a plea from and prayer session with Reverend Martin Luther King, Jr. I find it interesting that Lee does not probe further into the mother's reasons for not participating, letting her say only that plans were already made before she knew about the group funeral, which doesn't really explain why the family did not participate at all. Possibly, at the time, the mother did not want to get involved in the politics of the day or let the death of her daughter be a statement of some kind, but Lee has clearly established a relationship with each of the families and is unwilling to present them in a harsh or negative light. Several times in this day's viewing, we see family members holding and emotionally describing items belonging to the girls or, in Denise's mother's case, the piece of cement that had been lodged in her daughter's skull;

all of these scenes, of course, have been constructed by Lee, who obviously asked these individuals to show and speak about these remembrances. A number of well-known people (Walter Cronkite, Jesse Jackson, Bill Cosby, and others) weigh in on the importance of the bombing in the history of the civil rights movement, and Lee inserts a reason why it's still relevant today by including news footage about a rash of church burnings that occurred throughout the South in the 1990s. We then learn that fourteen years after the bombing, "Dynamite" Bob Chambliss was convicted of the bombing after extremely emotional and damning testimony in a trial that coincidentally ended on what would have been Denise's birthday. Even though Lee interviewed Chambliss's defense attorney about many topics, he chose not to include any comments relating to the evidence presented during the proceedings or any mention of his guilt or innocence, though several people state that Chambliss was a violent and evil racist. I do not have extensive knowledge of the case; I am only pointing out what Lee chose to include and what might have been included. The last interview contains the most interaction we have seen between Lee and one of the family members as he gently encourages her to continue talking. It is clear he is not doing a *60 Minutes*–type of "gotcha" interview. As the credits roll, we see home footage of young children playing and laughing, dressed in their Sunday best, as a song titled "4 Little Girls" plays on the sound track.

Key Sequence: 1:16:27–1:17:46

This short scene is cleverly constructed and emotionally affecting. We first hear a woman's voice, one we have not heard before, reading a letter addressed to the parents of one of the girls, Denise. The soft music we have heard at other key times fades in, and we learn that the reader is Coretta Scott King, Martin Luther King, Jr.'s widow. This letter would, of course, belong to Denise's parents, so it's clear that Lee has arranged to have Mrs. King read the letter. As she continues to read her husband's Christmas greeting, sent four months after the bombing and which describes the importance of family bonds, we see not only photos of Denise with her family, but also pictures of King with his own children. The sequence ends with photos of a funeral, making the connection between this incident—with its wrenching effect on these families—and the sacrifices that King, who would be murdered himself only five years later, and the rest of those in the movement have made.

Discussion Questions

1. Why do you think Lee spent so little time (less than ten minutes) on Bob Chambliss and his trial? Is that more or less than you expected or think is necessary? Why?

2. What other information would you have wanted included in this film? Why? Imagining that Lee had a time limit he had to meet, why do you think he included what he did?

3. Even as he explores the larger elements of the civil rights movement, Lee never loses focus on the girls themselves. How and why did he do this?

4. What do you think Lee wants his audience to come away with from this film? Why do you say this?

Closing Questions/Activities

1. Watch one of Spike Lee's fiction films (e.g., *Crooklyn*, *Get on the Bus*, *Malcolm X*, *Do the Right Thing*). What common themes do you find? What stylistic elements (shot choice, music, editing style, etc.) appear in both types of films?

2. Look at a fiction film that addresses the civil rights movement (e.g., *Ghosts of Mississippi*, *The Long Walk Home*, *Once upon a Time . . . When We Were Colored*) or the depiction of the former Alabama governor in the HBO film *George Wallace* and discuss how fiction and nonfiction films can treat the same topic in similar and in different ways.

3. The epilogue, included on the DVD, tells us that the federal government has recently indicted two additional men in the church bombing. Locate information to learn what has happened to these men and Bob Chambliss since the film was made.

4. Create, distribute, and tabulate a survey for students at your school that asks them about their knowledge of the bombing of the Birmingham church, the civil rights movement in general, and their feelings about racism today. Share these results with your classmates and even the school newspaper.

Six o'Clock News

1996, Not Rated, Directed by Ross McElwee

Summary

A documentary filmmaker who obsessively films his own life, Ross McElwee has recently become a father and begins to worry about the tragic and often violent images of the real world as seen on the local evening news. He decides to travel around the country to film people who have faced tragedy to see if the images on the news reflect the real world. (Approximately 100 minutes, currently available only on VHS)

Rationale

Ross McElwee is one of the most prominent documentarians working today and is certainly one of the most unusual. His style can be a little off-putting at first because it uses a form of documentary style with which our students have little experience. He films in a first-person approach in which the people being interviewed are really just a part of a conversation they are having with McElwee, with a scripted voice-over narration added later that reflects on what he captured on film. His family and friends are used to always seeing McElwee with a camera on his shoulder, so he probably captures realistic reactions at least somewhat unaffected by the presence of the camera. *Sherman's March*, his breakthrough film, started off as a project about Sherman's march to the sea at the end of the Civil War but quickly became a film about McElwee's own inability to find love; the digressions became the film. McElwee creates reflexive video diaries, extremely well shot, edited, and written, which are personal, funny, and revealing. Of McElwee's films, *Six o'Clock News* is the most appealing to high school students; with its emphasis on finding the truth behind the stories on the news, it would make a great addition to a unit on media studies or even on narrative or reflective writing. The challenging nature and structure of the film make it probably best for a twelfth-grade or college-level course.

Previewing

1. For the two days before students start watching the film, assign them to watch the first fifteen minutes of local evening news to keep track of the stories that air during that time. Try to determine the percentage of stories that deal with violence, disaster, or tragedy. Ask students why these stories are featured so prominently and what, if any, effect they might have on the audience.

2. Watching a McElwee film can be a challenge because there is usually so much to pay attention to. While his visual track has the look of our own home movies, the filmmaker frames his subjects with clear intentions and edits for particular purposes that appear to be simple but are quite complex. A second challenge comes with the audio track. There are always two levels of sound in a McElwee film: the diegetic sound

that he captures as he films and the nondiegetic voice-over that he writes and records long after. So every film includes present-tense (within the film) voices as well as this second layer of voice (outside of the film) that belongs solely to McElwee and that is sometimes spoken in the present tense and sometimes in the past; remember, though, that this second voice was recorded after the events depicted, so in a sense, what McElwee says in his voice-overs has the knowledge of future events. I recommend having students use a note-taking form like the one in Figure 4.18 to help them keep track of these different layers. You might want to practice with the opening of *Sherman's March* described next.

3. To introduce students to McElwee's style, consider showing them the opening four minutes of his *Sherman's March*, which is widely available on DVD. It starts as a traditional documentary with an off-screen voice-over, charts, still photos, maps of Civil War battlefields, and so on, until we hear a voice ask the narrator if he wants to do it over again. Then the film switches to a personal reflection on the film and the filmmaker's breakup with his girlfriend, as we see him pace back and forth in front of his camera on a tripod. After the title card, we see a framing that makes up the majority of shots in a McElwee film: he holds the camera on his shoulder and talks to people as if he were not recording. We also hear his narration recorded afterward. Ask students to comment on this style and approach.

Viewing Day 1: 0:00:00–0:30:00 (about 30 minutes)

- Begins with opening titles
- Ends with McElwee's decision to "plunge into the world"

Things to Notice

The film begins with an immediate awareness of itself as a film. McElwee's wife says that their new baby is probably affected by the presence of the camera, an idea that McElwee will return to often. A little later in the same room, the baby is playing with a mirror in his crib and tilts it so that it reveals McElwee with his camera. Including only the most violent and tragic stories from the evening news, McElwee creates a sense of anxiety for both himself and the audience. His first foray into exploring the reality of TV news is when he sees footage of Hurricane Hugo's damage of an area where a friend lives, and he decides to see and record the event for himself. He uses his friend's comments on the insecurity of life to reflect on his own childhood, especially about the tragic death of his brother, a victim of a boating accident, which he

Note Taking: *Six o'Clock News* Day 1		
As you watch, keep track of the information presented on the video track at the same time as the sounds on the two parts of the audio track.		
Video Track	**Audio Track**	
	During Filming	*Postproduction Narration*

Figure 4.18. Day 1 note-taking form for *Six o'Clock News*.

again links back to his own son. This stream of consciousness is typical of a McElwee film and has more in common with novelistic traditions than with documentary forms. After his experiences with a film crew (see the following key sequence), McElwee shows us more violent news clips and announces that he is leaving to explore the reality that is presented in the news, while the visual is of his wife and son waving goodbye.

Key Sequence: 0:23:32–0:29:00

As discussed in Chapter 1, a reflexive documentary is one that recognizes and comments on itself as a film and raises issues related to the nature of filmmaking and meaning. This sequence, in which a film crew comes to film McElwee as he films them filming him, is as clear an example of reflexivity as I can present to students. McElwee captures the reporter and film crew entering his apartment three times as they try to capture a "spontaneous" feel. Reflecting on the film crew's third entrance, he says that he never asks people to reenact moments for his films, so he wonders if his films are more "real" than theirs. But he also comments that both he and they will edit this sequence for their own purposes. McElwee, in fact, incorporates into his own film a shot of himself holding his camera that could only have come from the film crew's footage. As they interview him, McElwee blocks out his own diegetic voice in favor of his nondiegetic voice-over, which comments on his inability to articulate the points he would like to have made at the time. The sequence ends with shots of the final show as it aired on TV. All of his comments, editing, and visuals are designed to reveal the construction of reality that goes on, both in TV news and in his own film.

Discussion Questions

1. Describe McElwee's style. What does it remind you of? What is the purpose of his voice-over on the sound track?

2. In the sequence about the TV film crew, McElwee wonders whether his films are more "real" than theirs. Do you think this is true? Why or why not?

3. How has McElwee constructed his film up to this point? Is it all chronological? Thematic? What do you expect will happen in the next thirty minutes?

4. What point is McElwee trying to make about TV news so far? How has he edited the news segments to make this point?

Viewing Day 2: 0:30:00–1:02:00; (about 32 minutes)

- Begins in Jackson, Mississippi
- Ends with McElwee returning home from California

Things to Notice

Today's section can be broken down into three parts in which McElwee goes behind the news stories he's seen in order to meet and interview the real people involved in the events. I recommend using the new note-taking form (Figure 4.19) for this day's viewing to help students track McElwee's progress and reflections. First he meets Steve Im, whose face he saw on TV one night (which McElwee frames in an extreme close-up) when the murderer of Im's wife was convicted. McElwee spends several days with him, filming him at Im's various businesses, but is unable to ask him pointedly about his wife's murder until the last night, when Steve, who does not want to talk to the camera so we only hear him, confesses that he cannot believe in God anymore because God cannot control things on Earth any more. This last comment about things being out of control becomes the thesis that McElwee explores throughout the rest of his cross-country journey.

After watching more news coverage and especially a TV weatherman, McElwee decides to go to Arizona where a storm of "biblical" proportions has devastated the area. Once there he films "evidence" of the randomness of the world, with one trailer spared from damage while the one next to it is destroyed; he even films TV news crews filming the damage (see the following key sequence). Before he leaves Arizona, McElwee interviews a woman who believes that everything is in God's hands.

McElwee's last experience is actually an attempt to literally enter the news by joining a crew fighting a fire in California. His guide up the mountain echoes points made earlier in today's viewing by pointing out the randomness of the fire, but he also puts forward the idea that fighting fires can be restorative because it takes you out of yourself and allows you to see the cycle of life. McElwee, however, never gets the chance to see much of anything because the crew he was going to join is putting out the remains of a very little fire by the time he arrives. He was expecting an epiphany but instead got lost going down the mountain.

Note Taking: *Six o'Clock News* Days 2 and 3			
	What do we see?	**What do we hear?**	**What does he learn?**
Steve Im			
Trailers in Arizona			
Firefighting			
Salvador Pena and California			
Home and Charlene			

Figure 4.19. Days 2 and 3 note-taking form for *Six o'Clock News*.

Key Sequence: 0:49:45–0:54:06

Like yesterday's key sequence, this one is an example of the reflexive mode of documentaries. In this one, McElwee films a woman as she secures a neighbor's belongings after a storm, but then several camera crews show up and ask the woman to re-create what she had just done for McElwee's camera. He eventually gives up filming the residents and instead films the TV newspeople, for whom he has very little respect, referring to them as an "invasion" and accusing them of messing up "his laboratory." Afterward, he watches the news coverage with the woman, noting that there are actually three versions of the day's events: the nine seconds that show up on the news, the longer version he himself filmed earlier, and what he's filming right at that moment as they watch the coverage. Though McElwee doesn't say it, there is a fourth version, which is what we, the audience, are experiencing as we watch his final film with all of these segments edited side by side for us to see. This is the point of reflexive cinema: it forces us to question what we are seeing and where the truth might be found. McElwee himself suggests that none of these versions really reveals the truth.

Discussion Questions

1. How are McElwee's interviews different from those of the TV news reporters? How are his behavior and motivations similar to or different from those of a news reporter?

2. Though his film has the look of a home movie, it is clear that careful construction and editing have taken place. What evidence of construction do you find and why do you believe McElwee made these choices?

3. Is the world as random and out of control as McElwee is suggesting here? Why or why not?

4. Overall, what do you think McElwee learned from his journey across the country? What did you learn from his retelling?

5. What do you think is going to happen in the rest of the film? Why?

Viewing Day 3: 1:02:00–1:38:00 (about 36 minutes)

- Begins with McElwee's film students
- Ends with closing credits

Things to Notice

This section is mainly about the conflicts between fiction and nonfiction, as financial pressures cause McElwee to consider directing a Hollywood fiction film. The meeting for the movie takes place in Los Angeles, eight months after a devastating earthquake trapped Salvador Pena in the rubble until his rescue twelve hours later, which was thoroughly documented on the news. McElwee uses the opportunity to spend time with Pena, filming him at home, at church, going to the hospital, and learns that he still has faith in God even though the "act of God" keeps him from working. When McElwee finally meets with the star and producer of the prospective Hollywood film, the star seems quite put off by the presence of McElwee's camera, not knowing which "eye" he should look at, McElwee's or the camera's, just as McElwee appears to be uneasy with the idea of making a fiction film. The actor's discomfort is contrasted a little later in a scene in which McElwee films a woman in a church so deep in prayer that she is completely unaware of his camera. The last time we see Pena, he too is praying, clearly at peace with his accident, and McElwee himself feels affected by Pena's faith and stillness. Before he leaves L.A., McElwee goes to a giant camera obscura exhibit that, representing the earliest types of cameras, projects a reflection of the city below that is oddly disorientating and what he calls "fragile," meaning that even a true, nonfiction image is subject to distortion. This image makes McElwee miss his wife and son, who, now four years old, tells him when he returns home that he talks with God and asks McElwee to put down his camera and play with him, which McElwee does. After more scenes of crime coverage on TV news, this time much closer to his own home, McElwee decides to end his film back with his friend Charlene, whose house had suffered damage from Hurricane Hugo, and her new granddaughter. McElwee's questions about God, violence, the randomness of the world, and so on do not get answered; they seem less important in the face of a child who is loved. As the credits roll, we see Charlene and family in church with the baby. Has McElwee found an answer in religion? He does not say directly, but it's clear that he recognizes that people can find solace from the randomness of the world in God.

Key Sequence: 1:20:00–1:22:15

As he is considering accepting the fiction film job, McElwee happens on to a crew filming a scene for the TV show *Baywatch*, which gives McElwee an opportunity to see how the director has absolute control over every element of his production; he is not "encumbered by the fateful intrusions of real life." Just as McElwee reflects on this, a drunk or delusional man jumps right in front of McElwee's camera and asks him if he looks like Paul Newman. The point McElwee is making is that this type of intrusion *is* reality and without it, fiction films are just another episode of *Baywatch*.

Discussion Questions

1. What were the questions McElwee was seeking answers to? What answers did he find? Were they what you (and he) were expecting?

2. The film opens when his son is a baby and ends when he is four years old. How did McElwee present time in this film? Why do you think he did not include many time markers for us?

3. According to McElwee, what are the differences between fiction and nonfiction? Do you agree with his characterizations?

4. What is the purpose of McElwee's voice-over narration? How would the film be different without it?

Closing Questions/Activities

1. In a lot of ways, a McElwee film is similar to a well-edited and narrated home movie. Watch a short portion of a home movie that you or your family has filmed and write down on the left side of a piece of paper a description of what appears in the movie. Then, on the right side of the paper, write a voice-over narration (in McElwee's style) that reflects on and explains the on-screen action. Afterward, explain how the voice-over might affect an audience's feelings.

2. The Hollywood film that McElwee was offered never got off the ground. Choose a fiction film that you know well and describe how it might be filmed if it were directed by Ross McElwee. How would it be similar or different?

3. Michael Moore explored a similar idea about the role of the media in perpetuating violence and fear in his film *Bowling for Columbine*. Watch this section of the film (see page 208) and write a comparison between Moore's and McElwee's styles, purposes, and approaches.

The Thin Blue Line

1988, Not Rated, Directed by Errol Morris

Summary

This groundbreaking documentary tells the story of the 1976 murder of a Dallas police officer, the investigation, and the subsequent conviction of Randall Adams, who was then sentenced to death. Director Errol

Morris interviews the principals in the case, reenacts key events, and begins to question the facts and the interpretations that led to Adams's conviction. The film has been credited with getting him released from prison. (Approximately 100 minutes)

Rationale

The Thin Blue Line is as genuinely exciting as it is unique in documentary filmmaking. Morris, though clearly working in the expository mode here, has a style all his own. While appearing to be impartial (because he allows all sides to tell their stories), Morris deliberately withholds key information from the audience to create suspense and to allow us to question what we hear and see. But this film is most noted for its extensive use of reenactments that change depending on the person narrating the sequence, revealing the problematic nature of relying on witness testimony, not only in issues of justice but also in documentary filmmaking itself. While I like to show this film to students so that they can see how documentaries can take on the elements of fiction film—e.g., cinematic framing, lighting, musical score—it would also be worth showing in a unit on social justice or criminal issues such as the death penalty, rights of the accused, and so on. The structure and style of the film is complex and might be best suited for older high school or college-level students.

Previewing

1. Typically, documentary filmmakers capture the world that is presented to them and do not rely on acting, costumes, or scripts to tell their stories. Yet some documentaries, like this one, use reenactments—visual retellings of the action performed specifically for the camera—usually with actors. Why is this an ethical "thin line" for documentaries? Why do some documentarians reject all reenactments? What would be a case for including them? If possible, show a brief clip from the recent documentary *Touching the Void*, about a mountain climbing disaster (see the activity on narrative writing in Chapter 3). Why are reenactments used in that film? What do they add and what might have been lost without them?

2. Much of what is interesting about this film is the way Morris uses reenactments to illustrate how witness testimony is flawed and unreliable. To demonstrate this to your students, have a colleague or a student, ideally one with whom your students have had little contact, walk into your room in the middle of your lesson to say something that only

a few students can hear and to do some sort of odd behavior; he or she should then quickly walk out. Continue teaching for a few minutes and after some time has passed, ask students to write down what they noticed about this person: age, weight, height, mannerisms, clothes, what he or she said, did, and so on. Then students should compare discrepancies among their descriptions and discuss why witness testimony is so potentially flawed.

3. Errol Morris deliberately does not lay out the facts of the case initially, preferring that the interviews and reenactments do this for him. It's a great idea and it certainly works, but I always find that it's a little too confusing for some of my students. So, without ruining much of the story, I give my students the following information: *In November 1976, a police officer in Dallas, Texas, was shot and killed by the driver of a car that he had pulled over for a routine traffic violation. A month later, a sixteen-year-old boy, David Harris, was interviewed about the murder, and he named Randall Adams, a man he had picked up hitchhiking earlier on the day of the murder, as the killer. Adams was later tried for the crime and was sentenced to death.* Just these bare-bones, just-the-facts, Ma'am, seem to help a lot.

Viewing Day 1: 0:00:00–0:32:03; Chapters 1–8 on DVD (about 32 minutes)

- Opening credits
- Ends with discussion of car's damage

Things to Notice

The first thing I always react to in this film is the musical score by Philip Glass that begins as opening credits run; it is, like a lot of his work, haunting and somewhat detached emotionally. After cityscape shots of Dallas, we see interviews of two unidentified men, one dressed in a white shirt (later we will learn this is Randall Adams) and another dressed in red (David Harris, we will discover), talking about a time they had in Dallas; no context is provided, and the audience feels as though it has jumped into a story halfway through. Next we see the first of what we will see a number of times: a reenactment of the shooting of a police officer. It does not look real; it feels deliberately staged and theatrical, with dramatic close-ups and appropriately effective lighting. We start to learn about the facts of the case through interviews with Adams, Harris, the detectives assigned to the case, and newspaper headlines, though as discussed in the following key sequence, there are numerous contradictions and flaws in any conclusions based on disputed testimony. After the investigation leads to Vidor, Texas, Harris's hometown, and after we hear conflicting versions of the night of the murder, Morris includes a montage of cars that look like the one involved in the shooting transforming into another car, demonstrating the difficulty of relying on eyewitness testimony.

Key Sequence: 0:13:01–0:15:01; Chapter 4 on DVD

This second of the reenactments of the shooting focuses on the actions and behaviors of the partner, including the throwing of her milkshake, which Morris holds in a close-up so that it resembles the blood flowing out of the police officer's body. The license plates and taillights blend together in the reenactment. Not only does the partner not know the truth, but Morris has made it so that we do not either.

Discussion Questions

1. Most documentaries of this sort would identify those being interviewed, but Morris does not. Why do you think he made that choice and what is the effect on you as an audience?

2. You probably have seen reenactments on true-crime TV shows like *America's Most Wanted* that try to look as real as possible. Morris goes in the opposite direction for his reenactments, making them deliberately staged and cinematic. Why do you think he does this and what is the effect on you?

3. Morris is unfolding the facts of the case slowly and in a particular order. Does it seem as though he is withholding information from you? If so, why?

4. So far, what do you know about this case? What facts are in question and which are not in doubt? How does Morris demonstrate the differences between facts?

Viewing Day 2: 0:32:03–1:00:39; Chapters 9–14 on DVD (about 28 minutes)

- Begins with interview with defense attorney
- Ends with headline announcing that the jury begins deliberations

Things to Notice

This day's viewing mainly focuses on the trial phase of the case, continuing to highlight the conflicting versions of events. Even though Randall's defense team learned that David Harris went on a crime spree with the gun used to shoot the police officer, the judge in Randall's case does not allow the testimony. Morris shows that the judge may be predisposed to favor the police by including the judge's reminiscence about his father's work with the FBI, which Morris elaborates on by showing film clips of John Dillinger's arrest. We continue to see more reenactments of the shooting; pay attention to how they change depending on who is telling the story. When David is talking, a man with bushy hair, like Randall's, is driving, but when the original testimony of the slain officer's partner is discussed, the driver has short hair, like David's. Morris also reminds us of the contradictions in the partner's testimony by showing us the milkshake again, meaning that she could not have been where she testified she was. The reenactments take on another level of meaning at the end of the viewing day because now we learn that there were witnesses who say they saw Randall driving (see the following key sequence about Mrs. Miller's testimony), though Morris either allows them to discredit themselves or he makes it clear to us that they might not be telling the truth by interviewing other people who sound more credible. Today's viewing ends with the judge, whose father, remember, was an FBI agent, admitting that he was emotionally affected by the prosecution's final argument.

Key Sequence: 0:50:14–0:54:15; Chapter 11 on DVD

Always try to identify where Morris makes his own views about the case apparent. This is never as clear as in the sequence with Mrs. Miller, one of the witnesses who claim to have seen Randall in the car. First, as Mrs. Miller talks about how she likes to act as a detective, Morris cuts to footage of a TV detective show called *Boston Blackie*, which, along with the music, makes her seem more than a little ridiculous. We also see the reenactment several times in this sequence, this time from her point of view in a moving car. Morris shows us what the view into the assailant's car would look like, and it is clear that Morris thinks there is no way she could have positively identified Randall.

Discussion Questions

1. Why does Morris insert clips of Hollywood fiction films or TV shows as he interviews some of his subjects?
2. How have the reenactments changed during this viewing day? What is Morris saying with these multiple versions?
3. What facts about the case are still in conflict and on what do most people in the film agree?
4. What is your opinion of Randall's guilt or innocence at this point? Why? What do you think Morris thinks? Why?

Viewing Day 3: 1:00:39–1:37:09; Chapters 15–20 on DVD (about 37 minutes)

- Begins with announcement that Randall was convicted
- Ends with closing credits

Things to Notice

Once Randall has been convicted, his trial moves into the penalty phase, during which a psychiatrist, who interviewed Randall for only fifteen minutes, declares him to be without conscience or regret and that he should be executed. As Randall talks about death by electrocution, Morris shows close-ups of various parts of the electric chair, which is effective but a little misleading, since by 1977 Texas had already adopted lethal injection as its sole method of execution. When the U.S. Supreme Court determines an error in Randall's case and recommends a new trial, we do not learn why his sentence was overturned, but we assume it has to be because of all the discrepancies we have been seeing. Morris doesn't reveal that it was really due to a technicality about juror selection. While the film has been moving in a roughly chronological order up to this point (investigation, trial, sentencing), Morris moves into a more thematic approach by going back to previous interviews. He shows a portion of his interview with David in which David says he was essentially coached on his testimony and believes that the prosecutor deceived the jury; we learn that one of the three witnesses, Michael Randell, had someone else in the car and that he believes the jury was lied to by the Millers; and we learn that Emily Miller did not pick Randall out of a lineup, but was told by the police that someone (David, it turns out) had already done so. At one point in his interview, David appears to get a little confused and seems to say that he was the one driving away from the scene, which Morris supports by running the reenactment scene again. Morris then presents the most shocking part of the entire film: David clearly admits—on audiotape, not on film—that Randall is innocent of the crime. Morris shows this only through close-ups of a tape recorder and a transcript of their conversation on the text track. After one more shot of the spinning police lights, we learn that Randall is still in prison with a life sentence and that David is on death row for a different crime.

Key Sequence: 1:33:50–1:36:40; Chapter 20 on DVD

I almost always replay the confession for my students to see how cleverly Morris asks his questions of David, how evasive David is, and how simply Morris chose to present this scene. I ask students to imagine what other images Morris could have chosen, and we weigh the pros and cons of each. Typically, students decide that Morris's is most effective because here the words themselves are most important.

Discussion Questions

1. We learn quite a bit about David (his childhood, arrest record, etc.) but almost nothing about Randall. Why do you think Morris made this choice? Would you have felt anything different if you had learned more about Randall?

2. When the film was released, it was billed as a true-life murder mystery. What did Morris do to create and build suspense?

3. What role do the reenactments play in this film? What is Morris saying with their inclusion?

Closing Questions/Activities

1. Randall Adams was released from jail, in part due to the publicity of this film. Research his case since 1985 to find out what evidence in the case led to the charges being dismissed. Describe the Special Features section that would accompany the newest DVD release.

2. Since being released from prison, Randall has become an outspoken opponent of the death penalty. Conduct research on the issue and imagine a debate between Randall and an advocate for capital punishment. Write a transcript of this debate.

3. Watch *Mr. Death*, another film by Errol Morris, which is about a man who constructs the mechanisms for capital punishment. How is Morris's style in *Mr. Death* similar to and different from the style of *The Thin Blue Line*?

4. Some people have claimed that this film led to Adams's release. Can works of art really make a difference in people's lives? Research books, artwork, plays, or other films that have had an impact on politics, the law, or society.

High School and *High School II*

1968, 1994, Not Rated, Directed by Frederick Wiseman

Summary

Fred Wiseman is considered one of the most important filmmakers in the history of documentaries. In the late 1950s, when the technology finally allowed filmmakers to record sound and images simultaneously with relatively portable equipment, a movement called "direct cinema" began to emerge. Proponents of this style tried to become mere observers of the real-life dramas they filmed, resisting intrusion as much as possible. Wiseman's entire career has been spent observing the various institutions that make up our modern life, and films such *Law and Order, Welfare, Juvenile Court,* and these two films about American high schools drop us right into the middle of those institutions and show us what we ought to see every day around us, but often do not. Made in 1968, the first film presents Philadelphia's Northeast High School as an extraordinarily authoritarian institution where students, if heard at all, are repeatedly marginalized and degraded by the administration. Over twenty years later, Wiseman filmed at another school and found a totally different environment. At Central Park East Secondary School in Harlem, students are engaged in the curriculum, and the school clearly values communication, inquiry, and cooperation. Through remaining strictly observational, Wiseman demonstrates his point of view through selective editing, framing, and shot selection.

Rationale

I broke my number one rule by including these films: they are not widely available. Wiseman retains strict control of distribution of all of his films, and though they run with some regularity on PBS, and many specialty video stores and some libraries carry them, they are mainly available through his company Zipporah Films, Inc. (www.zipporah.com) at insanely high prices. I included them here because the films are so much fun to teach, especially to twelfth graders, who are so close to leaving high school and who have so many opinions on the subject that they are no longer afraid to share. Nothing else out there provides a slice of high school life without adornment or trivialization like these do. Students (and teachers) spend so much of their lives in school, and these films hold up a mirror so that we can recognize things about ourselves we might not normally see, or want to see. *High School,* for example, contains a scene in which an English teacher reads "Casey at the Bat" aloud to her class of bored teenagers. I cringe every time I see it because I (and every other teacher reading this) have had that experience. If I had to choose between the two films, I would choose the first one, and, in fact, the way I have constructed the following activities, students really only watch about half of *High School* (about 40 minutes) and about twenty-five minutes of *High School II.* Of course, if you need to rent or buy the film at Wiseman's prices, you might want to show the entire films, just to get your money's worth. (After I finish this book project, I am going to write to Wiseman and his company to plead for mercy on behalf of us all.)

Previewing

1. Ask students to describe the culture of your high school. What does your school seem to value and reward? How do you know this?

2. Discuss a typical day at your school. Students should imagine themselves in the following roles: student, teacher, and administrator.

3. Review the observational mode of documentary filmmaking. You might want to show a clip from an observational mode documentary (see Chapter 1) in order to identify the construction that takes place even in this mode. Students often think that the observational mode is somehow more "real" because of its style, but be sure to point out the editing that occurs in any clip you show.

4. Show students the note-taking form (Figure 4.20) that you might want to use with this film; it identifies various sequences Wiseman presents. Practice using it by asking students to examine your classroom for a minute, writing down whatever they see and hear. Afterward, ask them to draw some kind of conclusion from these observations about the class, the teacher, the students, etc.

Viewing Day 1 *(High School)*: **0:00:00–0:14:43 (about 15 minutes)**

- Begins with opening scene
- Ends with administrator in the hallway

Things to Notice

The students rarely talk at this school as represented by Wiseman, and the administrators wield the authority. The first scene with the administrator is a perfect scene for analyzing how Wiseman's editing and framing give the audience a sense that this school operates with deep authoritarian strains. Very quickly we learn that the student did not dress down for gym class, but the administrator does not let him speak and, in fact, moves out from behind his desk to further impose his will. When the boy agrees to do what he's supposed to, the administrator does not hear him and suspends him anyway. Throughout the exchange, Wiseman focuses on the administrator's mouth and his hands as examples of his power. Teachers and other authority figures are often framed this

High School (1968, Frederick Wiseman)	
Sequence: Opening Sequence	
Visual	**Sound**
Sequence: Daily Bulletin 0:01:30	
Visual	**Sound**
Sequence: Spanish Class 0:02:15	
Visual	**Sound**
Sequence: Band Class 0:03:10	
Visual	**Sound**
Sequence: Administrator—Gym Outfit Discussion 0:03:40	
Visual	**Sound**
Sequence: French Class 0:05:00	
Visual	**Sound**
Sequence: Parent Conference with Administrator 0:06:00	
Visual	**Sound**
Sequence: Administrator—Disruptive Student 0:09:40	
Visual	**Sound**
Sequence: Administrator—Hallway 0:14:00	
Visual	**Sound**
	continued on next page

Figure 4.20. Note-taking form for *High School* and *High School II*.

Figure 4.20 *continued.*

Pause to Reflect: "Wiseman's *High School* implies that this school is . . ."(Offer visual and sounds elements as support.)	

Sequence: Gym Class 0:14:58	
Visual	**Sound**

Sequence: "Casey at the Bat" 0:16:20	
Visual	**Sound**

Skip ahead to	

Sequence: Practice for Fashion Show 20:35	
Visual	**Sound**

Skip ahead to	

Sequence: Women's-Only Lecture 0:26:44	
Visual	**Sound**

Sequence: Administrator with Girl about Senior Prom Dress 0:29:03	
Visual	**Sound**

Pause to Reflect: What is Wiseman implying about how this school views women?	

Skip to . . .	

Sequence: Class Discussion on Simon and Garfunkel song 33:25	
Visual	**Sound**

Skip to . . .	

Sequence: Class Discussion on Civil Rights and Minorities 49:20	
Visual	**Sound**
	continued on next page

Figure 4.20 *continued.*

Skip to . . .
Sequence: Class Discussion on the Culture of the School 54:40

Visual	Sound

Skip to . . .
Sequence: Final Scene with Principal Reading Letter 1:11:44

Visual	Sound

Pause to Reflect: "Wiseman's *High School* implies that the culture of this school is . . ."

High School II (1994, Frederick Wiseman)

Sequence: Opening Titles

Visual	Sound

Sequence: Student Presentation on Socialism 0:00:45

Visual	Sound

Sequence: Student Presentation of Stock Market Internship 0:04:20

Visual	Sound

Sequence: Student-Parent-Teacher Conference 0:8:17

Visual	Sound

Sequence: Physics Class 0:10:28

Visual	Sound

continued on next page

Figure 4.20 *continued.*

Sequence: History Tutoring Session 0:12:44	
Visual	**Sound**

Sequence: Discussion with Failing Student 0:14:02	
Visual	**Sound**

Sequence: Administrator—Student and the Joke 0:17:05	
Visual	**Sound**

Pause to Reflect "Wiseman's *High School II* implies that this school is . . ." (Offer visual and sound elements as support.)

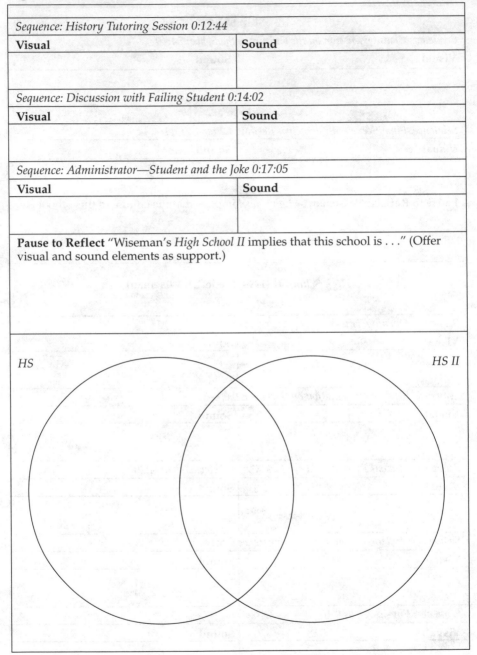

HS   HS II

way, and Wiseman loves to focus on their hands, which often are pointing or balled into fists. The administrators are unyielding, whether with disruptive students, parents, or kids using the phone.

Discussion Questions

1. Write a statement about what Wiseman is implying about this high school. Support that statement with details from your note taking. Refer to both visual and sound elements.

2. Wiseman's camera is not objective or neutral; his framing choices and editing may reveal his opinion about this school. Identify the construction Wiseman uses to present this opinion.

3. Wiseman could have ordered his scenes in any number of ways. Look back at the sequences you viewed today and describe the structure he uses. In other words, why does Wiseman put certain sequences next to others?

Viewing Day 2 *(High School):* **Various scenes (about 20 minutes)**

- Begins with gym class (fast forward to selected sequence)
- Ends with principal reading letter from soldier in Vietnam

Things to Notice

After the administrator stalks the hallways asking for passes, he looks into a doorway. Wiseman edits this to make it appear the administrator is looking into the gym where female students are doing stretching exercises. It is unlikely that Wiseman filmed the sequences in this order, but it sure feels like he's saying something about the exploitation of the young women at this school. The sequence with the girls in the gym is an extended one in which the faceless girls, just body parts, are dancing to "Simon Says." With the exception of the "Casey at the Bat" sequence, which is every English teacher's nightmare, the rest of the sequences identified on the note-taking form (Figure 4.20) until the next reflection deal with female representation. Listen carefully to the teacher running the fashion show rehearsal and notice how few complaints you hear from the students. After the reflection, we see three classroom discussions, in only one of which does any student try to express any individuality; notice how Wiseman captures that one student (the one with the sunglasses) quickly disengaging once the teacher again begins to dominate the discussion. Wiseman could not have scripted a better closing for his film (though of course with his editing this scene could have been among the first he filmed; there's no way to know). In the final scene, the principal reads a letter from a former student who is currently serving in Vietnam. In it, the student thanks the school for teaching him many things, including cooking, and he ends his letter with an admonishment not to worry about him because he is "not worth it" and "only a body, doing a job." After she finishes reading the letter, the principal says, "When you get a letter like this . . . we are very successful at Northeast High School." Well, sure, they are very successful at getting a student to think he has no individuality and is nothing but a body. All of Wiseman's selections highlight the school's desire for conformity and the students' willingness to surrender themselves to its power.

Discussion Questions

1. Describe the overall culture of this school? What does it value? How do you know? How does the letter the principal reads to the faculty support this?

2. According to Wiseman's representation, what does it mean to be a "man" or a "young woman" in this school?

3. How do you think the administration felt about the finished film? Why? How would you imagine the students felt? Why?

4. Without referring to the time period, how does your school compare to the representation of this school? Give evidence to support your opinion.

Viewing Day 3 *(High School II)*: **0:00:00–0:21:00 (about 21 minutes)**

- Begins with opening title
- Ends with discussion with student about a joke

Things to Notice

The first thing you and your students will notice is that in this school a kid is actually talking! Then you notice that the teachers are actually engaged in a dialogue with one another. Even when students are in trouble, as in the third and seventh sequences, the administrators ask about the feelings behind the students' actions and allow the students time and space to discuss the issues. Every time students are seen working with the curriculum, the materials appear authentic and the kids always articulate the how and why of what they're doing. It's a little frustrating for me and probably you, of course, to watch the one-on-one kind of interaction that this school's small class size allows. The students are clearly empowered to take responsibility for their actions, and the adults' role appears to be to guide students to reach their potential. This is a stark contrast to *High School. High School II* is much longer than the first, and I tend to show only this opening twenty minutes to make this contrast plain to my students, though the film includes many other compelling scenes, including ones of the students organizing a protest downtown.

Discussion Questions

1. Write a statement about what Wiseman is implying about this high school. Support your statement with details from your note taking. Refer to both visual and sound elements.

2. How does this school seem similar to or different from your own?

3. What does this school seem to value? Does Wiseman seem to agree or disagree with these values? How do you know?

Closing Questions/Activities

1. Create an observational documentary about your school. Describe the class periods, the hallways, or other school activities that in some way represent the culture of your school. If you are not able to film, create a storyboard for one or two scenes. You may want to consider the various perspectives of your school: student, administrator, parent, teacher, etc.

2. Imagine these films as interactive documentaries, in which the filmmaker is involved in the action on screen. Select any scene from either film and describe what it might look like in the interactive mode. You may want to storyboard a scene or two. How is the truth that is revealed in the imaginary one similar to or different from the truth revealed in Wiseman's films?

3. Compare *High School* with *High School II*. Focus on the students, teachers, and culture, but also on Wiseman's filming choices: framing, editing, sound, etc. How did he film the Harlem school differently? How much of the differences have to do with the differences in time periods? Use the Venn diagram to help you make the comparison.

4. Observational documentaries are not as popular a form as other types of nonfiction films. What are the challenges to an audience of an observational film? What are the unique challenges to a filmmaker working in this mode?

The Gleaners and I

2000, Not Rated, Directed by Agnès Varda

Summary

One of the most unusual, sophisticated, and intellectually challenging documentaries your students will ever see, *The Gleaners and I*, made by a well-known fiction filmmaker from the French New Wave movement, explores the notion of "gleaning," the act of using what has been left behind. Although she starts with the gleaners in Europe who follow the harvest season picking up stray potatoes and turnips, Varda then moves into other areas in which people use what has been cast aside, including documentary filmmaking, where she turns her lens on herself. (Approximately 82 minutes)

Rationale

This is the last film I wrote about for this book because I went back and forth for a long time about whether to include it. I have taught it only once, and my students found its style and topic vastly removed from any of their other experiences with documentary film. But probably because of this, and because my wife, whose judgment I trust above all others and who counts this as her absolute favorite film, kept leaving the DVD on my desk, I decided to take the risk. And I urge you to teach it, but with a group of sophisticated seniors or college students who have had at least some exposure to the nature of documentary filmmaking discussed in Chapter 1.

Previewing

1. First, you will need to define the term and the concept of a *gleaner*. A typical dictionary entry will say something about those who collect what remains after the harvest. You might want to show your students some of the paintings by Jean François Millet, who specialized in capturing rural peasant life, especially if you can project from your classroom computer. A number of Web sites have examples of his work, including one from 1857 called *The Gleaners*.

2. But this film also explores a second concept of gleaning, which is about the nature of using something left behind for another purpose. Ask students to identify people who glean in this manner. You will need to prompt them to go further than "homeless people" to be sure they are also thinking about recycling, people who shop in thrift stores, hand-

me-downs, etc. You can also discuss the idea of "waste" and how things can be reused so that materials are not wasted.

3. A way I like to get at this in a more abstract fashion is to hand out newspaper or magazine articles; the subject matter of the articles is not important. I ask students to skim through the articles and highlight all the interesting words or phrases they run across, which I then write on the board. Next I ask students to create a "found poem" on a topic that I select, but which they write using only the words on the board. Each student's poem is unique, though the words themselves were "harvested" from the same source. From this, students can see how gleaning can create art. Ask students how documentary films are like found poems or gleaning.

4. You might also want to provide your students with just a bit of background information on director Agnès Varda. She was part of the French New Wave of directors from the 1960s that included Truffaut and Godard. One of her most famous and groundbreaking films, *Cleo from 5 to 7*, follows two hours in the life of a woman awaiting her medical test reports. Also, since the subject plays a large role in the film, you might want to have a discussion about the differences between digital video and traditional movie cameras. You should try to get at the differences in size, weight, portability, and also in the look and style of video. There is still a home movie-ish quality to digital video, but it allows for more immediacy and can allow filmmakers to film where and how they might not have been able to before.

Viewing Day 1: 0:00:00–0:40:58; Chapters 1–11 on DVD (about 40 minutes)

- Begins with opening titles
- Ends with Louis Pons, the artist who gleans

Things to Notice

The film opens with a dictionary definition of *gleaning* (in French), but alongside the dictionary is the filmmaker's cat rubbing against the book. This should be a signal to us that this is going to be a personal and perhaps whimsical exploration of a topic. When Varda takes us to the museum where the Millet painting "The Gleaners" is exhibited, she speeds up the film to show the people who come to look at the painting as a sort of tourist attraction, but she animates the painting by overlapping it with the diegetic sounds (birds and wind rustling) from the next scene of a woman in the fields talking about gleaning. Varda cuts from this woman to black-and-white archival footage and still photos of gleaners and then to interviews of people who talk about gleaning as something of the past.

But it's clear that Varda does not agree with this view of gleaning, because she edits a montage of contemporary people in the "gleaner position," stooped over picking up trash, food, and other things in rural and urban areas. Interestingly, this montage is set to a rap song, which is a type of gleaning as well because rappers often use bits and pieces of other songs to create their own, new songs. One difference Varda notes between gleaners of the past and those of today is that today gleaning is a solitary experience instead of a communal one, which she illustrates with primary footage and still photos of paintings. We now start to be aware of Varda herself through her narration, and we get a sense that she is on some kind of investigation to learn about gleaning. She is also on a personal quest, as described in the following key sequence.

As if this were an expository film on potato farming, Varda gives us background information on the nature of the potato harvest and the tonnage collected each year. We soon see what she's up to, though, when we learn that a lot gets thrown away because modern machines cannot handle large or odd-sized potatoes, which are just dumped as trash in undisclosed places. This is the first we have seen of the other topic Varda explores: waste. She films people who find the potatoes, and she even gleans all the potatoes that are heart shaped. Notice that we see footage of her filming, so clearly more than one camera (and camera operator) is filming in this documentary.

After Varda meets a man who lives in a trailer near the potato fields who lost his job due to alcoholism, she tells a group of self-described gypsies that there are free potatoes available for gleaning. This is the second time Varda appears to use the film she is creating and the knowledge she is gaining to help people. She then follows the man as he gleans for food in dumpsters. A lot of the food they find is in great shape, but the stores have to get rid of it to make room for newer food.

At first glance, the cut from the dumpster gleaning to shots of a chef discussing a new lamb kidney appetizer appears to be a juxtaposition that makes a statement about the haves and have-nots in society, until we realize that the chef himself is a gleaner who uses all parts of the fish and meat so there is no waste and who forages for fresh herbs and fruit.

In between locations she visits, Varda appears obsessed with the trucks on the road. She includes shots of passing them by and will return to this motif throughout the film.

In wine country, Varda discovers deliberate wasting of the grapes in order to protect the wine growers' capital, which requires producing only a limited amount of wine, despite how many grapes have been grown. While some cheap table wine could be made from these grapes, the law prohibits gleaning of the grapes. Varda's camera shows a lot of fresh grapes going to waste on the vine. To transition back to the city, she includes a match cut from a couple in wine country talking about being married for fifty years to a couple in the city talking about how they met. Varda inserts herself again as she picks fruit directly from the tree and accuses those who do not allow gleaning of being stingy, after which she includes a clearly constructed scene in which a man dressed in law robes reads from a law book (that matches the red of the tomatoes) that seems to allow the poor and anyone in need access to gleaning opportunities once the harvest is over.

Returning to her implication that filmmaking is a type of gleaning, Varda films herself returning home from a trip to Japan (notice how she has changed the narrative structure on us; we no longer appear to be on the same quest that had her following the harvest) and reveals the results of her gleaning: the souvenirs she has collected. Looking at pictures she had taken of Rembrandt's self-portrait, Varda begins filming her hand again, looking at the beauty and the horror of it in a detached sort of way, her own self-portrait.

Varda is not alone in this idea of gleaning as art. We meet a man who scavenges for tools, metal, any objects left behind in dumps or in trash bins in order to recycle them into something beautiful. About the items he collects, he states what could be the theme of the film: the objects "have a past, they've already had a life, and they're still very much alive. All you have to do is give them a second chance."

At an antique shop, Varda sees a painting of gleaners that could be a symbol of the two types of gleaning Varda has depicted: some in the painting are standing proud and upright, while others are stooped in a submissive position.

After a visit to what could be called a shrine to gleaning, a castle constructed by a brick mason solely out of found objects, today's viewing ends with an interview of Louis Pons, a successful artist whose medium is made up of what he gleans. He says that while some people might call it a pile of junk, he sees it as a "cluster of possibilities" and that "the aim of art is to tidy up one's inner and exterior worlds."

Key Sequence: 0:04:28–0:05:54; Chapter 3 on DVD

This is where Varda first acknowledges that she, as a filmmaker, is a gleaner of sorts, which she demonstrates visually by standing in front of a painting of a female gleaner, striking the same pose (with props) as the subject of the painting. She drops the crops she has been holding and trades them for a video camera. What follows are shots of herself, digitized and distorted: her image is mingled with that of the painting and other images. She also introduces the topic of aging by showing us close-ups of her graying, thinning hair and her wrinkled, liver-spotted hands. At this point, we're not quite sure what she is making of this topic, but it shows her to be fearlessly facing her own image.

Discussion Questions

1. What are the most unusual forms of gleaning Varda presents in this section? What is Varda's tone toward the act of gleaning? How is this tone revealed in the images she selects?

2. Why does Varda keep returning to herself? What is the connection she is trying to make between gleaning and herself?

3. How would the film be different if it were a PBS documentary on gleaning? What would be added, changed, or removed? Why?

Viewing Day 2: 0:40:58–1:22:37; Chapters 12–22 on DVD (about 42 minutes)

- Begins with driving through a storm
- Ends with closing titles

Things to Notice

Varda's childlike game of "capturing" the trucks in her hand is a type of optical trick (see Figure 4.21) that she dismisses as "just fun," but it's another way to establish that gleaning is always a matter of perspective. Or it can be a matter of law or custom, as she learns from the people who glean oysters, all of whom have a different understanding of how much they are allowed to take.

The sequence on the Nenon family of grape pickers begins with a beautiful diegetic song by the family, created in part by the tools of their gleaning: buckets and pruning shears. Varda says that she got so carried away with the song that she forgot she was filming, and she includes the shots of her camera moving and lens cap swinging to a nondiegetic jazz song. The shot, however, continues for over a minute

Figure 4.21. This shot of the filmmaker's hand inserted in the frame from *The Gleaners and I* reminds viewers that what we are seeing is always a construction of reality.

and becomes dizzying and disorienting as the music increases in volume and pace. The shot and the music suddenly halt, calling attention to the film's construction. In a film about waste, Varda won't let many shots go unused, I suppose.

Filmmaking and gleaning coincide again when Varda interviews a winegrower whose great-grandfather was one of the earliest pioneers in moviemaking. She incorporates bits of his black-and-white films, mostly of animals in movement, into her film, accompanying them with music, and edits them, in proper gleaning fashion, to suit her own, new purposes.

Never one to prefer simplicity, Varda cuts from a short sequence on trash as art for children (with nicely cleaned and fresh artifacts) to real trash on the streets and garbage trucks, wondering if these kids have even shaken hands with a garbage collector.

Varda continues her connection between agricultural and urban gleaning by cutting from the lawyer we met earlier in the fields to a lawyer in the streets, also in black robes, who explains the city's salvaging laws. We then see a montage of all the abandoned items throughout the city that can be salvaged for scrap or other uses. Varda herself takes home things she finds on the street, including a clock without hands, which she says cannot show the passing of time; she films herself moving behind it, reminding us that in so many ways this is a film about Varda's own feelings about aging and her desire to remain useful.

At first glance, a long sequence about a man who scavenges for food after the market closes and outside of bakeries seems like just another of her profiles of urban gleaners, except that she follows this man for a number of days and eventually learns that he volunteers his time teaching immigrants to speak French; here again it is Varda's process of gleaning (filming) that allowed her—and us—to learn this about someone who might so easily be dismissed or discarded by us as unimportant.

The final scene of the film is a kind of return to the beginning in which Varda films another painting of gleaners, this one by Hedouin called *Gleaners Fleeing before the Storm*. The connection between art, film, and gleaning can once more be seen in the final shot, where Varda has the painting taken outside; we hear diegetic sound of a real storm starting as we see the storm brewing inside the painting.

Key Sequence: 0:50:21–0:53:40; Chapter 15 on DVD

In this section, Varda stumbles onto an interesting legal case of gleaning in which a group of homeless kids were charged with vandalizing a grocery store's trash cans. Notice how she assembles and briefly introduces each of the "protagonists" through crosscutting before she gets into the case itself and then quickly cuts back and forth between the authorities and the group of kids as they address each other's charges. The judge says it's simply a matter of law, but Varda, through beautiful and sympathetic close-ups of the kids, knows it's never that simple when you're talking about people who get their food from trash cans. To confirm this, we follow a man who gleans from trash cans for ethical reasons; he has a job and can afford to buy food but sees too much being wasted.

Discussion Questions

1. What are the main points Varda makes about gleaning? What is she saying about aging?
2. What documentary mode is dominant in this film?

3. How does Varda keep all of the disparate elements of the film together?

4. How is digital video used differently in this film than in others you have seen?

5. What connection does Varda make between film and gleaning?

Closing Questions/Activities

1. Conduct research on gleaning in the United States. Are there laws that govern who can glean and when? What are the differences in attitude toward gleaning in this country?

2. Ask each of your classmates to bring in one item from their homes that would normally be thrown out. From these artifacts, create your own gleaned artwork. Use some of the art you saw in the film as models.

3. Another possibility for those with access to video equipment is to film five minutes of footage of anything that interests you and then to exchange footage with at least two other people. Create your own gleaned movie by editing your footage together with theirs. Without any extensive equipment, you can create your own PowerPoint presentation with clip art images that you have gleaned and recontextualized.

4. Write a newspaper editorial about one of the following topics: waste, gleaning rights, recycling, aging. Then write a letter to the editor as though Varda were responding to your editorial.

Appendix A: Glossary of Film Terminology

The following are terms generally applied to *nonfiction films*. *Video Editing and Post Production* by James Caruso and Mavis Arthur was a big help in developing this glossary. Most of these terms are further described in Chapter 1 of this book.

Modes of Nonfiction Film

- *Expository:* documentaries that are intended to inform and/or persuade the audience about an issue.

  - direct address: uses narration and/or text track that clearly states the filmmaker's intent.

  - poetic: uses visuals and sound (and sometimes text) to allow the viewer to infer the film's intent.

- *Observational:* documentaries in which the filmmaker tries to minimize his or her presence as much as possible, acting as a "fly on the wall."

- *Interactive:* documentaries in which the filmmaker involves himself or herself in the on-screen action, often through interviews and narration.

- *Reflexive:* a film that is aware of itself as a film and often presents the dilemmas or the contradictions associated with documentary filmmaking.

Parts of Nonfiction Films

- Visual Track

  - *A-roll:* also called primary footage; contains all the original footage (audio and visual) captured by the filmmaker.

  - *Archival (found) footage:* visuals—or sound—that the filmmaker him- or herself did not create: e.g., news broadcasts, home movies, newspaper headlines. These can be moving or still images.

  - *B-roll:* the secondary shots used to cover or to cut away from the A-roll and/or voice-overs. The B-roll can come from the primary footage and/or archival footage.

  - *Cutaway:* a shot specifically inserted that takes the audience away from the primary footage. This is often used to explain something on the A-roll or as a transition to the next scene.

- *Cut-in:* a shot inserted that highlights a specific part of the primary footage. An example might be a close-up of a hand tapping nervously during an interview.

■ Audio Track

- *Diegetic:* any sound (music, dialogue, . . .) that could logically be heard by someone within the film, at the time of recording.

- *Nondiegetic:* any sound (music, voices, sound effects) that could not logically be heard at the time of recording and has been added by the filmmaker afterward.

- *Narration:* some films will use a third-person narration (the "voice of God") delivered by someone who does not reveal him- or herself either by name or by appearance, while other films use a first-person narration ("I") by someone who identifies him- or herself (oftentimes the filmmaker), and the narration can be delivered on screen or it can be recorded afterward and added on a B-roll audio.

■ Text Track (or Graphic Track): written information that appears on screen added by the filmmaker in postproduction. Examples are subtitles, identifications, charts, and graphs.

Other Terms

- *Cinema verité:* literally "film truth," it refers to a type of interactive documentary that tries to present a version of reality by documenting the encounters between subject and filmmaker. A popularized form of the term refers to the handheld camera style of filmmaking.

- *Direct cinema:* though similar in many ways to *cinema verité*, direct cinema describes those films in the observational mode that have little interaction between filmmaker and subject.

- *Mockumentary:* a fiction film that intentionally takes on the style of a documentary, often for humor's sake.

- *Docudrama:* a fiction film that is based on real-life events.

- *Ethnographic filmmaking:* similar to the work of an anthropologist, an ethnographic filmmaker has a goal to observe a "culture" (broadly defined) and present his or her findings to an audience unfamiliar with the culture.

- *Montage:* editing together several different types of shots, each of short duration, for a particular effect. Typically, a montage in nonfiction film will include visuals and music (sometimes with text), though often without voices.

- *Realism:* although all nonfiction films are in most ways considered "real," this term is used to describe the feelings and degree of reality the filmmaker chooses to include. For example, obvious reenactments, though "real," do not have a high realism quotient, whereas raw, unedited footage feels more real to the audience.

The following are terms regularly associated with fiction films, but they are frequently relevant to documentaries as well.

Framing/Shots

- *Long shot* (LS): a shot taken from some distance; shows the full subject and perhaps the surrounding scene as well.
- *Establishing shot* (ES): often a long shot or series of shots that sets the scene or shows the space of a scene.
- *Close-up* (CS): the image being shot takes up at least 80 percent of the frame. There is also the extreme close-up, which would show one part of the body or a portion of an object.
- *Medium shot* (MS): in between LS and CS; people are seen from the waist up.

Camera Angles

- *Low angle* (LA): camera shoots subject from below; has the effect of making the subject look larger than normal—strong, powerful, threatening.
- *High angle* (HA): camera is above the subject; usually has the effect of making the subject look smaller than normal—weak, powerless, trapped.
- *Eye-level* (EL): accounts for 90 to 95 percent of the shots seen because it is most natural; camera is even with the characters' eyes.
- *Dutch angle:* shot that is tilted sideways on the horizontal line; used to add tension to a static frame, it creates a sinister or distorted view of a character.

Lighting

- *Low-key:* scene is flooded with shadows and darkness; creates suspense/suspicion.
- *High-key:* scene is flooded with light; creates bright and open-looking scene.
- *Neutral:* neither bright nor dark—even lighting throughout the shot.
- *Bottom/side:* direct lighting from below or from one side; often

dangerous or evil looking, may convey split personality or moral ambiguity.

- *Front/rear:* soft, direct lighting on face or back of subject—may suggest innocence.

Editing Techniques

The most common is a "cut" to another image. Others are:

- *Fade:* scene fades to black or white; often implies that time has passed.
- *Dissolve:* an image fades into another; can create a connection between images.
- *Crosscutting:* cut to action that is happening simultaneously.
- *Flashback:* movement into action that has happened previously; often signified by a change in music, voice-over narration, or a dissolve.
- *Eye-line match:* a shot of person looking, then a cut to what he or she saw, followed by a cut back for a reaction.

Camera Movement

- *Pan:* stationary camera moves left or right.
- *Tilt:* stationary camera moves up or down.
- *Zoom:* the camera is stationary but the lens moves, making the objects appear to grow larger or smaller.
- *Dolly:* the camera itself is moving with the action—on a track, on wheels, or held by hand; often called "trucking" when the camera moves left or right.

Appendix B: Blank Activity Charts

	Parts of a Documentary
	Title: _____ Year: _____ Director: _____

Visual Track	*Primary/archival footage, still pictures, etc.*
Audio Track	*Voices, music, sound effects, etc.*
Text Track	*Identifications, subtitles, information, etc.*

On the back, in a topic sentence, identify the key visual, sound, and/or textual elements used, and in a paragraph explain the *effect* of these elements on the viewer.

Modes of Nonfiction Film
As you watch each of the following clips, try to determine which documentary mode is most prevalent; the modes certainly overlap, but which one seems dominant? Then provide a reason for your choice of mode and describe some of the stylistic choices (shot type, editing style, use of sound, etc.) that this film demonstrates.

Title	Dominant Mode	Stylistic Elements of the Mode

To consider: What are the stylistic elements for each mode? In other words, how could you recognize each mode by examining how the information is communicated to the audience? Why do some modes use elements that others do not? Do any of the modes feel more "real" to you? Why is this?

Reading in the Reel World: Teaching Documentaries and Other Nonfiction Texts by John Golden © 2006 NCTE.

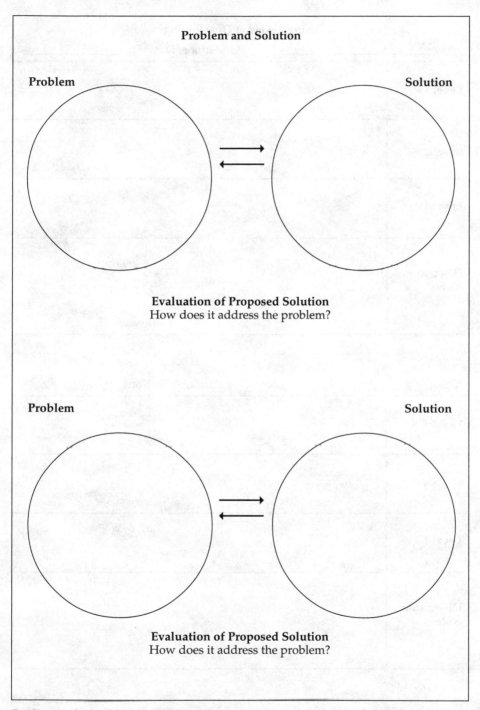

Problem and Solution

Problem

Solution

Evaluation of Proposed Solution
How does it address the problem?

Problem

Solution

Evaluation of Proposed Solution
How does it address the problem?

Using Levels of Questioning	
Title: _____	Author/Director: _____

Level 1	
Level 2	
Level 3	
Discussion Notes	

Title: _____	Author/Director: _____

Level 1	
Level 2	
Level 3	
Discussion Notes	

Reading in the Reel World: Teaching Documentaries and Other Nonfiction Texts by John Golden © 2006 NCTE.

Using SOAPStone	
Text 1:	
Speaker	
Occasion	
Audience	
Purpose	
Subject	
Tone	
Analysis:	
Text 2:	
Speaker	
Occasion	
Audience	
Purpose	
Subject	
Tone	
Analysis:	

Reading in the Reel World: Teaching Documentaries and Other Nonfiction Texts by John Golden © 2006 NCTE.

Tone Analysis

Title: _____   Director: _____

As you watch the following clip, circle words that could describe the tone of the piece. Add other words in the space below as they occur to you.

frustrated	angry	humorous	satirical	reverent
enthusiastic	detached	formal	informal	serious
bitter	critical	kind	lighthearted	ironic
mocking	outraged	disgusted	loving	emotional

Also, keep track of the words, phrases, music, and sounds used on the audio track and the key images on the visual track that might point toward the filmmaker's attitude toward the subject.

Audio	Visual

Now write a statement that uses the following model: "Director _____ uses a _____ tone in order to _____."
Write a paragraph that supports this statement by referring to specific words, phrases, music, images, or text from the clip.

Reading in the Reel World: Teaching Documentaries and Other Nonfiction Texts by John Golden © 2006 NCTE.

Perspective in Nonfiction Texts	
Title: _____ Director/Author: _____ Topic: _____	
What information is presented?	
How is information presented?	
What is NOT included?	
What is the perspective?	

Now imagine that you were going to create a nonfiction text on the same topic, but with a different perspective.

What information would you present?	
How would you present the information?	
What would you NOT include?	
How would you summarize this new perspective?	

Reading in the Reel World: Teaching Documentaries and Other Nonfiction Texts by John Golden © 2006 NCTE.

Persuasive Appeals

Title of film: _____ Director: _____ Year: _____

	As presented	How effective? Why?	Could be added
Logos			
Pathos			
Ethos			

Title of film: _____ Director: _____ Year: _____

	As presented	How effective? Why?	Could be added
Logos			
Pathos			
Ethos			

For your own topic: _____

	What you know already	What you want to find	Why it will be effective
Logos			
Pathos			
Ethos			

Reading in the Reel World: Teaching Documentaries and Other Nonfiction Texts by John Golden © 2006 NCTE.

Nonfiction Film Treatment		
Visual: *What will the audience see?*	**Audio**: *What will the audience hear? Key dialogue?*	**Commentary**: *What do you want the audience to feel?*

Reading in the Reel World: Teaching Documentaries and Other Nonfiction Texts by John Golden © 2006 NCTE.

Nonfiction Storyboard		
Title: _____ Director: _____ Sequence #: _____		
Visual/Text Track	**Audio Track**	**Notes/Editing**

Reading in the Reel World: Teaching Documentaries and Other Nonfiction Texts by John Golden © 2006 NCTE.

Appendix C: Other Documentaries by Topic

All of the following films are widely available on Amazon.com or other similar source:

Sports

The Life and Times of Hank Greenberg

Riding Giants

The Endless Summer

When We Were Kings

Dogtown and Z-Boys

Baseball

Murderball

Go Tigers!

Mockumentaries

This Is Spinal Tap

Waiting for Guffman /Best in Show

Series 7

The Blair Witch Project

Science/Nature

A Brief History of Time

Winged Migration

Microcosmos

March of the Penguins

Music/Film/the Arts

The Decline of Western Civilization

Metallica: Some Kind of Monster

Fellini: I'm a Born Liar

DiG!

Baadasssss Cinema

F for Fake

Crumb

Gimme Shelter

Don't Look Back

American Movie

Lost in La Mancha

The Kid Stays in the Picture

The Celluloid Closet

Politics/Social Issues/Crime

Gunner Palace

The Corporation

Outfoxed

The War Room

Roger & Me

Manufacturing Consent

Harlan County, USA

Dark Days

Brother's Keeper

Paradise Lost

Devil's Playground

U.S. History

Liberty

The Fog of War

The Civil War

Hearts and Minds

Chisholm '72:- Unbought & Unbossed

Incident at Oglala

The Weather Underground

"Reality" Experiences

The Up series (*Seven Up!, 7 Plus Seven, 21 Up,* etc.)

World History/ Politics

Gaza Strip

Control Room

The Sorrow and the Pity

Triumph of the Will

One Day in September

Bus 174

Children Underground

Hotel Terminus

Documentaries and fiction film on the same subject

Incident at Oglala and *Thunderheart*

Blind Spot: Hitler's Secretary and *The Downfall*

Dogtown and Z-Boys and *Lords of Dogtown*

Rock School and *School of Rock*

Aileen: Life and Death of a Serial Killer and *Monster*

The Brandon Teena Story and *Boys Don't Cry*

Appendix D: Annotated List of Resources

The following are the best texts that I have read about documentaries. You'll notice that some analyze the documentary form itself, whereas others are about the creation of documentaries and are written by professional filmmakers. Both types helped me to write this book, though none is really targeted for high school students.

Books

Barnouw, Erik. 1993. *Documentary: A History of the Non-Fiction Film.* 2nd rev. edition. New York: Oxford University Press.

Along with the Nichols's texts, this book must be on your reading list if you are interested in understanding documentaries. As he traces the historical development of nonfiction film, Barnouw ascribes different attributes to documentary filmmakers depending on their era, philosophy, or intent. Documentarians can be, according to Barnouw, explorers, prophets, reporters, poets, catalysts, and so on. These classifications helped me tremendously in considering the reasons that filmmakers make the choices they make.

Brenton, Sam, and Reuben Cohen. 2003. *Shooting People: Adventures in Reality TV.* London: Verso.

Finally, people who watch more reality TV than I do; even better: they make my voyeurism seem academic. Not only is this book perfect for wrapping one's mind around the reality TV phenomenon, but it is also extremely readable in its psychological approach to the documentary form as a whole. It gave me great ideas for trying to answer the question: why do we like to watch nonfiction?

Grant, Barry Keith, and Jeannette Sloniowski, eds. 1998. *Documenting the Documentary: Close Readings of Documentary Film and Video.* Detroit: Wayne State University Press.

This is a collection of more than twenty essays on specific films, ranging from the earliest to the most recent and from the widely known to the somewhat obscure. I specifically used the chapters on *Night and Fog, Nanook of the North,* and *Triumph of the Will,* but there are sure to be sections on many of the films that you might choose to teach.

Nichols, Bill. 2001. *Introduction to Documentary.* Bloomington: Indiana University Press.

Nichols, Bill. 1991. *Representing Reality: Issues and Concepts in Documentary.* Bloomington: Indiana University Press.

By all accounts, Nichols is "the man." Since he is the acknowledged expert in documentary form, style, and content, conquering these two texts should be your first step. I say "conquering" because these are dense books. Nichols can pack a sentence so chock full of information that it usually takes me two or three read-throughs to get his point. But these texts will reward your effort. They especially helped me to understand the different modes of documentary expression and to see how ethical issues are so important to nonfiction filmmaking. I wouldn't have had a prayer of writing this book if it weren't for Nichols's books.

Stubbs, Liz. 2002. *Documentary Filmmakers Speak.* New York: Allworth Press.

This is a great read and extremely informative. Stubbs conducts one-on-one interviews with some of the most influential documentarians (D. A. Pennebaker, Albert Maysles, Barbara Kopple, Ken Burns, Ross McElwee) and some who clearly deserve more recognition than they have received so far (Joe Berlinger, Liz Garbus, Bruce Sinofsky). While some of the material gets technical (aspect ratio?), most of the interviews reveal a great deal about what motivates nonfiction filmmakers to choose their topics and about the ethics they apply in their films.

Rosenthal, Alan. 2002. *Writing, Directing, and Producing Documentary Films and Videos.* 3rd edition. Carbondale: Southern Illinois University Press.

Caruso, James R., and Mavis E. Arthur. 1992. *Video Editing and Post Production.* Englewood Cliffs, NJ: Prentice Hall.

Millerson, Gerald. 1992. *Video Production Handbook.* 2nd edition. Oxford, England: Focal Press.

These are some of the books I stole from my wife, who uses them regularly in her job as a video editor and producer. They are, of course, technical in nature, but they are especially useful, particularly the first one, if you want to adapt video creation projects in your classroom.

Internet Sites

The following are some key Internet sites of tremendous value for teaching the documentary. Each has been around for a while, so I imagine that addresses will stay the same by the time this goes to print.

Movie Review Query Engine (www.mrqe.com)

> I use this site all of the time to get quick access to reviews of thousands of films. The search engine links to such sites as the *New York Times, Washington Post, Salon,* etc.

The Internet Movie Database (www.imdb.com)

> This is the quickest way to get that title of that one movie with that one guy in it. The database has information on seemingly every film ever made, often including those not yet released.

Reality Film (www.realityfilm.com)

Documentary Films.net (www.documentaryfilms.net)

> These are two fairly new sites that showcase reviews and news about documentary films. The former contains a collection of definitions from various sources about nonfiction films, and the latter has an excellent links section.

DocuSeek (www.docuseek.com)

> DocuSeek is a search site for independent documentary, social issue, and educational videos available in the United States and Canada. This is a good place to get those hard-to-find films.

Women Make Movies (www.wmm.com)

> Women Make Movies is "a multicultural, multiracial, non-profit media arts organization which facilitates the production, promotion, distribution and exhibition of independent films and videotapes by and about women." You can also locate and purchase films directly from this site.

Documentary Educational Resources (www.der.org)

> Documentary Educational Resources produces, distributes, and promotes ethnographic and documentary films from around the

world. The prices for purchase or rental are steep, but these films are unavailable elsewhere, and the Web page also has a fantastic "links" section.

Appendix E: Index of Films Discussed

Title	Director(s)	Rating	Activity	Page
Amandla!	Lee Hirsch	PG-13	Complete film	165
The Atomic Café	Jayne Loader, Kevin Rafferty, and Pierce Rafferty	Not rated	SOAPSTone	82
Baraka	Ron Fricke	Not rated	Modes, tone	37, 107
Born into Brothels	Zana Briski and Ross Kauffman	R	Editing, tone, complete film	30, 107, 172
Bowling for Columbine	Michael Moore	R	Theme, complete film	103, 201
Cane Toads	Mark Lewis	Not rated	Cause/effect	79
Celsius 41.11	Kevin Knoblock	R	Perspective	110
Fahrenheit 9/11	Michael Moore	R	Editing, modes, perspective, persuasive writing	27, 38, 110, 114
Fahrenhype 9/11	Alan Peterson	Not rated	Persuasive writing	115
The Fog of War	Errol Morris	PG-13	Cornell Notes, tone	92, 105
4 Little Girls	Spike Lee	Not rated	Cornell Notes, complete film	92, 221
Girlhood	Liz Garbus	Not rated	Complete film	152
The Gleaners and I	Agnès Varda	Not rated	Complete film	252
High School and *High School II*	Frederick Wiseman	Not rated	Complete films	242
Hoop Dreams	Steve James	PG-13	Complete film	157
Jackass	Jeff Tremaine	R	RAFT	121
The Kid Stays in the Picture	Nanette Burstein and Brett Morgen	R	Narrative writing	116
Koyaanisqatsi	Godfrey Reggio	Not rated	RAFT	121
Mad Hot Ballroom	Marilyn Agrelo	PG	Levels of Questioning, complete film	88, 143
March of the Penguins	Luc Jacquet	G	Cornell Notes	94
Night and Fog	Alain Resnais	Not rated	RAFT, complete film	120, 184
Outfoxed	Robert Greenwald	NR	Parts of a documentary, problem/solution	23, 78

Powaqqatsi	Godfrey Reggio	G	Editing	29
Roger & Me	Michael Moore	R	Cause/effect	80
Six o'Clock News	Ross McElwee	NR	Modes, complete film	38, 227
Spellbound	Jeffrey Blitz	G	Compare/contrast, complete film	73, 137
Super Size Me	Morgan Spurlock	PG-13	Parts of a documentary, modes, problem/solution, complete film	24, 35, 78, 191
The Thin Blue Line	Errol Morris	Not rated	Complete film	234
This Is Spinal Tap	Rob Reiner	R	RAFT	122
Touching the Void	Kevin Macdonald	R	Narrative writing	116
Triumph of the Will	Leni Riefenstahl	Not rated	Propaganda	58
The True Meaning of Pictures	Jennifer Baichwal	Not rated	Complete film	212
Tupac: Resurrection	Lauren Lazin	R	Levels of Questioning	85
The War Room	Chris Hegedus and D. A. Pennebaker	PG	Modes, RAFT	37, 122
Why We Fight series	Frank Capra (Producer)	Not rated	Propaganda, compare/contrast, persuasive writing	61, 76, 114

Works Cited

American Dialect Society. 2005. 2005 Word of the Year Nominations. Retrieved 12 April 2006. http://www.americandialect.org/ADS_WOTY_Nominations_2005.pdf.

Barnouw, Erik. 1993. *Documentary: A History of the Non-Fiction Film.* 2nd rev. edition. New York: Oxford University Press.

Brenton, Sam, and Reuben Cohen. 2003. *Shooting People: Adventures in Reality TV.* London: Verso.

Ehrenreich, Barbara. 2001. *Nickel and Dimed: On (Not) Getting by in America.* New York: Metropolitan Books.

Golden, John. 2001. *Reading in the Dark: Using Film as a Tool in the English Classroom.* Urbana, IL: National Council of Teachers of English.

Hewitt, John A. 2005. "A Habit of Lies—How Scientists Cheat." Updated 5 October 2005. http://freespace.virgin.net/john.hewitt1/pg_glossary.html.

Jones, LeAlan, and Lloyd Newman, with David Isay. 1998. *Our America: Life and Death on the South Side of Chicago.* New York: Pocket Books.

Nichols, Bill. 1991. *Representing Reality: Issues and Concepts in Documentary.* Bloomington: Indiana University Press.

Nichols, Bill. 2001. *Introduction to Documentary.* Bloomington: Indiana University Press.

O'Brien, Tim. 1990. "How to Tell a True War Story." *The Things They Carried.* Boston: Houghton Mifflin.

Orwell, George. 1950. *1984.* New York: New American Library.

Pauk, Walter. 2001. *How to Study in College.* 7th edition. Boston: Houghton Mifflin.

Power, Samantha. 2002. *A Problem from Hell: America and the Age of Genocide.* New York: Basic Books.

Schlosser, Eric. 2001. *Fast Food Nation: The Dark Side of the All-American Meal.* New York: Perennial.

Sontag, Susan. 1975. "Fascinating Fascism." *New York Review of Books.* February 6.

Stubbs, Liz. 2002. *Documentary Filmmakers Speak.* New York: Allworth Press.

Author

Photo by Laura Lull.

John Golden has taught English at public and private high schools in Virginia and Maryland and currently teaches at Grant High School in Portland, Oregon. He has presented strategies for using film in the classroom for hundreds of teachers around the country and is the author of *Reading in the Dark: Using Film as a Tool in the English Classroom* (2001). You can reach him at goldenlull @hotmail.com.

This book was typeset in Palatino and Helvetica by Electronic Imaging.
The typefaces used on the cover were American Typewriter, Avant Garde,
and Berling.
The book was printed on 50-lb. White Williamsburg Offset
by Versa Press, Inc.